YAMAHA DIRTBIKES

OSPREY
COLLECTOR'S
LIBRARY

YAMAHA DIRTBIKES

All off-road, motocross, enduro and dual-purpose motorcycles, both two- and four-stroke—1968 onwards

Colin MacKellar

Published in 1986 by Osprey Publishing Limited
27A Floral Street, London WC2E 9DP
Member company of the George Philip Group

British Library Cataloguing in Publication Data

MacKellar, Colin
    Yamaha dirtbikes.
    1. Motorcycle racing—History   2. Yamaha
    motorcycle—History
    I. Title
    796.7′5   GV1060
ISBN 0-85045-660-6

Design Gwyn Lewis

Filmset and printed in England by
BAS Printers Limited, Over Wallop, Hampshire

Contents

Foreword

It seems like only yesterday that I was riding the GP motocross circuits of the world on the YZR500 Yamaha and winning more often than not! Reading Colin MacKellar's account of the development of Yamaha's motocross and other off-road motorcycles brought back many fond memories of the days when the combination of Mikkola and Yamaha was the one to beat. Although I already had two world championship titles when I joined the company, the two that followed in 1977 and 1978 were especially pleasing, since my great rival Roger de Coster could do no better than second and third respectively.

When I signed that contract for a year's employment racing Yamaha motocross machines in December 1976, there had already been two false starts to my relationship with the company. At the end of the 1972 season, Yamaha were a week too late with the offer of a contract to ride the first monoshock machines. In the summer of 1975, I was asked if I would be prepared to ride for the company for the next year, but later Yamaha changed their minds and pulled out of the sport for a year. Perhaps it was a pity for both of us that we didn't get together sooner.

My relationship with Yamaha did not, however, get off to a good start on the racetrack. Racing for the first time on the YZR500 in a frozen Hechtel in Belgium, with a large contingent of big-shots from the European Yamaha HQ there to see me win, a bad case of 'Yamahop' from

the rear suspension threw me off when I landed from a jump and I badly dislocated my shoulder. Fortunately the rest of the year turned out to be more successful.

The secret to winning in the motocross sport lies not only with the need for a good machine but also a good team. That is what we had, with Lucien Tilkens, the father of the monoshock suspension, caring for the development of his child, Minoru Tanaka running the team efficiently and Heikki Pentilla taking good care of the bike. The fact that I only had machine trouble three times in three years says a lot for Heikki's ability as a mechanic.

This book contains a wealth of information on the development of the Yamaha YZ series of motocross machines. It is now clear to me how the YZR500 I first rode in Japan in December 1976 had come into existence and what part it played in the development of the YZs of the 1980s. When I have the opportunity to throw my leg over one of the latest YZ490s, I still have the feeling that it is related to the bike that took me to 27 GP race wins in three years. Yamaha created the off-road revolution and helped develop it into the important branch of the motorcycle industry it has become. This superb book tells us exactly how it all happened.

Heikki Mikkola
Läyliäinen, Finland
September 1986

Introduction

Motorcycle sport has fascinated me since my first interest in motorcycles and I have always admired Yamaha for their firm commitment to motorcycle competition on both the dirt and racetrack. Clearly a motorcycle company is in business to sell motorcycles and racing is the medium that Yamaha have chosen to achieve this. But a feeling I had while writing *Yamaha Two-Stroke Twins* has been reinforced while writing this book. Yamaha's success on the racetrack, and hence in streetbike sales, is primarily due to the efforts made by Yamaha's international and not domestic organization. The company's attitude towards enthusiastic owners of their products is at best lukewarm and at worst one of total disinterest.

My own encounter with this incomprehensible attitude of Yamaha in Japan occurred when I requested copies of a number of photos from the company archive, that I had previously been told were available. After numerous unanswered requests on my behalf by the European Yamaha HQ, I was informed that they were 'too busy' to locate and send the dozen or so photos I wanted. In contrast, Allyn Fleming of *Cycle* magazine spent what must have been a considerable amount of time locating and clearing the copyright of some 66 photos from the magazine's archive. Fran Kuhn of *Dirtbike* magazine responded immediately to a panic call for some shots of Broc Glover and Ricky Johnson, which were in my hands within ten days. It would

be easy to attribute this attitude to a difference in culture, but I don't think this is the cause. I believe it is a poor PR department that presents an unattractive side of the Yamaha corporate personality which should be improved.

Fortunately, most of the people I encountered during the writing of this book were more positive in their reaction and helped as best they could. Vital background information was provided by riders who were involved in the Yamaha European motocross team during the 1970s. Jaak van Velthoven, Gerard Rond and, in particular, Torsten Hallman were able to recall the details of their time with Yamaha, and Sten Lundin talked of his involvement with the Hallman and Lundin four-stroke 500 cc motocross bike. Heikki Mikkola is thanked for his willingness to write the Foreword and the speed with which he got the job done.

Several people at the Dutch and European Yamaha HQ in Uithoorn helped in the difficult task of tracking machine development. David O'Neill was able to loan me some Yamaha parts books and service manuals and kindly supplied data for the machine specifications. Cor Soetens allowed me to rummage through his spare parts warehouse and measure up as many YZ cylinders as I could find, as well as helping with my endless search for parts books. Anneke Meijerink did her best to help me with my fruitless communication with Yamaha Japan and provided some photos of the more recent Yamaha models. In the US, Yamaha International racing team manager Kenny Clarke threw some light on the early days of Yamaha's involvement with the National motocross series. Bob Pritchard kindly supplied me with copies of the excellent 'wrench report' series of newsletters, detailing performance modifications for Yamaha competition models since 1979.

Early on in the project, it became clear to me that the only photographs that were accessible for many of the models that I was describing were to be found in the archives of US magazines. These would be so crucial to the completeness of the book, that it would have been meaningless to produce it without them. It was therefore with some trepidation that I made my first contact with Allyn Fleming of *Cycle*, with my enormous list of the photographs I wanted to borrow. I needn't have worried; she couldn't have been more helpful. The quality of the photographs was especially high and the copyright owners, Dave Hawkins, Robin Riggs, Steve Broadday and Scott Darough, are thanked for their permission to use them. In the UK, Brian Woolley of two-stroke tuning fame and now faced with the massive task of bringing some order to the 80-year-old *Motor Cycle Weekly* files, helped me locate a few unexpected gems.

In the Netherlands, Derk Evers once again generously gave me *carte blanche* to ransack the rich archives of *Motor* magazine and to come and go as I pleased. A drawing is worth a thousand words and Piet Cornet exercised his considerable artistic talents by drawing the five stages in the Yamaha monoshock rear suspension design evolution, thereby illustrating the indescribable. Finally, Jan Heese responded to my request for a jacket shot of a Yamaha in action, with a flood of high-quality slides, that made the choice extremely difficult.

The accuracy of the story of the development of Yamaha's dirtbikes is directly related to the quality and quantity of the research material that would act as my source. Many people deserve credit for the enviable collection I was able to accumulate. Meko Books of Haarlem kindly donated a number of service manuals for the early T series. Thanks go to Neil Collins of South Australia, who supplied me with a number of parts manuals, which I had been unable to obtain, out of his comprehensive archive of Yamaha documentation. My friend Fedor van de Pol helped me sort through his ten-year-old collection of US magazines, which resulted in some 300 plus Yamaha dirtbike-related articles. In fact it was these articles more than anything that provided the most useful information and consequently a special thank you goes to the US motorcycle journalists of the past 15 years who have so conscientiously tested and critically reviewed Yamaha off-road models, recorded their results so articulately and still managed to have a good time.

Peace and quiet are essential ingredients to the successful completion of any book and with a year-old baby daughter in the house, they are often both in short supply. Marian was instrumental in keeping her happy and contented despite Cara's involuntary donation of the attention she rightly felt she should be getting from me. Without their sacrifice, I'd still be writing this book now.

Colin MacKellar
Hilversum, The Netherlands
July 1986

1 | The DT1—an American vision

Above **This YDS3-CM is a rare beast, being a TD1-B road-race engine in a YDS3 chassis, with upswept exhausts and a bash plate the sole concessions to off-road riding. Note the twin-leading-shoe front brake**

Left **Fumio Ito on the rough stuff during Yamaha's first international 'road-race' at Catalina in 1958**

Yamaha's links with the world of off-road competition, in fact, date back to the days of their first participation in motorcycle competition of any form. During 1954, construction had begun of the first production-line Yamaha motorcycle. The YA1, or Red Dragonfly as it was affectionately named, was a 125 cc two-stroke single modelled heavily on the most influential 125 of the period, the DKW RT125. At the time of the YA1's launch on to the market, its success was not assured. In fact, the odds were against it competing successfully in a market swamped by the products of more than 40 native manufacturers. Many of these companies placed their hope of survival not only in the production of what they felt to be high-quality machines, but in the demonstration of their superiority over the others through the emerging medium of racing.

In 1953, the first post-war Japanese road-race had been held on the slopes of Mount Fuji. The term 'road-race' was a bit of a misnomer as the track surface was actually of hard-packed volcanic ash, with not a trace of tarmacadam to be found. The philosophy behind the event had been to foster and encourage the home motorcycle industry with the view that racing improved the breed. To this end, the entry was restricted to standard Japanese machines. The race was a huge success, although not able to prevent the manufacturers of the winning Autobit from slipping into oblivion not long after their triumph.

The following year two classes were introduced and Suzuki started their roll of honour with a win in the 90 cc lightweight class. The same 90 cc and 250 cc class divisions were to be used for the 1955 event, putting Yamaha at a large capacity disadvantage. Their 125 Red Dragonfly would have to do battle against machines twice its size. The company was so anxious to prove their product in the public arena that they took the chance and entered the race. They needn't have worried, for the power-to-weight ratio of the YA1s seemed to be perfect for the muddy surface and a Red Dragonfly flew round the track to take it and Yamaha's first race victory.

A second race was planned for 1955, at a change of venue. A track similar to that on Mount Fuji was found on Mount Asama, just north of Tokyo. The Nippon Motorcycle Race Association wanted to stage regular events at this location and 1955 would herald the first. Yamaha were anxious to confirm the quality of the YA1 by again defeating all-comers. What ensued was the now legendary Asama race, for which the Yamaha team had achieved a couple of hours' practice on the actual circuit while the competition was still in bed! The first four places were taken by the Yamaha team members. The famous link between the company and motorcycle competition had been forged.

The race victories in 1955 had the desired effect. Sales of the YA1 were very strong and provided enough income to enable the company to grow and begin development of what was to be their first twin, the YD1. The second Asama Plains race meeting was to be yet another Yamaha triumph with the first two places in the newly introduced 125 class for the YA1 and first three in the 250 class for the YD1. Although not billed as such, these were really dirt-track events, for Japan didn't get a tarmaced road-racing circuit until Honda built their Suzuka test track in 1962. The only concession that was made to the inhospitable terrain was the provision of knobbly tyres for improved traction, and flat handlebars for better control. The first bikes raced in the US were similarly kitted, but it wasn't long before they began looking more like the road-racers they were.

While the company fought to establish itself as a major motorcycle manufacturer, development was concentrated on the production of good streetbikes and their road-race equivalents. The overriding priority was to establish a range of street machines that would sell in enough numbers to allow the company to expand. Only then would it be possible for the company to explore the peripheral fields of motorcycling, such as motocross. While this was undoubtedly Yamaha's philosophy for the first half of the 1960s, they did not waste the occasional opportunity that arose to produce street-based or road-racer-based machines that were intended for off-road riding.

The first of these was the Ascot Scrambler machine that appeared in 1963. It was basically a hybrid machine constructed from the YDS2 streetbike. This was Yamaha's first real worldwide-selling street 250 twin, from which had been derived their first production road-racer, the TD1. The Ascot Scrambler was an amalgam of the two. The chassis came straight from the streetbike, with most of the street electrics removed and a fully tuned road-race engine was slipped into it complete with chromed expansion chambers. Yamaha produced the machine in very small numbers for use on half-mile oval tracks and for desert races and American TTs over hard-packed smooth surfaces. There were no modifications made to help the machine perform better in the dirt, and it cost Yamaha virtually nothing to develop. The few that were produced were quickly sold, since it was undoubtedly the fastest, if not the most reliable, 250 machine available at the time.

When the next 250 twin appeared during 1964, Yamaha went one step further, by producing the first of their 'Street Scramblers'. This was a concept that gave the first indication of the growing movement towards dual-purpose motorcycles in the US. Street scramblers were street machines through and through, but an impression was carefully nurtured that the bike could actually perform on the dirt, by fitting it out with upswept exhaust pipes and a bash plate under the engine. In 90 per cent of the cases this was all that was changed on the machines. Understandably, they were hardly suited to anything but the gentlest trail ride, which could as easily have been ridden on the standard street machine. Where they did perform well, was in the building of an image for the owner, and for that reason they sold well.

Interestingly, Yamaha's YDS3-based street scrambler did have a slight tune-up over the pure street engine. A higher compression head was fitted and the exhaust port timing was raised by means of a slot cut on the exhaust side of the piston. The extra power this generated would have been useless on the dirt with the weight of the YDS3 to haul around. But Yamaha had thought of that one as well, for it was possible to buy a YDS3CM kit, that basically converted your street scrambler into a TD1-B road-racer-based machine. Almost half the engine was replaced in the kit, with different cylinders, heads, carburettors, pipes and ignition included. The resulting power output would have been around 35 bhp, but the excess weight of the rig would have severely compromised the kit's effectiveness.

Yamaha continued to produce street scrambling variants of some of their twins up to the end of the 1960s, but these were limited to the cosmetic changes of upswept exhaust pipes and were intended for the boulevard posers and not the true dirtbike enthusiast. A completely separ-

A typical example of the 'Street Scrambler' concept was this 1965 YDS3-C, although this one has been stripped of electrical equipment ready for competition

ate range of motorcycles had been developed for him marking one of the most stunningly successful developments of a motorcycle genre the industry had ever experienced.

Like many of the earth-shattering decisions that were made in the motorcycle industry, there is a very simple human story behind it. It is told very well by the current editor of *Cycle*, Phil Schilling, in his book *The Motorcycle World*. The story is so important in showing how successfully the knowledge of a group of Western experts could be combined with the enormous drive and resources of a Far Eastern company, that the salient facts are repeated here.

The concept of a dual-purpose motorcycle crystallized around the contact between two men working for the US Yamaha concern in 1966, Jack Hoel and Dave Holeman. Hoel was Yamaha International's head of research and development and in a unique position to be able to influence the Yamaha product line. The mid-1960s was the golden time of proliferation for all the Japanese manufacturers and it was their success in the US market that was largely responsible. Any ideas for new products that were likely to improve their market share in the US would be guaranteed a receptive ear. Hoel's meeting with Holeman sparked off just such an idea. Holeman, then head of technical publications with the company, was in the process of picking up a new sport—desert racing.

This was a minority sport if ever there was one. Basically classified as enduro riding, the term encompassed two very different forms of off-road competition that had evolved due to the startling environmental contrasts encountered in the continental US. In the north and east of the US, enduro racing had developed in the European style of timed trials through rocky woodland, where the skill lay in matching the time allocated for sections rather than going Wide Flat Out (WFO) to get to a given location first. In many of the southern states, the more erudite skills of balance and pacing had been rejected

for the more physical skills of controlling 150 kg of raw power as it flew over the wide open spaces of the desert surface. The two environments had led to different machines being developed as most suitable for the riders of each type of enduro. Desert sleds, as they were termed, required two main qualities that took complete priority over everything else: blistering speed and tramline stability. In contrast, the woods enduros needed lightweight machines with quick steering and an engine that would lug them out of trouble. The resulting machines were big four-stroke twins based on street models in desert racing and smaller two- or four-stroke singles, that were close to trial machines, for the woodland enduros.

Interestingly a change was taking place at the beginning of the 1960s, that was most evident in the desert racing world. More and more lightweight motocross-based machines were finding their way into leading positions in desert races, where their slight lack of top end performance was more than compensated by their agility and ease of riding, causing the rider less fatigue than the white-knuckled wrestling match often encountered with the monster desert sleds. The ground between the two variants of enduro racing was beginning to close as Dave Holeman began his initiation into the sport.

Hoel was curious enough to tag along a couple of times when Holeman went to his desert race meetings. After seeing the machinery being used, he became increasingly convinced that a market would exist for a machine that was a perfectly respectable street machine from Monday to Friday, and could easily be turned into a reasonably competent rough-terrain vehicle at weekends. Anxious to bounce his idea off someone possibly more tuned into the domestic Yamaha attitude, he shared his concept with two native Japanese on detached duty at Yamaha International in Los Angeles. Both Mike Sekine and Ike Kono considered the idea worthy of being brought to the attention of the long-range project team in Japan. So at the next project planning meeting in Japan, Hoel put his case for starting a development of a dual-purpose motorcycle capable of being used in both environments. He left the meeting with the commitment for production of an initial prototype, based on input he would provide. Mindful of the development method of 'design by emulation' that had so successfully produced the first Yamaha single and twin, the best initial input to the design was considered to be suitable machines that already existed.

This was a tricky point, since nothing quite like the intended machine existed at that moment. The closest any came to the concept were the Spanish dual-purpose machines that had begun appearing a couple of years before. Montesa had produced a 250 cc Scorpion in 1964, and Bultaco had followed with the 153 cc Campera in 1965 which was enlarged to 175 cc for 1966. In 1967, Bultaco added the 250 cc Matador, a four- (later five-) speed 250, that was close to the design objective of the Yamaha machine. But they were doomed to failure. Without the support of a comprehensive dealer network, they would never sell to anyone but die-hard enthusiasts who were happy enough if there was a dealer in their state, let alone city. Needless to say, apart from the Japanese, there was only one group of motorcycle manufacturers that might have been able to make the idea work, and that was the large British companies. With their extensive dealer network, and with their reputation still surprisingly intact, they would have been well placed to have made the idea work. But one can easily imagine the derision with which such a suggestion would have been greeted in the company boardrooms back in the UK. As it was, all the Europeans could do was look on impotently as their machines were plagiarized to produce a new generation dual-purpose motorcycle.

In mid-1966, the first prototype arrived in the US for analysis, having been built based on the information gleaned from the European mach-

ines Hoel had sent to Japan. It could hardly be said that it was right first time, but at least the engine was all right. Fortuitously, the company had started to develop a 250 cc single-cylinder engine with which they had intended to power their first attempt at producing a motocross machine. A detuned version of this was an ideal power unit for the new dual-purpose machine. The chassis was not quite so suitable, but that could be more easily developed in tests in the wastelands of southern California. In order to help with the development, Neil Fergus, a successful desert racer, was brought into the team and together they set about producing a chassis that had the special qualities necessary for the rigours of off-road riding. Weekly reports were sent to Japan detailing the changes that were being made and recording the results. Although the development was being done in the US, Yamaha Japan was holding the budget purse-strings and wanted to be kept right on top of the progress being made.

The story goes that the team completed the tests towards the end of 1966, and crated the finished product up and despatched it to Japan for analysis. Two days later, the first pre-production models arrived from Japan. Based on the reports sent back to Japan, prototype models had been assembled and would be used as a model for the production of the first model year. Japan had not waited for the final machine before committing themselves to a production model. The version they had built was not as good as the final team product but adequate enough to justify production. The first DT1s had been assembled.

Despite the startling impact the bike would have on the motorcycle world, the DT1 was not a remarkably radical machine. It was a soundly engineered motorcycle employing contemporary two-stroke technology, in which, it must be admitted, Yamaha were world leaders. The engine had the largest displacement cylinder Yamaha had ever built, but this caused no prob-

lems. Although the cylinder dimensions of 70 mm × 64 mm represent an engine with a slightly short stroke, the DT1 was not built to rev. With a conservative compression ratio, and a simple exhaust pipe, the peak power was delivered at a lowly 6000 rpm. For this range of engine speed, the engine was really over-engineered. The result of this safety margin was an absolutely reliable, completely bullet-proof, mill, which was just as well when it is considered how hard it was thrashed.

The crankcases were split vertically, as was always the case with single-cylinder machines. The alloy cylinder had a shrunkfit iron liner into which the ports had been cut before assembly. Four long-reach studs screwed into the crankcases and held both barrel and cylinder head in place. The combustion chamber featured a spark plug whose position was offset towards the left-hand side of the cylinder. It is difficult to understand the reasons for this since it would not have eased the thermal loads on the piston crown, the usual reason for moving the plug from its central

position. Four rubber pellets were inserted between the fins of the cylinder head in an attempt to reduce their ringing. The fresh charge was fed to the engine by a 26 mm round slide Mikuni carburettor, fitted with a choke lever that enriched the fuel/air mixture via an extra starter jet, as was standard Mikuni practice at the time. The air filter was not easily accessible behind the exhaust pipe. The pipe exited straight from the exhaust manifold for about 20 cm, before sweeping up and to the right-hand side of the bike, keeping well out of harm's way. The matt black pipe was fitted with a heat guard along its length under the fuel tank and seat to protect the rider's legs from its high surface temperature. Since the exhaust design was not too critical for the generation of high-power outputs, Yamaha were able to tuck the pipe well out of the way by flattening the sidewalls in the section passing under the rider's legs. It was a well-designed piece of equipment, and full credit to Yamaha for resisting the temptation to chrome it!

The pressed-up crankshaft ran on two main

Left and right **One of the final DT1-prototypes stripped for competition in the way Hoel and Holeman envisaged many DT1s would be used**

ball bearings, with a roller bearing at the big end of the conrod and a needle bearing at the small end. Initially, two flat rings were fitted to the piston and the first 3000 engine units were assembled without expander rings but after some seizure problems these were added. Later, the Keystone ring, that Yamaha so wholeheartedly embraced, was used. Ignition was by magneto with the flywheel keyed to the right-hand end of the crankshaft. On the opposite end was the helical primary drive, and the gear for the Autolube oil pump. Autolube had first started appearing on Yamaha motorcycles in 1964, as Yamaha attempted to make the two-stroke more socially acceptable. It was quite simply a small oil pump driven from the crankshaft, that passed oil from a tank under one of the side covers via a banjo bolt to the inlet tract of the cylinder. The amount of oil that flowed was dependent on the engine speed, and hence a more accurate and much simpler means of lubricating the engine was provided. By 1966, its use had become universal.

The clutch was of conventional design with an actuation rod running the length of the transmission mainshaft to free the 14-plate sandwich of friction and metal plates. Somewhat wary of the kind of shock loads the transmission might be exposed to by the abuse of the clutch so often performed during off-road riding, Yamaha included a cush drive in the clutch basket/ primary gear connection by means of six short springs arranged in the same plane as the primary gear. Five well-chosen ratios were used in the gearbox, with a high first gear and top gear providing moderate overdrive for street use. Three forks were used in the selection mechanism, two running along a rail, driven by pins following the track cut in the surface of the selection drum, and the third fork mounted on the drum itself and running along its length driven by an internal guide pin. Primary kickstarting, allowing the bike to be started in gear with the clutch in, showed the thought that had been put into the functionality of the machine.

The main frame consisted of a large diameter

The premier of the DT1 took place at the October 1967 Tokyo Motorcycle Show

single backbone tube running from the top of the headstock above the engine, before curving down behind the engine, and a duplex engine cradle running down in front of the engine, under and behind to join the backbone. The rear sub-frame to which the seat and top of the rear shock absorbers were attached, was a single loop of rail from the backbone of the main frame, with two rails running from the main frame behind and under the engine to the damper mounting lugs. A bracing tube tied the backbone to a plate between the two front downtubes just under the headstock. Extensive gusseting was used around the headstock. Constructed from mild-steel, the diameter of the tubes was a little excessive, adding significantly to the overall weight of the DT1. A steel bash plate protected the bottom of the engine from any rocks encountered on the trail.

The massive box-section swinging-arm pivoted on a plain bush without any provision for *in situ* lubrication. A sheet aluminium chainguard helped protect the exposed section of chain from low-level branches that might otherwise derail it. Ceriani-style front forks were provided but no attempt was made to extend the amount of wheel travel above the standard 100 mm or so available on streetbikes. Three-way adjustable spring preload was possible on the rear dampers. Both front and rear wheels used full-width hubs running on ball bearings with single leading-shoe drum brakes. The rear brake was full-floating with the brake shoe backing plate tied to the frame by an aluminium rod. A second transmission cush drive was provided in the rear hub with the rear sprocket mounting plate meshing with six rubber segments in the hub.

The miscellaneous equipment was all solidly designed. The footrests were spring-loaded and the brake pedal had a serrated surface to improve grip with a muddy boot. A grab-rail was provided to help lift the 105 kg machine out of quagmires or to help the passenger hang on to the rather short dualseat. Actual passenger footrests were not provided as standard but optional extras that were bolted on to drilled and tapped holes in the swinging-arm. Full electrical equipment included a 35-watt headlight and a tail-light. No indicators were fitted. Both speedo and tacho were mounted above the headlight, with a resettable odometer located within the speedo. The first DT1 came decked out in white with a lettered Yamaha badge on the sidewall and as the DT series progressed it was always referred to as the 'white tank' model. A decal on the left-hand sidecover proudly announced the capacity and enduro function of the DT.

The performance of the DT1 was quite satisfactory, with a top speed on the open road of 70 mph and sufficient torque to allow all-day chugging along the trail. Clearly there were serious limitations to the abilities of the standard DT1 in the dirt, but it performed better than any other street-based motorcycle ever produced.

Yamaha quickly realized the potential of the DT1 in amateur-level motocross competition and US-style TT and scrambles. A Genuine Yamaha Tuning (GYT) kit was hastily assembled, which added a whacking 10 bhp to the power output and a further 1500 rpm to the top end. It consisted of a chromed cylinder, head, piston, 30 mm Mikuni and a properly designed exhaust pipe. The piston had a single thinner ring in place of the two standard rings. As the engine was expected to turn faster, the thinner ring would reduce power-sapping friction and be less likely to start fluttering at the 7500 rpm engine speed. The chromed cylinder was lighter, lowered piston/wall friction and had longer exhaust and inlet period port timing. The compression ratio had been raised by reducing the capacity of the combustion chamber by 27 per cent. A large selection of drive and rear wheel sprockets were available to allow changes in gearing according to the application. As Jack Hoel and Dave Holeman had expected, DT1s started showing up in open country enduros with good results, culminating in Mike Patrick and Phil Bower's victory in the 1969 Mint 400 desert race, when they headed the 24 finishers home from a starting field of more than 200. Hoel and Holeman's vision had been confirmed.

When announced at the beginning of 1968 in the US and Australia, the demand was simply staggering, catching Yamaha completely by surprise. The initial 8000 machines exported to the US were snapped up within a couple of months. Production was stepped up from the initial 1500 per month to the 2500 maximum that the plant was capable of. Export orders were given priority leaving a starved domestic market with three-month waiting lists developing. The unit sales figures over the first model year were never exceeded before or after by another Yamaha model. Jack Hoel deserved Yamaha's Medal of Freedom or promotion to Official Yamaha Oracle, or something. Instead he simply continued in his function as head of Yamaha R & D in the US, working on the conception of another DT1 success story.

Appearing to recognize the significance of the introduction of the DT1, *Cycle World* placed this photo on the cover page of their February 1968 issue

A touch of the DTs

The DT1-B of 1969 was primarily a cosmetic update and the first DT to appear in Europe in any numbers

With the DT1 selling like the proverbial hot cakes, Yamaha realized they had struck gold and rushed to extend the range to other capacity classes. The first machine development to reach fruition was the 125 and by the beginning of 1969, the first AT1s were arriving in the US and Australia.

It was immediately christened the kid brother of the DT1, and indeed the design was almost identical. The single-cylinder engine, with vertically split crankcases, had the time-honoured dimensions of a 56 × 50 mm bore and stroke, exactly as found on the cylinders of the YDS 250 cc street twins and the TD road-racers. The five-port cylinder design was common to almost the entire range of Yamaha machines by the end of the 1960s. In contrast to the DT1, the spark plug was located in the centre of the cylinder head, which provided a conservative compression ratio. A 24 mm Mikuni performed the carburation, with the air cleaner nestling behind the oil tank under the sidecover on the left-hand side of the bike. The upswept exhaust looked like a scaled-down version of the DT1 pipe.

The engine layout was identical to that of the DT1, with magneto on the left-hand end of the crankshaft and the primary transmission and Autolube drive on the other. The ten-plate clutch borrowed many components from other machines, but did not use the spring-based cush drive of the DT1. Instead the pins connecting the transmission primary gear to the clutch housing were rubber mounted. A five-speed transmission was fitted with a very low first gear and a large jump to second, the rest of the ratios being fairly equally spaced, with top gear offering overdrive for street use. The shift mechanism differed slightly from the DT1, in that the fork which was mounted on the drum on the DT1, now ran along its own rail.

Although appearing to use the same chassis design as its bigger brother, there were a few subtle differences between the two. On the frame of the AT1, the main backbone member extended down behind the engine to join a pressed-steel box that connected the single backbone tube to the twin rails of the engine cradle and provided the mounting point for the swinging-arm. In fact it was a very similar frame to the YAS1 125 street twin, except this used a single downtube and the engine as a stressed member of the frame. The rake of the AT1 was a fairly steep 29·5 degrees. The other unusual feature of the bike was the use of a half-width rear hub. Yamaha's intention was to reduce the amount of unsprung weight on the rear end by using a narrower width drum brake to stop the lighter machine. The performance of the brake did not suffer as a consequence, proving in fact to be rather too powerful and locking the wheel.

This was to be a curse that dogged many of the dirtbikes in Yamaha's range for the next ten years. It was not, however, a floating design as on the DT1, since the tie rod for the brake backing plate was attached to the swinging-arm and not the frame. In theory this would result in extra compression of the spring under rear wheel braking, and, if travelling over rough ground while braking, the rear wheel would have a tendency to hop under the torque reaction forces. In practice, other deficiencies of the AT1 prevented it from being ridden on the kind of terrain where this would be a problem. Except for the addition of traffic indicators, the rest of the machine was almost a mini-clone of the DT1, with the same equipment coming as standard.

High plains drifter—the CT1-C of 1970

Much as the DT1 before it, the AT1 performed quite well in both environments, although the 145 mm of front and 110 mm of rear wheel travel meant that the rider had to take it easy on the rough stuff. The rear dampers had the usual three-position spring preload adjustment but whenever the suspension worked up a sweat, the poor rebound damping characteristics became very noticeable. First gear was low enough to get the 11 bhp bike up almost any incline, but the gap between first and second was too wide. Weighing in at 94 kg dry, the AT1 was significantly lighter than the DT1 and so would appeal to those looking for a light machine. The AT1 was competent for its time, and if anybody needed a last attraction to convince them to buy one, it must surely have been the price tag. At US$480, it was a bargain.

As with the DT1, a GYT kit was available for aspiring motocross or serious enduro riders. The kit contained the same components as for the DT1, including a chromed cylinder, single-ring piston, a 26 mm carburettor and a racing magneto. The increase in performance was just as impressive with a claimed 18 bhp output at the higher engine speed of 8500 rpm. The accuracy of these figures is now unknown, but if they were, and it is considered that the early YZ 125s were only producing around 20 bhp, the AT1-M was a pretty potent machine. Unfortunately, there was no feasible means of bringing the suspension up to the same standard as the engine.

The next of the T series to be announced was produced with zero development costs. The CT1 arrived on the market towards the end of 1969, with a total of about 30 original components. It was quite simply an AT1 bored out from 56 mm

to 66 mm, with the same stroke, giving a capacity of 171 cc. The rest of the engine and transmission were AT1 items. Even the exhaust pipe was borrowed from the new version of the AT1 with an electric starter, the AT1-B. The chassis was identical. The increased capacity of the engine added 4 bhp to the power output, and, since the weight had only increased slightly, produced a noticeably quicker machine. No GYT kit was available for the CT1, although it was possible to make use of some of the components of GYT kits for other models if extra power was required.

Towards the end of 1969, came the first reports of the machine everyone had been waiting for since the DT1's introduction in 1968. At the beginning of 1970, production started of the 351 cc RT1 machine, a DT1 with more power. The similarity between the DT1 and RT1 was very apparent but there were more differences than the AT/CT comparison. Rather than simply bore out the 250, Yamaha developed a new engine

The RT1-B big-bore black beauty was a better machine

based on the design used for all the T series. The new cylinder dimensions were an 80 × 70 mm bore and stroke, once again a slightly short-stroke engine, but with a 6000 rpm maximum engine speed, no attempt had been made to get the engine to rev. Where possible, components from the DT1 were used, differences only occurring when it was felt safer to strengthen a component. A slight change was made to the way the cylinder head was fastened. A total of eight studs were used, four short studs bolting the head to the cylinder and another four long-reach studs extending from the crankcase halves up to the cylinder head. This was a rather unnecessary modification, since the compression ratio was scarcely altered from the DT1, and four bolts had been adequate then. Clutch and transmission were carried over from the 250, although a heftier kickstart lever was provided. The carburettor grew to a 32 mm throat diameter and a different exhaust pipe was used.

The chassis remained largely untouched, varying in only a few minor details. An extra bracing tube was added to the frame behind the engine. The swinging-arm was of conventional circular-section tubing and not box-section. The front forks were of the same design, but with thicker, stronger stanchions and secured to the steering stem with double pinch bolts. The rear wheel was a mixture of AT and DT designs, with a half-width hub as on the AT, but the rear brake was fully floating. In contrast to the white DT1, the RT1 was offered with a jet-black colour scheme, that was equally attractive.

Claimed output of the RT1 was 30 bhp, which was eight more than the DT1. The powerband extended from about 3000 rpm up to the maximum 6000 rpm engine speed, and under this range the engine was a little too docile. On steep inclines this could be a problem, since the engine would either stall or the rear wheel would spin. On the tarmac, the machine was good for 80 mph, and the handling was reasonable, in the dry at least. The semi-knobbly tyres were not so effective on a wet road surface, as could be expected. One problem the early RT1s suffered from was quite serious pre-ignition, which manifested itself with kickbacks when being started and 'pinging' once under way. The starting problem was solved on the RT1-B which appeared in 1971, by the provision of a compression release mechanism linked to a lever on the handlebars. As the lever turned, a cable linked to it pulled out a small valve located above the exhaust port in the cylinder, thus reducing the cylinder compression. The standard cure for the pre-ignition when under way was to add a second copper cylinder head gasket. A redesigned head on the RT1-B solved the problem for good.

With the introduction of the RT1, Yamaha decided to extend their GYT kit contents to include some alternative transmission components. The new ratios for the first three gears were all higher than those fitted as standard. The effect of this was to close down the gaps between gears and result in a close-ratio gearbox. The alternative ratios were most suitable for the desert type of enduro where the standard lower gears would have been of little use. Heavier clutch springs were also available. Since the transmission of the 350 was common to that of the DT1, these items could also be used by the 250 riders. The rest of the kit was virtually identical to the other GYT kits in the T series. One slight difference was the use of an alloy cylinder with an iron liner instead of the chromed cylinders offered before. While a chromed cylinder wall reduces the piston/cylinder friction somewhat, it is not possible to rebore, so a seizure means that the cylinder is ruined. By using the conventional iron liner, it was possible to perform rebores and the difference in performance was not significant. Brackets were also offered to mount a wider front mudguard to the bottom of the headstock where it would provide more protection to the rider. Highlight of the year for the RT1-M in 1970 was its win of the Mint 400

YAMAHA 125 MOTOCROSS
AT1-M

A lightweight Motocross machine featuring outstanding performance. Even the roughest, without losing vetes to the power of this ATM. Primary kick starting in any gear for extra convenience. Authentic 5-speed transmission operation extra smooths for super-fine changes at any speed. Extra-high ground clearance with skid plate for complete protection from damage on any terrain. Yamaha's exclusive auto-proven Autolube oil injection system keeps engine performance smooth. Double clutch horse design. The tough yet light weight of the Motocross class.

YAMAHA 250 MOTOCROSS
DT1-M

This big 283 has all of the guts to get across the roughest country with all the ease of cruising down the turnpike. Built to take the shock and punishment has no other machine its size. Famous 5-port engine delivers exciting power under all conditions. Has powerful torque for unequalled GO power. Now looped hood and plug for compression release. Special long-stroke front forks engineered to take all the bounce and shock of cross-country riding. Super-smooth wide-ratio 5-speed transmission works with amazing ease in any speed range. A machine unequalled in its class.

YAMAHA 360 MOTOCROSS
RT1-M

This husky machine has a frame design which will withstand all of the brute power and punishment of the Motocross and stands ready for more. The amazingly powerful short-stroke engine makes the roughest terrain seem like a Sombre ride. The smooth 5-speed transmission and incomparable handling ease make this machine a beauty to operate. Special non-slip knobby tires for superior traction. And, even on the wildest terrain, the front fork and rear suspension make the riding almost as comfortable as the smoothest highway.

The 1971 M variants of the T-series machines were almost identical to their road-going brothers

in the Nevada desert near Las Vegas, following in the footsteps of its brother, the DT1, which had won in 1969.

Not content with a range of large-capacity trail machines, Yamaha also started a number of minibikes of less than 100 cc capacity. The first of these was the HT1, which was a 90 cc capacity single modelled very closely on the AT1 and indeed sharing a number of components with its larger relation. The engine produced a claimed 8 bhp at 7000 rpm and used the same transmission and frame as the AT1. A GYT kit was also available for the tiddler. In 1971, a 100 cc variant was produced, the LT2, based very closely on the HT1 and HT2, and with a GYT kit that resulted in 16 bhp at 10,000 rpm. This was the forerunner of the YZ100 that was to be produced into the 1980s. During 1970 two more minicycles were announced, the 58 cc JT1, which fell out of the mainstream of the T-series development by being powered by a utility rotary valve engine and not equipped with lights.

The machine was later to develop into the GT80, with a piston port engine, and it was manufactured through to the 1980s but was purely a fun bike. A 50 cc version, in the form of the FT1 was also offered, and this became the GT50 and followed the same path as the GT80.

So by the end of 1970, Yamaha had a comprehensive range of dirtbikes varying in capacity from 50 cc to 350 cc. The sales in the US, Australasia and Japan remained buoyant and the series was turning into a real cash-cow. A number of minor updates had been made to the original DT1, in the model years since its introduction. The year 1970 saw it receive an upgrade with some of the parts from the RT1, and attention to a few of the problem components that had been identified in the previous two years. In addition revised port timing liberated 2 bhp from the engine. Cosmetic changes were made to the complete series for 1971. But Yamaha had something more interesting in the pipeline and they considered it important enough to increment the model number as the new machines were produced in the summer of 1971. Yamaha christened the new concept

'Torque Induction' but for the more knowledgeable in the motorcycle world, it was simply the resurrection of the reed valve.

Reed valves had first been used in anger by DKW, the pioneers of the two-stroke racing engine. Back in the 1930s they had fitted a single petal reed to their split single 250 and had achieved a respectable 25 bhp power output at 4500 rpm. However, the theory had outstripped the material technology and valve breakage forced DKW to move on to other engine designs. On marine engines reed valves began to appear more often and after World War 2, the Mercury engine company started using reeds on all their engines. During the 1950s, the appearance of two-stroke reed-valve chainsaw engines from Mercury and McCulloch led to their widespread use in the newly established world of go-kart racing. Inevitably unhappy with the performance of the industrial engines, extensive experimentation by backstreet tuners led to the development of the type of reed valve Yamaha were to use.

Yamaha had decided that the improvement the reed valve brought in terms of mid-range torque were exactly what was needed for serious off-road engines. The basic problem of the two-stroke engine is the need to use asymmetrical inlet timing to produce the most power. During the intake phase of the cycle, it is desirable to open the inlet port as early as possible in order to give the engine plenty of time to fill the crankcase under the rising piston. The more the charge that can be induced and burnt, the more the power that will be produced. During the exhaust phase of the cycle, the inlet port should be closed as soon as possible to avoid significant blow-back of the charge out of the engine. If both these results can be achieved, the engine will pull like a tractor. The only problem is that a single component is responsible for both conditions and one is achieved at the expense of the other. If the skirt of the inlet side of the piston is cut away, the inlet port opens early, plenty of charge gets into the engine, only to be blown

back out again as the piston descends. This blow-back is resisted initially by the inertia of fresh charge flowing into the crankcase and inlet tract resonances, but fresh charge will be lost.

The concept of the reed valve seems simple when considered superficially. Place a uni-directional valve in the inlet tract and the problem of blow-back is solved. The practical implementation of the concept is not so easy. The valve must be designed so that it responds instantaneously to the vacuum forming under the rising piston to open and provide no impediment to the flow of fresh charge into the crankcase. It should remain open for as long as possible, closing only as the pressure rise in the crankcase threatens to blow the charge back out of the engine. The resulting design was inevitably a compromise.

Yamaha's reed valve consisted of a base plate to which was fastened a wedge-shaped aluminium die-cast block. Four pairs of metal strips were attached at the base of the block, each pair consisting of a thin stainless steel petal and a thicker strip curved out and away from the block. There were two pairs of petals on each face of the block

A typical Yamaha reed valve of the 1970s, although the earliest versions used only four petals

and the base plate bolted to the barrel with the wedge pointing down into the cylinder. The block was cut away underneath the metal strips. As the vacuum grew in the crankcase and assisted by resonances in the inlet tract, the free end of the thin reed of stainless steel would snap open against the curved metal stop, allowing the charge to flow down into the crankcase. As the vacuum dropped, the tension of the reed would cause it to snap back closed, preventing any flow back from the engine. A thin coating of neoprene on the reed stop and base block acted as a cushion for the violent motion of the reed.

Complementary changes to the inlet side of the engine were necessary. A window was cut in the inlet skirt of the piston. This served two functions. As the piston descended on the downstroke, it uncovered an extra port that had been cut in the cylinder wall above the inlet port. In fact it was not so much a port as a gully, that passed down to the inlet tract between the reed valve and the cylinder. At the moment the port was uncovered the windows in the piston skirt were open to the inlet port and so charge in the crankcase was drawn up through the extra boost port. Yamaha had been searching for a way to make use of the cylinder wall above the inlet port since the days of their disc-valved racing engines. They had claimed that their five-port system in use at the end of the 1960s had achieved a similar effect, but they had clearly not been satisfied. The secondary function of the windows was to expose the reed valve to the crankcase vacuum as soon as possible on the upstroke. The sooner the reeds cracked open the more the charge would be flowed into the crankcase.

Windows were used rather than pistons with a shorter skirt because the piston would not have been adequately supported by the cylinder wall, and would have failed quickly. There were now a total of seven ports in the cylinder, four conventional transfer ports, inlet and exhaust port, and the extension of the inlet port that aided the scavenging process. Later, Yamaha were to use the 'seven-port engine' and 'Torque Induction' slogans to the full as more of their two-strokes, both road and race machines, adopted the same configuration.

The first of the T series to undergo conversion to reed-valve operation were the DT and RT entering production in June 1971, followed a month later by the AT. A conversion was exactly what it was, since the machines were left largely untouched except for the addition of the reed valves and the corresponding engine updates. These changes included cylinder, head, piston rejetted carburettor and pipe, but apart from a strengthened fifth gear in the transmission nothing else was altered. An attempt was made to improve the chassis slightly by providing rear suspension with dual-rate springs. This would improve the damper's compliance over small bumps without increasing the chance of bottoming out on the larger bumps. Also two sets of optional springs were available, softer and harder than standard. The frame design was unaltered, but tube diameter increased and extra gusseting was provided around the steering head in an attempt to eliminate any flex. The maintenance of the swinging-arm was improved by the provision of a grease nipple in the hollow pivot bolt, allowing *in situ* lubrication. The position of the footpegs was raised 50 mm to keep the rider's feet well away from the rough stuff.

The reed valves seemed to do their job very well, with a noticeable increase of power across the entire range of engine speeds. Unfortunately this was negated by the enormous increase in weight as a result of the chassis changes. Consequently street performance was slightly poorer than the last of the T1 models and the extra weight made itself felt on the trail. Realizing that this would be unacceptable on any serious motocross bikes, no GYT kits were produced for the DT2 or RT2. Instead a competition model was offered as a complete machine under the designation M for Motocross. With a lighter frame, wheels and some engine components, the com-

The snake in the grass. The first contemporary reed-valve-equipped road bike was the DT2 of 1972

Top of the range DT360A at rest at the 1973 Amsterdam Motorcycle Show with an Astro-turf carpet thoughtfully provided to help it feel at home

petition machines were a handy 18 kg lighter than their standard counterparts! This weight reduction coupled with 32 bhp of the DT2 and 39 bhp of the RT2 made them real flyers. One interesting feature of the RT2-M was its use of CDI ignition, marking Yamaha's first use of this superior system on a production dirtbike. Bultaco had been using CDI for several years. Suspension was reasonable, but incredibly unsophisticated in comparison with the units available just a few years later. Rear wheel travel was totally inadequate for serious motocross competition.

The initial changes made to the AT2 in 1971 were limited to the application of the reed valves. As on the other machines this resulted in an increase in power, especially at the low and middle range. An AT2-M was also available with a significant weight reduction and a claimed 20 bhp at 8500 rpm. A year later, with the introduction of the CT2, a number of other improvements were made, such as new front forks, rear swinging-arm, a more efficient air filter and an uprated crankshaft for the combined starter/dynamo that was used on the electric start variant. The CT2 remained simply a bored-out AT2.

Not too much changed in the transition from the 1972 DT2/RT2 series to the 1973 models known as both the DT3/RT3 and DT250/DT360. In fact, it was purely the replacement of the 19-inch front wheel for a 21-inch item. The larger front wheel had been fitted to the motocross models in 1972 and it was felt that the extra stability this would produce due to the accompanying increase in rake would be beneficial on the street. Unfortunately it seemed to do more harm than good to the cornering capabilities of the bikes, since the front end felt twitchy and oversensitive.

1973 also marked the year of division between the development of the DT series as all the dual-purpose machines were to be designated, and the competition models in the form of the MX and YZ models. Initially the MX models bore a very strong resemblance to the pre-1973 M variants, but they were soon phased out by the top-line YZ series that bore less resemblance to their streetbike cousins. The true enduro riders also moved on to the motocross models before the introduction of the IT series in 1976. Consequently, with more suitable machines available for the serious off-road rider, the DT series became more oriented to the very casual trail rider. Effectively they were the street scramblers of the 1970s.

The LT3, AT3 and CT3 were all given the DT designation and offered for sale in Australasia, Europe and the US. The HT1 became the DT90 and remained a domestic model. The A and B model years for the small DTs passed uneventfully, with literally only cosmetic differences indicating the arrival of a new year. For 1976, minor updates were performed, with a slight increase in the compression ratio, revised carburation, steeper rake, the infamous Thermal Flow rear suspension units and a fraction more suspension travel. In 1977, the 125 and 175 once again marked time, without even a cosmetic change, the C models remaining for sale through the year. The DT100 underwent another minor update, giving a slightly higher compression ratio and revised front suspension. It was to remain in this form until withdrawn from the Yamaha range as a mass-production model in 1981. It all seemed like the small-capacity DTs were being allowed to drift away into obscurity. That was until 1978.

The DT125E and DT175E were totally new machines, with a design based very clearly on the YZ125D of the previous year. In 1977, the YZ125 and newly introduced competition enduro IT175 models had also been very close in design and a year later more of the small-capacity two-stroke dirtbikes could be given Yamaha's latest technology. Power output remained approximately the same, although a radial head was used. The main engine change was the addition of an extra gear in the transmission. With the comparatively low power output of these machines, the extra gear enabled the gap between the gears to be closed down and allowed the engine to be kept on the boil. In addition, the 175 was the recipient of a CDI

Above **Typical of the uniform DT series of 1973 was the DT175A, differing little from the CT3**

Above **This 1980 DT175-MX is typical of the small range of DT models that survived into the 1980s**

Right **This YZ lookalike was created in 1984 and in 12 bhp restricted form ended up being the best seller in its class**

ignition, the 125 retaining the old magneto unit. The frame was now of the latest monoshock design with the De Carbon rear damper located within the backbone of the frame. In contrast to the YZ unit, no damping adjustment was possible. The little DTs were extremely competent dual-purpose machines and justifiably received *Cycle World's* vote for the best dual-purpose machines of 1977, despite being 1978 models.

This 1978 redesign was to mark the last big change for the two DT models. As the DT100, they were to remain for sale in the US until 1981, when the Environmental Protection Agency (EPA) anti-pollution regulations forced them out of the market. In Europe they were to remain for sale as the MX models and received one or two new components such as an aluminium box-section swinging-arm. In the UK, the 125 was to be transformed into a YZ replica complete with liquid-cooling, power-valve, YEIS, Mono-cross suspension and a 12 bhp restriction. The machine was intended for youngsters before they obtained their driving licence. Various DT clones continued to be offered in various parts of the world right up to the mid-1980s, but the bloodline was broken in 1981.

The story of the large DT models is much the same. For 1974, the DT250A and DT360A shared many components with the MX motocross models. Most important were the new frame, with a slightly different backbone arrangement, and the front and rear suspension. The increase in wheelbase of 35 mm improved the straight-line stability. In the engine, the reed-valve assembly was widened and a total of six petals used. The increased flow of the inlet tract was accompanied by an increase to a 28 mm diameter carburettor on the 250 while the 360 retained the old 30 mm unit. The gearbox on the European models had different ratios for second, third and fifth, whereas the models for the rest of the world were not altered. CDI ignition made its appearance on the DT360, but the 250 had to make do with the conventional magneto.

For the following year little changed on either bike. The cylinder head was of a radial design but of the same volume. The gear ratios for the rest of the world were used on the European machines as well. Both machines benefited from the use of a half-width front wheel hub and a slightly larger front brake. Crankcase sidecovers were magnesium alloy replacing the previous aluminium items. The bore of the 360 was enlarged by 5 mm and produced a total capacity of 397 cc resulting in the DT400B. The increased capacity was accompanied by the move to the next size Mikuni, namely 32 mm.

The last year of the MX versions of the 250 and 400 was 1975, so from this time on the DT models were on their own. As if to indicate this, the 1976 versions were identical to the B models. With the introduction of the XT500C that year, the days of the 400 seemed numbered, although it was lighter and more manoeuvrable on the trail. But the DTs were not finished yet.

As if they had been harnessing their strength, Yamaha produced a major update for the 1977 DT250 and 400 by giving them a monoshock-equipped frame. Being the keymark of the YZ motocross models it was logical that the design should be applied to all Yamaha's dirtbikes. The frame design was essentially the same as that found on the YZs, with a massive backbone frame member in which the De Carbon rear shock absorber was mounted. A rather strange feature due to the street-based functionality of the DTs was the provision of a quickly detachable rear wheel as found on the IT series of pukka enduro models. The geometry of the frame was the same with a 30·5-degree rake and the wheelbase was unaltered. A number of engine changes were made to improve the mid-range power, resulting in a lot of new components. Most significant was the move to an eight-petal reed, pre-empting the YZ series by five years. Also the 250 was provided with CDI ignition, bringing it in line with the 400. A very smart styling update was applied to the DTs emphasizing the substantial upgrade over the previous models. A number of functional changes completed the package with rubber-mounted traffic indicators, plastic mudguards and sidecovers, an oil tank that swung out for refills and a lockable toolkit box.

The 1977 models were the last time that the larger DTs received a significant upgrade. The E series was unchanged and the 400 didn't make it to the F series in the US. On the chassis of the DT250F, the rake of the frame was brought down to a quicker 28·8 degrees after this had been successfully used on the IT series. The engine of the US 1979 DT250F only underwent changes that were essential to allow the engines to meet the increasingly stringent US EPA regulations. The Pulsating Air System, as Yamaha christened it, was a small air filter clamped to the

Above **The DT250B ready for business. The remote reservoir rear shocks were a spin-off from the motocross development**

Below **Although more suited to road-riding, the DT250B had enough of everything to provide some fun out on the trail**

frame backbone, which was attached to the cylinder just above the exhaust port via a short hose. Inside the air filter was a four-petal reed that allowed air to be drawn into the exhaust manifold, via a drilled passageway, when the exhaust port opened. The fresh air oxidized some of the unburnt hydrocarbons and reduced their percentage in the exhaust gases. The set-up was enough to meet the EPA's regulations for 1979 and 1980 but for no longer. In the rest of the world the DT250 and 400 struggled on into the 1980s, but by 1981 the number of sales, under strong pressure from Yamaha's own XT, TT and IT ranges, were insufficient to justify continued production and the bike, directly related to the machine that had started the off-road revolution, slipped into history.

Above **The monoshock rear suspension hit the streets with the DT series of 1977**

Below **One of the last with one of the first. The writing was on the wall for the DT400D, and the XT500D next to it was due to take its place**

3 | Factory fame and fortune

An incognito works Yamaha 250 that won the Japanese National championship in 1967

The best thing that ever happened to Yamaha's racing department was the decision by Husqvarna's motocross team manager to put Torsten Hallman out to grass at the end of the 1970 season. Hallman had been with the company since 1958 and brought them four 250 World Championship titles. They were anxious to cut the 250 team to two riders, hoping that the higher per capita expenditure would enable them to successfully take on the Suzuki steamroller that had landed the first three places in 1970. So Heikki Mikkola and Hakan Andersson were chosen. Ironically both were later to play leading roles in Yamaha's onslaught on the GPs. But what to do with Torsten? They couldn't fire him—14 years with the same motocross team is a lifetime in the racing world. Husqvarna and Hallman were synonymous. There was only one solution, make him an offer his pride wouldn't allow him to accept, and maybe he'd leave on his own accord, buy himself a motorcycle business in some quiet corner of Sweden and settle down with his memories of past glory.

And it almost worked. They made him an offer for support in the 1971 season that he couldn't accept and he left of his own accord. But he didn't settle down and slip into obscurity. Knowing his age counted against him, Hallman realized that his most valuable asset was his experience and he had a shrewd idea who might want to make use of it—Japan.

At the end of the 1967 season Suzuki were

Hideaki Suzuki hurrying his GYT-kitted DT1 to a win in the 1969 Japanese junior 250 championship

One of the factory Yamahas that were campaigned in Europe during 1970. This shot was taken at the Isle of Man TT race motocross meeting in June of that year

looking for a European rider to develop their RH 250 machines that had been campaigned without success for two years. As they had done six years before in the road-racing world, they didn't hesitate, but went straight to the 1967 World Champion, Torsten Hallman. They were two days too late, for Torsten had just re-signed for Husqvarna. Disappointed at the lost opportunity, Hallman nevertheless recommended that they contact Olle Pettersson, who subsequently joined Suzuki and helped develop the machines into the championship winners they were to become.

At the 1970 Italian GP, a squad of Yamaha engineers armed with cameras and endless supplies of film had swept through the paddock photographing and noting everything there was to be seen. A couple of weeks later, Hideaki and Tadao Suzuki turned up at the motocross events held at the Isle of Man during the road-racing TT week, with two factory DT1-MXs and came away with a third and sixth place in the international field. Clearly the factory were considering an entry into world championship motocross

competition. But why in Europe? Surely with the enormous growth in off-road sales in the US and the expectation of a similar explosion in off-road competition, the people to be impressed by factory successes were on the other side of the Atlantic. To understand why Europe was so important, the state of motocross competition in the two continents should be considered.

With a heritage dating back to a time before World War 2, European motocross had matured into a rider's sport. The initially slow development of pure off-road machines had led to the need for riders to compensate by honing their own skills to enable them to master the cut and chopped roadsters that were to pass as motocross motorcycles for so long. Even with the introduction of more suitable machinery from the beginning of the 1960s, these skills lived on, passed from old to young in the continuous process of renewal which all sports undergo. In contrast, US motocross racing was in its infancy at the start of the 1970s, undoubtedly gathering momentum in its rush towards fully-fledged acceptance in the US world of racing, but without the pedigree to be found in Europe. US riders were still in the process of developing from gifted amateurs with a stack of enthusiasm into cool hard-headed professionals. The European riders that toured the US in the famous Trans-AMA series of the early 1970s were treated as demigods capable of miraculous things on a dirt-track. Typically, the young Americans were quick to learn and as the sport blossomed their skills kept pace until by the end of the 1970s, their ability had matched, if not surpassed, those of the Europeans they had so admired. But it was professionals that the Japanese needed when they entered the sport at the end of the 1960s. Only they had the experience to turn the drawing board specials into championship winners. Success in their hands would be respected on both continents, and with respect would come sales of the mass-produced race-replicas.

The phone call Hallman made to the director of Yamaha's new European HQ, Kuramoto, when he realized he must leave Husqvarna, must have seemed like manna from heaven. Not realizing the work required to produce a good machine, Yamaha were initially only interested in a one-off analysis of their machines, but Hallman convinced them that a full-time long-term development rider was essential if they were to stand any chance of success. One month after his initial contact with Kuramoto, Hallman left Yamaha Motor NV with a three-year contract to develop the machines that were to become the YZ series.

Within a couple of weeks two pairs of machines arrived in Sweden. Hallman's contract had been to develop the complete range of Yamaha motocross machines and he received the 125 and 250 immediately. At the time, the beginning of 1971, the only Yamaha machines that could be considered motocross bikes were the MX versions of the AT, DT and RT series. Expecting to have to start with these mediocre packages, Hallman was surprised to find completely new engine units. Not only new, but of a radical new

Above **The factory AT1-MX that was delivered to Torsten Hallman at the start of 1971, which Tommy Jansson used to win the Swedish championship**

Above **The DT2-based 250 that Torsten Hallman received from Japan to develop into a world championship-winning YZ**

design. The reed valve had made a reappearance on racing motorcycles. Later that year the DT and RT machines were to appear with the first mass-produced reed-valve engines.

Clearly a lot of work had gone into the design of a totally new power plant for the new motocross machines, with very promising results. Hallman did a little work on the engines

Above **Note the lack of oil pump on the clutch side of the 250 engine block**

Above **In true contemporary two-stroke fashion, dual spark plugs were provided on the works 250 to allow a switch when the first one oiled up**

to see if he could improve the power, but soon decided that the engine was good enough as it was, if only the power could be used. Typical of most Japanese motorcycles of the time, the handling left a lot to be desired. Hallman decided that the machines would be competitive, if the chassis was improved.

Showing that little had changed in the inter-mediate five years, the factory were quick to respond to the call for redesigned parts. Minoru Tanaka was assigned to act as contact man between Hallman and the factory. He had been one of the first Yamaha employees to come to Europe as a mechanic for the road-racing team in 1963. His role was crucial in communicating, quickly and concisely, the design changes required for new parts coming from Japan. It took the factory just two weeks to redesign, produce and dispatch a new rear hub after both of the original hubs failed. Yamaha had bought into the motocross world and were placing their full weight behind the endeavour.

Not long after the start of the 1971 season, the bikes were considered to be competitive enough to enter some of the non-GP international meetings that were held throughout Europe. The 125 was entered in the Swedish National championships, where it was raced by Tommy Jansson to a championship win. Despite the fact that in the years before the 125 class was awarded GP status there was little factory interest in this class, the championship win was a considerable achievement, coming in the machine's development year. The 250 class was a lot more difficult. Hallman gave the machine its racing début at Steyr in Austria, being flagged off as the winner only to be disqualified for cutting the course. By the middle of June, Hallman was confident enough to enter the 250 in the Dutch GP. Riding in pouring rain on the sand circuit of Bergharen, Hallman brought Yamaha their first GP points with a 9th place in the first leg backed up by an 8th place in the second, to take 7th overall. This confirmed Hallman's own feeling that the development was heading in the right direction and demonstrated to the Yamaha management that their trust in Hallman's development skills was not misplaced.

In the meantime, two new crates had arrived in Amsterdam for the attention of Hallman and Tanaka. The open class machines were ready for analysis. The two machines were very different.

Above **Tanaka making last-minute adjustments to Hallman's machine prior to the 1971 Dutch 250 GP**

Right **Hallman getting his head down in the pouring rain to finish seventh and bring Yamaha their first world championship point in Holland in June 1971**

One was an RT1-MX power unit slotted into a frame very similar to the one being used for the 250. The engine was not 100 per cent standard, with a re-ported cylinder and more efficient exhaust pipe. The other bore no resemblance to any existing machine, with sandcast magnesium crankcases, a totally new diaphragm clutch, identified by the reinforced ribbing on the engine covers and the external worm gear operating mechanism, and reed-valve induction. The barrel was base-mounted to the crankcases, allowing fuller use of the cylinder for the transfer ports. No Autolube oil pump was provided, the lubrication being provided by pre-mix as was usual in the race world. Capacity was around the 400 cc mark, producing about 40 bhp transmitted to the rear wheel through a five-speed gearbox.

It was decided to race the two new arrivals back to back in a Dutch international meeting at Lichtenvoorde. Hallman asked Arne Lindfors, a successful Swedish national rider, to help him out. Lindfors used the 400 special and finished an overall 3rd behind Husqvarna riders Gerrit Wolsink and Christer Hammargren. Hallman took 4th place in the first leg, after a split exhaust

Above and above right **The two open class machines that arrived in Holland in the summer of 1971. The first was clearly derived from the RT1, whereas the second was a completely new machine. Note the compression-release mechanism operated from the left-hand handlebar**

had relegated Lindfors to 5th place, but in doing so aggravated an old back injury that prevented him finishing higher than 9th in the second leg. An encouraging début for the machines, which then disappeared behind closed doors for further development work, not to reappear that year.

Yamaha management were satisfied enough with 1971 as development year to decide to officially enter the motocross GPs of 1972 with two riders in each class. Once again the factory went to the top riders of the period to solicit their services at Yamaha. Runner-up to the all-time great Joel Robert, World Champion in the 250 class, was Hakan Andersson, one of Husqvarna's works team members. Flying in the face of his extremely conservative nature, Andersson was persuaded to leave the Husqvarna fold and to lead Yamaha's attack on the 250 title, supported by Lindfors. For the open class, Husqvarna were again robbed of two of their riders, Swede Christer Hammargren and Jaak van Velthoven of Belgium. The 250 was very similar to the one rid-

den by Hallman the year before at the Dutch GP, although a winter's development had brought the power up to a very respectable 35 bhp at 8000 rpm, comparable to the Husqvarnas and Suzukis of the time.

Again, two machines were available for the 500 class, a 351 RT1-MX clone, with 40 bhp on tap at 7000 rpm and a full 490 cc version of the 400 that had appeared the year before. This was a monster of a bike said to produce the incredible figure of 50 bhp at 6000 rpm, a full 10–15 bhp more than the other works machines in the class. Despite the enormous power output, the engine power delivery was flat enough to allow a four-speed transmission to be fitted. Jaak van Velthoven was given the unenviable task of wrestling the machine through the GP season.

In an attempt at improving the race-long consistency of the rear suspension, new shock absorbers were used with an external oil reservoir to assist in the cooling of the damping oil. This was the eternal bugbear of motocross suspension since the oil in the shock absorbers used to damp out the resonances of the suspension spring reaches very high temperatures under race conditions. The higher the temperature, the lower the viscosity of the oil and the poorer it does its job of damping. The external

The 1972 360 machine that Jaak van Velthoven was happy to race and win on

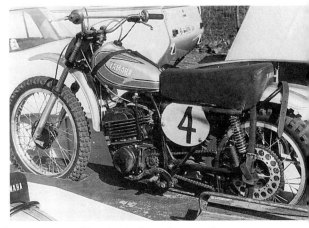

The 1972 490 machine that Jaak was happy to leave on the trailer, even with a 420 cylinder mounted

reservoir helped in two ways, it enabled more oil to be present in the suspension unit and it kept it cooler. The disadvantage of using such a unit lay in its vulnerability to damage during a crash and its addition to the total unsprung weight of the machine. The shocks were also rebuildable with the possibility of adjusting compression and rebounding damping separately, by the use of different jets within the body of the unit.

The year 1972 turned out to be unbelievably successful for Yamaha, after an initially disastrous start. While training in Belgium at the end of March, before the first of the GPs, Hakan Andersson crashed heavily and broke his right wrist. He was unable to ride in the first two rounds in Spain and France and was only able to circulate slowly, way off the pace at the Dutch GP. But then he started getting into his stride; a 3rd and 8th in Czechoslovakia, a 5th and 8th in West Germany, 2nd in Poland, 4th in Russia, 3rd in Finland and finally, the triumph of his home GP. Racing at the track in the town of Husqvarna, a stone's throw from the factory, Andersson brought Yamaha their first motocross GP victory, adding insult to injury by beating Husky-pilot

Arne Kring in the process. Continuing to ride well and getting good results meant that Andersson finished second in the world championships in Yamaha's first year of competition. A tremendous achievement, only shadowed slightly by the performance of the World Champion for 1972, Joel Robert. Riding for Suzuki, he was already World Champion by the middle of the season. The combination of Robert and Suzuki was almost unbeatable.

The 500 class produced less sensational but quite satisfactory results. Pre-season testing of both the 490 machine and a sleeved-down 420 convinced van Velthoven that he would be better off sticking to the proven 360 engine. The first two GPs were disappointing, with Hammargren finishing just within the points and van Velthoven retiring. From the third round in Sweden, van Velthoven began to feel more confident on the 360, and started turning in some good solid rides into top five places. He even took the 420 out for an airing in the UK and West Germany, taking 3rd place overall at both GPs. Back on the 360 for the last GP at Luxembourg, on a mudbath of a circuit, he came home second in both legs to win the Grand Prix. The date 13 August, the time 17.00, a couple of hours after Hakan Andersson had brought Yamaha their 250 GP victory in Sweden, making it one of the most important days in the annals of Yamaha's competition history. Final position in the world championship was a solid 5th place, a very satisfactory start to Yamaha's challenge for the 500 crown.

While Andersson and van Velthoven were busy racing the machines developed during 1971, Hallman was working on the next season's bikes. In particular he was concentrating on a new suspension system that would result in the most radical change in motocross chassis design ever witnessed: the monoshock suspension. In

Above **Scarcely recognizable after a particularly muddy meeting in 1972 is Hakan Andersson's pre-monoshock YZ**

Below **Hallman discovering that the 1972 360 machines needed a little more rear-end travel**

the world of off-road competition, the chassis has always played as large a role, if not larger, in the success of a machine as the engine. An underpowered machine with a good chassis can often outperform a powerful machine in a poor chassis. It has always been a question of usable power and on the arduous motocross circuits of the world it is the chassis that holds the key to success. The 50 bhp 490 monster of the factory had proved the point.

Power can only be transmitted to the ground when the rear wheel is in contact with it. On the rough terrain of a motocross circuit, the profile of the surface can only be followed by the rear wheel fitted with soft suspension, which would then bottom out on jumps making the machine uncontrollable and exhausting the rider. In order to allow a reasonably soft spring but to reduce the chance of bottoming of the suspension units, designers were tempted to increase the stroke of the suspension by fitting longer units. However, this raised the height of the rear subframe on which the rider was sitting, making it more difficult for him to reach the ground as needed to stabilize the bike. The result was the inevitable compromise, offering reasonably sensitive springs and a manageable seat height.

Lucien Tilkens thought he had a better solution. Recognizing that the limitation on suspension stroke arose from the upper mounting of the rear dampers, he developed a cantilever system reminiscent of that used on the Vincent roadsters of the 1950s. The conventional swinging-arm was topped by a wishbone-shaped second fork that ran up from the rear axle at 45 degrees and whose apex was a point behind the rear wheel. A bolt passed through bushes welded to the end of the upper fork and acted as pivot mount for the lower end of the suspension unit. Both upper and lower forks had cross-bracing just behind their pivot mounting points. Additional vertical bracing ran between the two forks a few inches from their join and between each

Above **The monoshock revealed. A chassis design that was to become very familiar to production YZ owners during 1974 and 1975**

Right **Hakan Andersson flying to the 1973 250 World Championship aboard his monoshock YZ250**

fork's own cross-bracing, making the rear swinging-arm assembly fully triangulated. Initially circular-section tubing was used, later to be replaced on the upper fork by square-section to improve the rigidity further. The pivot shaft for the lower fork ran on roller bearings, a departure from Yamaha's usual practice of using bushes. The suspension unit extended from behind the wheel to be fixed to the bottom of the headstock by a rose joint. Total wheel travel increased by 100 per cent for the same seat height, making softer springs possible, thus helping to keep the rear wheel in contact with the ground. In addition, the triangulation greatly improved the lateral stiffness of the swinging-arm, prevented the rear fork from twisting under the high lateral forces experienced when diving into and driving out of a berm. It had to be a winner.

Hallman was convinced that the monoshock system was better than the conventional twin Girlings so universal at the time. Having

thoroughly tested the 250 using Tilkens' original frame, he ordered up a copy in Reynolds 531, which cut back some of the excessive weight of the first prototype. With this frame, Hallman felt ready to go GP racing. There was just one small problem: the complete system was patented by Tilkens, who was asking what he felt was a reasonable amount of money for the patent rights. Despite being an insignificant amount for a company Yamaha's size, they wanted to be certain they were getting value for money. So towards the end of 1972, a series of top managers beat a path to Hallman's door, armed with stopwatches to measure how many tenths of a second the new suspension would knock off his lap times! More importantly, they asked Hallman as an experienced motocross rider whether the system really was better. Yes, was the answer every time and finally they agreed to buy.

Having convinced Yamaha management of

Hideaki Suzuki had the joint honour of débuting a monoshock-equipped Yamaha in 1973 when he and his brother Tadao wheeled out their 125s at a Japanese meeting in March of that year

the advantages of the monoshock system, the real work began—convincing the riders. The team riders did not consider themselves to be development riders. They had been hired to win races and they expected the means to this end to be ready and waiting. Andersson was reluctant to use the new machine. He had been doing well at the end of the 1972 season on the conventional twin-shock bike and he wanted to continue with it. Even after back-to-back tests, just prior to the start of the 1973 season, he remained unconvinced. He used the conventional machine at the first two rounds in Spain and Italy, finishing 4th in both GPs.

The delay in débuting the 250 meant that the world's first glimpse of a monoshock-fitted bike came when the Suzuki brothers, Yamaha factory riders, wheeled out two 125 prototypes for the first Japanese national race of the year. Tadao won, but then left for Europe to contest the first season of official FIM European 125 motocross GPs. At the next 250 round in Belgium on 2 May, Hallman, supported by Yamaha management, insisted that Andersson use the monoshock machine. The result was a 3rd place in the first leg and a win in the second to take an overall win. A week later in Switzerland it was a double win, and from that moment wild horses couldn't have separated Andersson from the monoshock machine. With overall wins in the next five GPs including three double-leg victories, Andersson romped away with the 250 World Championship title. In only their second year of serious competition, Yamaha, relying heavily on the development skills of Torsten Hallman, and the riding skills of Hakan Andersson, had produced a world-beating machine. The intense rivalry between the Japanese companies must have made it an especially sweet success, as it was from Suzuki they stole the crown.

Works specials for the common man

The MX range of 1973 was cosmetically identical, this 250 virtually being indistinguishable from the 360

By hiring Torsten Hallman in 1971 to develop competitive motocross machinery, Yamaha had taken the first step on the path to what they surely hoped would be glory on the European circuits. There was only one reason why they were so anxious to produce championship winning GP racers, and that of course was publicity. Just as they had ten years before in road-racing, they were entering factory specials in the GPs in order to win races, gain publicity and sell bikes. Whereas the intention at the beginning of the 1960s had been to sell roadsters through road-racing success, it was now Yamaha's intention to sell off-road bikes through motocross GP success.

In Europe the sales of the T series had been disappointing in comparison with the explosive sales that had occurred in the USA. GP victories would undoubtedly bolster the European market for off-road machines, especially if it were combined with a concentrated sales drive from the European importers. Also Yamaha had decided that yet another lucrative market was awaiting exploitation throughout the world. Having pushed the idea of the dual-purpose motorcycle for five years, and noticing the good sales in the US of their race-kitted T-series machines, the factory decided that the world was ready for mass production of single-purpose motorcycles, off-road competition bikes.

As always, the success of the factory-prepared machinery would have a direct effect on the sales of mass-produced versions from the same factory. The advertising concept of the factory machines in the winners' circle being linked to the company's mass-produced product always worked, especially if technology identified with the factory machines could be adapted for mass-production without a long time-lag. 1971 was to see both the first year of factory-supported GP competition, and Gary Jones' first US 250 championship win for the factory and 1972, Jones' second title and the launch of the company's first out-of-the-crate motocross racers, the MX250 and 360 and the SC500.

The two MX machines were newly developed machines, departing from Yamaha's policy until then of producing a limited number of race-kitted DT or RT machines within the factory walls. A casual inspection would have suggested that the 360 was purely a bored and stroked version of its little brother, but in fact it contained a number of significant differences. The basic construction was the same. The matt black barrel of both machines contained a cast-iron liner with the seven-port system introduced on the T series. Six-petal reed valves were used with a 30 mm Mikuni on the 250 and a 34 mm for the 360. The foam air filter was tucked out of harm's way in a plastic housing bolted to the rear mudguard. An upswept spring-mounted exhaust was used on both models, something that was not universal on all motocross machines of the time, since it was thought that the resulting shape seriously compromised the production of the resonant waves that were so vital to the correct functioning of the pipe. A demountable stinger was provided for the pipe, leaving it to the discretion of the owner as to whether or not it would be used.

There were two threaded holes in the cylinder heads of both models. One came with the spark plug installed and the other with a blanking bolt. This was a hangover from the 1960s when riders had fitted two plugs to the head so that a quick swap of the plug cap could put the bike back in action on the all too frequent occurrence of an oiled plug. Ignition systems had improved enough to make the precaution redundant. The 360 was fitted with a compression-release valve that was activated by the throw of the kickstart lever. A cam mounted on a dowel pin in the right-hand crankcase half followed a profile in the kickstart ratchet gear, and secured one end of a braided cable. The cable passed up and over the engine to the front of the barrel where the compression-release valve was located. As the kickstart lever descended, the tension of the cable pulled out a small plug in the cylinder wall just above the exhaust port. The plug passed through a small bleed valve that screwed into the barrel, resulting in a drop of pressure inside the cylinder dependent on the size of the venturi in the bleed valve, until the piston rose above the valve and sealed the combustion chamber. It worked quite well, making the pressure required on the kickstart about equal to that of the 250, something a tired rider with a stalled engine at the end of a 40-minute moto would appreciate.

All crankcase bolts, including those joining the vertically split crankcase halves, were Allen bolts, a thoughtful gesture to the mechanic, making the engine assembly/disassembly easier. Conventional Japanese crankshaft design was utilized, with full-circle flywheels running on roller bearings. The conrod ran on a big-end roller bearing and the single ring piston ran on a needle bearing. Primary transmission was taken off the right-hand end of the crankshaft by means of a helically cut gear. In addition, on the 360, two extra sprockets were splined to the crankshaft just inboard of the primary transmission gear. Their purpose was to drive the 'Omni-Phase Balancer' weight running at the top of the gearbox behind the cylinder.

Yamaha were really getting into the spirit of christening any change made to the basic design of a motorcycle with a hi-tech inane name. Joining the 'Torque Induction' (reed valves) and the

'Thermal Flow' rear shocks (external oil reservoir) was the Omni-Phase Balancer, whose purpose was to eliminate crank-induced vibration on the MX360.

This system had been first seen on the ill-fated TX750 which preceded the introduction of the MX350 by a couple of months. The TX750 was Yamaha's entry in the Superbike class, although it hardly lived up to that description. A parallel four-stroke twin based on the 650 released in 1970, it was fitted with a contra-rotating weight that was intended to smooth out the legendary vibrations immortalized on big British twins. Due to the difficulty of installing the drive for the contra-weight without compromising the layout or size of the engine block, a reflected L-shaped drive was necessary. Two idler gears ran on the inside of the duplex chain at the heel and toe, while the chain passed on over the crankshaft sprockets to drive twin sprockets keyed to the end of the contra-weight shaft. Supported by roller bearings at both ends, the weight was profiled to provide an equal and opposite reaction to the forces generated by the rotating mass of the crankshaft assembly. A spring-loaded tensioner was also needed to ensure full contact between the crankshaft sprockets and the chain. It was a sound theoretical solution to vibration damping that proved disappointing in practice.

Inevitably, Autolube lubrication was also provided, driven from the right-hand end of the crankshaft. At this time in Yamaha's history, *all* two-stroke machines they made were fitted with Autolube, whether practical or not. This resulted in the strange sight of road-race and motocross machines fitted with this neat little accessory that had done so much for the street-based two-stroke machines. It was out of place on a racetrack, as Yamaha realized after a couple of years.

On the left-hand end of the crankshaft was the rotor for the CDI ignition. The clutch was of the design adopted by Yamaha from the end of the 1960s. A pushrod passed down the length of the transmission mainshaft to bear up against the outer clutch pressure plate against the tension of six clutch springs and allow the friction plates and clutch plates to freewheel. The clutch basket was spring mounted to the primary transmission gear which acted as a cush drive.

Identical five-speed gearboxes were used on both models although the overall gearing on the 250 was a little lower due to different primary and final drive ratios. The transmission shafts ran on ball bearings on the drive end and rollers at the other end. Primary kickstarting was provided allowing the bikes to be started in gear, an essential feature for all dirtbikes but not universally adopted for some years. The activation mechanism for the drum gear selector differed slightly from that found on the T series. The double gear-change pawl mechanism was replaced by a single pawl operated via two interleaving gear-change quadrants, one splined to the gear-change shaft and the other turning on a shaft on which one of the selector forks ran. The gear-change pawl was clipped to this quadrant. The use of a single pawl for moving up and down the box should, in theory at least, have produced more accurate and smooth changes. All three selector forks ran along rails, with pins following the tracks cut in the surface of the drum.

Both MX250 and 350 models made use of the frame of big brother, the SC500. The general design was similar to that used on the T series, with a number of detail changes. It consisted of a double loop cradle with a short backbone of considerably wider diameter tubing, supported by a pipe running from a crossbar under the headstock to its end. The 30-degree rake fell in line with the geometry of contemporary motocross machines. The front suspension used conventional oil-damped telescopic forks with 32 mm diameter stanchions. The rear swinging-arm with Yamaha's usual plastic bushes was fitted with the Thermal Flow rear suspension units. These were production versions of those used on the works bikes in Europe, offering five levels of preload adjustment and an external reservoir of damping oil. Both brakes were single leading-shoe drums, 130 mm at the front and 150 mm at the rear. Aluminium alloy rims were used on both wheels with security bolts fitted to prevent the tyres turning on the rim during hard acceleration or braking. The finish of the machines was in a distinctive silver grey with a red stripe on both sides of the petrol tank highlighting its shape.

Going into production at the end of 1972, the MXs reached the US and Europe at the beginning of 1973 and were received enthusiastically. The 250 proved to be the better of the two machines, with a far smoother power delivery up to its limit of 7500 rpm, with usable power coming in around 4000 rpm. In contrast, the 360 was pretty docile under 5000 rpm, after which power came in with a bang getting the front end a little light. This coupled with the weight problem suffered by both bikes, made the 360 a bit of a handful. The front brake was about right but the rear locked up too easily, which would also cause some rear wheel chatter revealing a weakness of the rear suspension. Berm bashing was not too easy on an MX mainly due to its excessive weight as well as a rather high centre of gravity, caused by a tall seat height. But with a price in the US of a little over $1000 for the 250 and $150 more for the 360, they were considerably cheaper than the European alternatives and almost as good.

Actually, a third motocross machine was introduced at the same time as the two MX models, but its appearance on the market is one Yamaha would like to forget. Still supposing that the US market adhered to the philosophy that 'a lot is good, but more is better', Yamaha went for a full 500 dirtbike, using the MX360 as baseline. The stroke was kept to 70 mm but the bore was opened out to 95 mm, giving a displacement of 496 cc. The bore of the carburettor was raised to 38 mm, the gearbox lost one speed, but little else changed in the engine. On paper a reasonable-looking bike pushing out 44 bhp—

5 bhp more than the 360. But a combination of poor-quality control and basic design flaws emphasized by the size of the bike turned it into a horror story on two wheels that earned the distinction of being included in the list of *Cycle World*'s ten worst motorcycles of the decade.

For some reason it was given a different series classification and went under the title SC500, some speculating that the SC stood for 'Scrambler'. From the start it was plagued by seizures. This was quickly traced to the first batch of pistons, whose skirts had not been correctly machined, and a service bulletin issued. Other frequent causes of complaint were failed ignition systems, cylinder base gaskets poorly matching the transfer ports, terminal detonation and a miscellany of minor problems. Even when running correctly, there was little that the SC500 could do well. Hampered by an enormous gap between first and second gears, slow corners were taken either with the engine revving madly or way out of the powerband, requiring excessive clutch slip. The handling didn't help at all in corners, for with a high centre of gravity and badly flexing front forks, the bike ended up seriously oversteering. As on the MX models, the rear brake locked the rear wheel at the slightest touch, although the front brake was a lot better. Despite the Omni-Phase Balancer a lot of vibration made its way to the handlebars tiring the rider prematurely, a state that was aggravated by the excessive compression damping in the front forks causing the transmission of most of the jolts straight to the handlebars.

All in all, the SC500 turned out to be a good example of one of the bad apples all motorcycle manufacturers seem to manage to turn out at one time or another. To their credit, Yamaha quickly realized this and the SC disappeared into welcome obscurity at the end of 1973.

With the introduction of the MX machines, Yamaha had produced bikes that would appeal to what they expected to be the largest market for motocross competition, the novice and

The big bad apple of Yamaha's early motocross line-up, the SC500, trying to pass itself off as a more docile 360

junior groups and possibly with a little help the intermediate class, all of course being at amateur level. But the way the sport was expanding in the US at the beginning of the 1970s it was becoming clear that a substantial professional group of motocross riders was developing for which the MX series would be totally unsatisfactory. The company decided that the only machines that would attract this group of riders would be replicas of the factory team machines, built as close to the real thing as possible, with only minor concessions to mass production. It would be a limited series due to the size of the market Yamaha anticipated and the high price that would have to be paid for such competitive machines. Only one name was suitable, the one used already to describe the factory team's machine—YZ.

Although of similar design to the MX series, there were virtually no common components. The few YZ components borrowed from their tame brothers came from the SC500. Engine dimensions were the same, the 360 having a bore and stroke of 80 mm × 70 mm, the 250 measuring 70 mm × 64 mm. The iron liner of the MX-series cylinders was rejected in favour of a chromed cylinder wall that reduced friction without compromising the oil-retention properties of the surface. This technique had been perfected by Yamaha during the 1960s on their TD and TR road-racers. The most serious disadvantage of chromed cylinders was that they were usually only good for junk after a seizure, adding to the cost of racing. The same double-securing of cylinder and head was used as on the MX series, but there was only a single central plug hole.

Crankshaft design was the same as for the MX series, with the addition of circlips to position and retain the oil seals and bearings. Both 250 and 360 used the big-end fitted to the MX360, which actually dated back to the RT1. The con-rod had extra oil grooves milled in the big-end eye, to improve lubrication. Windows were not cut in the skirts of YZ pistons. Instead, to gain the maximum intake period free of obstacles in the inlet tract, the skirt was cut away on the inlet side. The cost to be paid was shorter piston life due to the lack of support in this area as it slapped against the cylinder wall in a reaction to the pressure generated during the combustion process.

Primary transmission take-off was on the right-hand crankshaft end and the CDI unit of the same design as on the MX machines was keyed to the left-hand crankshaft half. The 12-plate clutch no longer had the spring cush drive and was activated slightly differently. The actuation mechanism was housed within the left-hand crankcase cover, and was accessible for adjustment via a small window. A short shaft with a worm thread cut in its outer surface was attached to a flange that enabled it to turn in its housing in the left-hand crankcase cover. A stud passed through its centre to butt up against the pushrod of the clutch, and was locked in place by a nut. Hence, as the shaft turned the pushrod would be pushed along the transmission mainshaft to free the clutch. Identical ratios were used in both the 250 and 360 gearboxes, with the gap between first and second reduced considerably with respect to the MX gearing. The old double pawl selector mechanism was retained for the YZs although all three selector forks ran on rails running under the gear clusters.

On the intake side, 34 mm Mikuni carburettors were used on both the 250 and 360 machines, with six-petal reed valves from the SC500. Access to the air filter was restricted due to its position behind the sidecovers and under the upswept exhaust pipe. Both had to be removed before the air filter cover could be loosened and extracted. In acknowledgement of the fragility of the exhaust pipe and the consequences a damaged pipe could have to a race, the pipe was spring mounted in three places.

The basic chassis design was unchanged from the MX series, although the tubes used were thicker-walled and of smaller diameter, resulting in the saving of a few pounds. The Thermal Flow rear shocks were cast in an aluminium alloy that also contributed to the dramatic weight difference between the MX and YZ models. The front wheel remained unchanged for the YZ series, but the rear brake shoes were widened

10 mm to increase the swept surface area, although more attention should have been paid to improving the sensitivity—it was as bad as ever. Probably the most distinctive feature of the early YZ series was the inch-wide rubber band round the petrol tank, securing it to clips on the headstock gusseting. While it certainly was distinctive, it was probably not so practical in view of the damaging effect petrol has on rubber. Capping the peaked filler on the tank was a breather pipe that passed under the front of the tank to a spot not easily accessible to dirt and mud. All components that were expected to be sources of heat, including the reservoir of the rear shocks, were painted matt black to increase their degree of radiation and hence improve their cooling. With the silver petrol tank highlighted by the red flash in Europe and the bright competition yellow in the US, the YZs were the cosmetic equal of any other machine on the track.

But were they the functional equal, or better still, superior? As soon as it became known that a batch of race replicas were to be offered for sale, Yamaha dealers were inundated with orders, especially in the US. Gary Jones' championship win in 1972 had prepared the path for the YZ series and from May 1973 they were available over the counter, in theory at least. In fact Yamaha had only manufactured a comparatively small batch of both models expecting the demand for the milder MX machines to be greater and the price to be too high. At $1700 for the 250 and $100 more for the 360, the price was a good $600 higher than the MX models, and $600 could pay a lot of entry fees and full gas tanks. But the YZs were clearly superior to the MX machines. The 250 weighed in at 94 kg, a saving of 9 kg over the MX250. Without the complications of Autolube oil pump, Omni-Phase Balancer and decompression-release mechanism, the 360 lost a massive 17 kg and this, combined with the extra 4 bhp both engines developed, brought the handling and speed up to the same level as the Husqvarna, Bultaco and

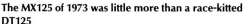

The MX125 of 1973 was little more than a race-kitted DT125

The MX100 appeared in the US towards the end of 1973 and set a standard that was to help its successors to survive for ten years

CZ competition. Although considerably better than their stable mates, the YZs were far from perfect. The powerband on the 250 was too narrow, requiring a tap dance on the gearchange pedal to keep the engine on the boil. Both bikes tended to fall into corners due mainly to the high centre of gravity, and there was always that rear brake. . . . So Yamaha had manufactured a good first attempt at an expert's machine, but there was plenty of room for improvement.

During the same month as the YZs began arriving in the US and Europe, another two MX models began running off the assembly lines, the 100 and 125. Just as their larger brothers, they were derived from the T-series MX variants, but qualified for a separate code due to their assembly as fully-fledged motocross machines. The general design differed little from the MX250, except for the lack of CDI ignition; breaker points and a magneto were considered adequate for the tiddlers. Only the four bolts to the crankcase studs were used to secure the cylinder head. A Mikuni carburettor, 24 mm for the 100 and 26 mm for the 125, fed the four-petal reed valves and the exhaust pipe was spring mounted at the

exhaust manifold. A five-speed gearbox, Auto-lube lubrication and Thermal Flow rear shocks completed the spec. Neither available in Europe, the MX100 produced 12 bhp at 10,500 rpm whereas the MX125 produced 15 bhp at 8500 rpm. To catch the attention of the younger riders Yamaha expected the MX125 to appeal to, the petrol tank was decked out in the factory's US racing colour—bright yellow.

In fact Yamaha needed to use every trick in the book, if they were going to enter the 125 class seriously, for, of all the classes, this was the one with the most choice of machines for potential customers. Not only were the other Japanese companies interested, Suzuki already producing TM 125, Honda a CR125 Elsinore and Kawasaki about to introduce the KX125, but European and US competition was still strong. Husqvarna, Bultaco, Penton (KTM), Monark, Rickman and DKW were all established in the market. Yamaha hit them where they knew it would hurt most—price. At $800, the MX125 was anything from $150 to $400 cheaper than the European competition. Only the other Japanese manufacturers could compete in this area.

With so much activity on the motocross area, it took the factory until the end of the year to produce the parts required to transform the MX125 into a YZ125. A higher compression-ratio cylinder head along with revised porting and a new pipe resulted in a 4 bhp increase. The mechanical ignition was discarded in favour of a CDI unit. The gearing was lowered for all except first gear, to improve acceleration and give the rider a chance in the race to the first corner. The suspension was firmed-up front and rear, including the light alloy Thermal Flows used on the larger YZs. In fact a comprehensive weight-saving exercise was adopted on the YZ125, with new frame, alloy wheel rims and hubs and magnesium backing plates for the single-leading-shoe drum brakes at both ends, helping to drop the weight by 12 kg. In line with its increased performance the YZ retailed for $960, not only a lot more expensive than its brother but also more than the Japanese competition.

If it had been a lot better than the Kawasaki and Honda, its most serious competitors, it might have been worth the extra $100. But it wasn't. The main culprit was the suspension which was way too hard and of course that rear brake. The two combined to make braking on a bumpy approach to a corner not far short of trying to ride a steer that had just been stung by a hornet! The rest of the bike functioned quite well with a 2000 rpm powerband from 7000 rpm and reasonable gearing, although perhaps a shade too low. It was a fair start to the 125 series, but the price was too high and the ride too harsh.

The MX variant of the 125 was not to remain in the Yamaha range for so long. With only cosmetic changes being performed in 1975, it was 1976 before any significant update was made to the machine. The power plant of the YZ125C was grafted into the original MX125 chassis and the rear suspension improved by the use of twin Kayaba gas shocks, laid down at 30 degrees from vertical and inverted to reduce unsprung weight. The package worked pretty well and offered a machine that was as good if not better than the Honda and Kawasaki 125s, but not of the same standard as the YZ and Suzuki. But for the $890 retail price it was an absolute bargain. Despite this, there were no MX125s included in the factory line-up again.

During 1973, the Yamaha works teams on both sides of the Atlantic did well. Hakan Andersson took the 250 world title on his monoshock machine, and Dutch exile Pierre Karsmakers took the open class title in the USA. Karsmakers campaigned the 250 Monocross during 1974 with considerable success, taking the Supercross 250 title, but was deprived of a championship win in the AMA National championship due to the introduction of regulations requiring US citizenship for all competitors. But the bright yellow Karsmakers/Yamaha monoshock combination was the talk of the US motocross world in 1974 as Hakan Andersson had been in Europe, the year before. With the new models for 1974, Yamaha would make total use of the publicity their works teams had created and completely in keeping with their philosophy of offering last year's works technology on this year's production machines, the monoshock YZ250 and YZ360 machines were introduced.

Yamaha were cautious in their introduction of the monoshock models. They restricted the changes to the machines mainly to the redesign needed to fit the single rear shock absorber and new swinging-arm. The only engine change was the use of a cylinder head that raised the compression ratio slightly. This, coupled with the new pipe that was needed to route around the rear shock, broadened the powerband slightly making the YZs, in particular the 250, somewhat easier to ride.

The exhaust pipe followed a route any rollercoaster would have been proud of in an attempt to maintain the volume and dimensions

Jaak van Velthoven was Yamaha's most successful 500 cc class rider from 1972 to 1975

necessary for efficient engine combustion, while passing through a maze of engine and chassis components seemingly determined to prevent it. In order to simplify removal, the header was spring mounted to the rest of the pipe, with a copper gasket to provide a good gas seal. The complete assembly looped down to the left-hand side of the machine, round the outside of the duplex cradle frame members, up and crossing over the engine, and was bolted to the right-hand frame member behind the sidecover. A separate stinger silencer was clamped to the end of the pipe and bolted to the upper rear sub-frame rail.

Another component that suffered from the use of the monoshock was the air filter box. It was no longer possible to mount the air filter vertically behind the carburettor with access under the seat. The new design used a twin element filter lying horizontally behind the carburettor with access via both sidecovers. This was in fact a far better arrangement, simplifying and speeding up the most frequent chore required for any dirtbike, the cleaning of the air filters.

The general design of the frame didn't change much but the area around the headstock was beefed up in expectation of the extra stress to which it would be exposed with the top of the monoshock bolted to it. The reinforcement took the form of extra gusseting between the backbone of the frame and the front downtubes, as well as double bracing rails between the front and back of the cradle. Access to the upper end of the monoshock was via a hole cut in the gusseting behind the headstock. The swinging-arm assembly looked pretty much like the works component, with round tubing for the lower fork and square section for the upper. The production version was made from chrome-molybdenum, the factory item was aluminium.

The rear shock absorber was fully rebuildable, although it was not a task to be attempted by the home mechanic. With the reservoir moun-

Above **After an injury-plagued season in 1974, Hakan Andersson took this works YZ250B to second place in the 1975 World Championships**

Right **The YZ125C was the best machine in its class and Yamaha's first really proficient motocrosser**

ted on the base of the body of the unit, it made use of compressed nitrogen gas to provide the damping. The aluminium reservoir contained a neoprene rubber membrane that separated the oil from the compressed gas. The body of the suspension unit contained two sets of jets through which oil passed on compression or expansion. One set was always open and provided the low speed, small deflection damping, the other, normally capped closed under the tension of a leaf spring, opened up when the oil pressure exceeded the spring tension. As the oil flowed into the reservoir, the gas would be compressed further, increasingly resisting the further compression of the suspension. By separating the gas and oil in this way, the problem of frothing of the oil experienced with conventional shock absorbers disappeared.

Nitrogen was chosen in place of air since it does not expand as much as air when heated and could not form a combustible mixture if the membrane were to fail and the oil and com-

pressed gas were to mix. A measure of damping adjustment was possible by altering the pressure of the compressed nitrogen but it was hardly a trackside task. It was not possible to change the preload of the spring, but three different rate springs were listed as official parts. The new system was also no lightweight, the combination of swinging-arm and suspension unit weighing twice that of the conventional dual-shock A model.

Despite the shortcomings in adjustability, the new rear suspension was far better than the conventional dual-shock systems of the time. Offering 165 mm of travel, the suspension did not respond too well to small stutter bumps, feeling rigid and unresponsive. But the faster you went and the nastier the bumps you took on, the smoother it seemed. Neutral steering, quick turning, good straight-line stability were all characteristics of the new monoshock machines. While most of the credit for this improvement could be given to the rear suspension, the front had also undergone an upgrade. With thicker stanchions and less compression damping, it proved to be far more sensitive than it had been on the A models.

Although clearly distinguished by the rear suspension, the B models also got a cosmetic update, with new chequered decals on the petrol tank symbolizing the racing environment in which the machines were expected to be used. Also the capacity of the bike was shown on a decal on the yellow petrol tank to distinguish the two models. The first real Yellow Zappers were on the loose.

Meanwhile the pint pot class was running a model year behind. The YZ125A had first been available in any numbers at the start of 1974, just before the B models of its bigger brother began arriving in the dealers. Some bright spark decided to get them back in synch by leaving out the 125B designation and going straight on to the YZ125C for 1975. Fine. Only trouble was that no large-capacity YZs appeared in 1975, so

the 125 was now a model in front instead of behind its brethren. Tricky things model codes. Anyway, December 1974 saw a new YZ125 rolling off the assembly lines and no mistakes were made with the design; this one was on top from the moment it was born.

The YZ125A had suffered severely at the hands of the Suzuki and Honda opposition. Both engine power and handling finesse had been lacking and the 125 class was proving to be the one with the largest sales volume. The company were determined to get back in 1975 any ground they had lost to the Japanese competition. Major development work went into the engine design resulting in the most powerful 125 available on the market with an output close to 18 bhp at 10,500 rpm. A new cylinder head lowered the compression ratio a fraction and the chromed cylinders were rejected in favour of the conventional iron liner in an alloy muff. The piston was cutaway just above the gudgeon pin, as had become common practice in the road-racing two-stroke engines. This reduced the friction between the piston and cylinder wall, minimizing the heat produced from their contact and consequently preventing the breakdown of the oil film clinging to the cylinder wall.

The transmission gained a ratio bringing it up to a full six-speed gearbox. First gear was a little higher than on the A model and the gap between first and second had grown. The oil pump for the Autolube was discarded, bringing it in line with the rest of the YZ range. The carburettor was provided with a proper choke lever after persistent complaints from YZ owners of the pokiness of the tiny rod parallel to the slide housing on the carburettor that had previously been used to choke the engine. At 30 mm, the carburettor bore was also a size up on the previous model.

A complete monoshock chassis was constructed for the YZ125C, the layout of the frame remaining unchanged except for the modifications to the headstock area to allow access to the upper mounting position of the shock absor-

ber. The design of the monoshock suspension and rear swinging-arm was identical to that of the YZ250 and 360 B models, scaled down for the smaller 125, while the front forks and drum brakes were YZ250B items. The rear brake was unchanged from the A model. In Europe, the paint job on the petrol tank heralding the arrival of a new model was white with black pin-stripes just above the lower tank edge and 5 cm high YAMAHA in red letters. In the US, the mustard yellow of the racing team was continued from the MX125, with speed stripes along the lower edge of the petrol tank.

As on all the YZ models, the change to monoshock suspension had resulted in a weight increase, in the 125's case, 3.5 kg. But the new engine design produced so much more power, and the handling was so improved, it was a price the 125 could afford to pay. When it came to the track, the YZ was the leader of the pack, literally. The only other bike to measure up to the YZ was the new RM from Suzuki, who had tackled the problem of long travel rear suspension by fitting twin laid-down shocks. This worked at least as well as the monoshock and also gave a slightly higher rising rate of spring stiffness. It was only the 3 bhp power advantage of the Yamaha that kept the Suzuki at bay. By contemporary standards the YZ125C was difficult to fault and was Yamaha's first truly successful production motocross machine. *Cycle* included it in their ten best of the year in 1975, although it must be said, Yamaha had pulled a fast one on them and passed a semi-works machine through for testing. Despite this, the YZ125C was a worthy entry in the list.

Top left **The YZ125C engine conformed to standard contemporary YZ design. The bulge on the engine cover hides the CDI rotor pick-up**

Left **With a second place on his YZ125C at his home GP in 1975, Dutchman Gerard Rond broke into the world championship scene from nowhere**

Meanwhile, the MX models had marked time since their introduction at the beginning of 1973. In March 1974, the 100, 125, 250 and 360 bikes had been joined in the US by a 175. The 175 class was quite popular and at the time devoid of Japanese machinery, no doubt leading Yamaha to think they could easily exploit the small market for this class. The 175 was almost identical to the 125, with a 10 mm wider cylinder bore, CDI ignition and a 50 mm longer swinging-arm. Far from dominating its class, it turned out to be a dog of a bike, staggeringly under-powered and under-suspended. Pushing out a feeble 16 bhp, with a ridiculously narrow power-

Below **Despite its poor performance, the MX175 was a reasonable bike for novices, forcing them to learn the basics without intimidating them by its performance**

Above **Despite belonging to a different series, the similarity between the engine of this MX175B and the YZ125C was striking. So was the difference in performance**

band of less than 2000 rpm preceded by a 1000 rpm-wide glitch in the power curve, the springs on both front and rear suspension were far too stiff, giving a very harsh ride. The increasingly famous competition yellow paint job worn so proudly by other Yamaha motocross machines, seemed little more than a bad joke on the 175. Since the competition, CanAm, Bultaco, Penton and Puch, sold better bikes for a similar price, the MX175A was a dead duck. A year later the B appeared, with few changes except a new coat of paint and revised carburation that smoothed out the power delivery, making the machine a little better, but still not a shadow on the competition.

Surprisingly enough, the 175 motocross machines did not disappear so quickly from the

Yamaha range as might have been expected. The class seemed to be dying fast throughout the country, yet for 1976 the factory introduced a full-blown YZ175C, borrowing much from the YZ125, including the complete chassis. With around 22 bhp at 10,500 rpm and a fair amount of torque, the YZ proved to be at the top of the small group of 175 machines commercially available.

Only available for one year, there was no YZ175D in the motocross line-up for 1977. End of story, you might think. Not just yet; 1979 saw the reintroduction of the MX175, now being offered as a mildly tuned off-road playbike, which was exactly what it was. A cross between the on-road DTs and the off-road ITs, it was equipped with the usual reed-valve, CDI, Autolube engine in a monoshock frame. It fitted the bill quite acceptably, although suffering a little from the lack of basic equipment required for street legality. Enough of the MX175 were sold in 1979 and 1980 to justify continued production but it disappeared from the Yamaha range once and for all at the end of 1981.

Price rather than performance had sold the other MX bikes in the US at the local level, and the machines were becoming increasingly in need of an upgrade. But Yamaha were questioning the wisdom of the double range of motocross machines. The original idea of a cheaper, easier-to-ride bike being available alongside its full-blooded brother was a sound one. There were just two factors that worked against this. Someone entering motocross competition usually wants to win, and that was almost impossible on an MX. Worse still, while being considerably cheaper than a YZ, they were not a lot cheaper than the equivalent Suzuki and Honda mounts. Would the MX series be able to maintain a segment of the motocross market in the future? Yamaha were not convinced they could. They decided instead to try getting the price of the YZ models down towards that of the Japanese competition and at the same time produce

The MX175 as it reappeared in 1979. Technology had moved fast in the MX's years of absence and it seemed a dinosaur in comparison to contemporary machines

engines whose power was easier to use for expert and novice alike.

Strangely enough, Yamaha's first step in the direction of unification of the MX and YZ was to skip the 1975 update to the YZ series. The MX250 and 400 were significantly improved for 1975 and the YZ series for 1975 were in fact identical to these bikes. The factory's philosophy seemed to be that now the previous concept of limited-production YZs was to be discarded, the identity of the YZs more common brother should be used. It only took them a year to realize that the works connotations of the YZ designation was a valuable selling point.

Both bikes were fitted with cylinder heads with radial finning, giving the impression that high compression ratios were being used. Despite a new head design, the extra offset sparkplug hole was still present. The 400 maintained the use of the decompression valve operated by the kick-

start pedal. An alloy cylinder with iron liner was provided as standard, but for the guy on the block who had to have the trickiest bike in town, chromed cylinders were available as alternative parts. Rubber wedges were used on both the cylinder and head to cut the noise from ringing cooling fins.

The helical primary gear was no longer splined, but keyed to the right-hand crankshaft half. Autolube went missing on both 250 and 400 and the larger machine was also relieved of the infamous Omni-Phase Balancers that had so stifled its predecessors. The clutch on the 250 was inherited from the YZ, while the 400 continued to use the clutch basket with the spring-

The last and best of all the MXs was the 1975 MX400B. Despite reliability problems it became the desert rider's first choice in the US

mounted primary transmission gear. Transmission, ignition and carburation were largely unchanged, although the adoption of the monoshock forced the air filter arrangement of the YZ B series to be used. The transmission ratios from the 250 also came from the YZ B series whilst completely new gearing went into the 400. First gear was very low, with a large jump up to second. In fact the gears were all spaced slightly further apart than on previous big-bore models, culminating in a high top gear. The engine would have to produce good torque and have a wide powerband if the transmission was to be effective.

The monoshock chassis was inherited from the YZs, the only notable change being 34 mm diameter stanchions and the availability of front fork springs of different stiffness. However, what had proved to be so successful on the YZs did not perform so well on the new, more powerful MXs, particularly the 400. The larger machine had gained 5 kg over the YZ360B and the extra weight made itself felt on rough courses and in slow turns. In heavy, boggy ground and sand, the front suspension seemed far too soft, with a tendency to flex that gave the rider a lot of work wrestling with the handlebars to prevent the wheel digging in and high-siding him. The 400 seemed more suited to enduro riding and desert racing where it was used to win the 1975 Mint 400, as well as a lot of local amateur-level desert races. The chances to let rip with that gutsy motor and not too many tight turns suited it fine. The 250 was a slightly better MXer, with a good engine seeming to cause the suspension less

Above **Despite the magnesium engine covers, the MX400B was overweight, but this was compensated for by the gutsiest engine on the block**

trouble although at 100 kg it was also a little overweight. Rear brake on both machines needed to bed in before a measure of sensitivity was achieved, a carry-over from the bad old original MX machines. On the 400, pistons started cracking after only a few hundred miles of use. This was caused by a combination of too wide inlet and boost port on the rear cylinder wall and the square cutaway on the inlet side of the piston skirt.

The MX250 and 400B models were the last of their type in these two classes. Effectively, 1975 was the last year of the MXs; another 125 model appeared in 1976 and the 175 was resurrected at the end of the 1970s. The works machines had provided the publicity for Yamaha, the MXs had provided the introduction for many riders, and it was left to the YZ series to build on this foundation and put Yamaha at the top of the motocross tree.

Above **In Europe, Ake Jonsson was provided with this YZ400 for 1975, but it was an uneasy relationship and fourth place in the world championships was the result**

5 | The path to excellence

The YZ80 first appeared in 1974, but it was to take Yamaha a couple of models before it arrived at the top of the class

By the start of 1976, all four Japanese companies were locked in battle for the motocross manufacturers' crown, in all of the three main classes. Kawasaki was lagging behind the other three a little despite Jim Weinart's US 500 class crown in 1974 and Olle Pettersson's earlier efforts on the racetracks of Europe. Honda had concentrated on the US and thumbed their noses at those that had labelled them as incapable of making a competitive two-stroke, by producing the Elsinore series. Success was achieved at both national and local level. For 1973, Gary Jones was bought in, after two seasons as National 250 champion with Yamaha. A clear winner in 1973, Gary was pushed hard by Marty Tripes riding Husqvarna in 1974, but still took the title for the fourth consecutive year. In the first 125 series held in 1974, Marty Smith ran away with the championship for Honda and repeated the performance for 1975. For 1973 and 1974, the 125 and 250 Elsinores were virtually unbeatable at local level, but by 1975 Suzuki and Yamaha machines were getting the edge over the Hondas. Motocross competition in the US was about to enter the era of Yamaha's total domination of the 125 and Supercross classes and a see-saw battle in the 250 and 500 class between the factory and one of the other Japanese manufacturers. Glorious days for the company.

The 1976 line-up consisted of six YZ models — 80, 100, 125, 175, 250 and 400. The 80 cc class was fast becoming the most oversubscribed class in the US for the under-14s dreaming of bigger and better things in the future. Yamaha had produced the first YZ80A back in 1974 and it had been a competent machine putting out 7 bhp at 9000 rpm. The conventional piston-port engine was equipped with Autolube lubrication and was slotted in a duplex cradle frame with conventional dual-shock rear suspension. Unfortunately the Honda XR75 was quicker than the Yamaha and typically the US concern put out a comprehensive Genuine Yamaha Tuning (GYT) kit consisting of a new pipe, cylinder, head, piston, carburettor and main bearing that raised the output to a Honda-beating 10 bhp. For 1975, the GYT parts were incorporated into the stock machines and little else changed. For 1976, the suspension travel was increased at both ends, the front with longer stanchions, the rear with laid-down shocks increasing the arc of the rear wheel. The use of reed valves improved the low end of the engine enormously while the 24 mm carburettor and new cylinder porting helped push the output of the little machine to 12 bhp at 9000 rpm. The YZ80C was the fastest stock machine in its class.

The YZ100C and 125X (the X was used to get the model designations in line) were essentially the same bike. Apart from the obvious differences due to capacity, it was only the front suspension that distinguished the two. The 100 used conventional coil spring front suspension. The 125, 250 and 400 were all fitted with new front forks in which compressed air was used to cushion the rider.

Air has always been a tempting medium for fork designers due to its and any gas's progressively increasing resistance to compression. Unfortunately, the simple application of compressed air to provide the front fork cushion, resulted in either too little cushioning during the initial fork compression or too great a resistance to movement over the last part of the fork compression. Yamaha came up with a solution to the problem. An aluminium cannister was screwed

to the top of each fork leg. On the top and bottom of the cannister were two separate air valves that controlled the pressure above and below a floating piston that was located inside. Conventional Ceriani-type dampers were attached to the bottom of the stanchions.

There were therefore three adjustments that could be made to the forks, oil level, air pressure above the floating piston and air pressure below, which effectively meant within the stanchion. The air pressure under the piston regulated the initial movement of the fork, in much the same way as spring preload. The pressure above the piston was set to approximately double the stanchion pressure in order to define a point at which the floating piston would move and ease the stanchion pressure, much like a safety valve. A change of oil level would result in a change in compression ratio between the air and oil in the fork, similar to changing the spring rate of the fork. With the nitrogen-charged monoshock on the rear and air forks up front, the new Yamahas had infinitely adjustable suspension, in theory at least.

A few changes had been made to the excellent, if disappointingly poor-selling, YX125C of 1975. Inevitably the ports had been breathed on, with narrower, higher transfers intended to broaden the powerband a little. A change across the board for the YZs was the rounding of the cutaway on the inlet side of the piston skirts. The MX and YZ models of 1975 had suffered from drastically reduced piston life, due partially to cracking at the corners of the square cutaway. Carburettor diameter grew 4 mm to 34 mm and the CDI unit had an internal pulse generator for triggering the spark. The primary gearing was changed slightly to allow the use of a larger $\frac{5}{8}$ in. pitch chain after it was found that the correct drive sprocket would foul the cases with the new chain. The rear swinging-arm was lengthened 30 mm, the longer wheelbase improving straight-line stability. Some work was done on the monoshock unit to increase rear wheel travel

Air was used to suspend the 125, 250 and 400 motocross machines in 1976 and these aluminium cannisters provided infinite tuning capabilities

Although appearing to differ little from the MX400B engine, the YZ400C had been updated to improve reliability

to 200 mm with less spring preload.

Both the 100 and 125 worked well on the track, once some attention had been paid to the rear suspension. As delivered it was too stiff, resulting in a very harsh ride. A softer spring eased the problem considerably. With 18 bhp on tap, the 100 was a lot more powerful than its only significant competitor, the Suzuki. But the Suzuki's suspension was better and steering more precise making the two a pretty even match. The same was true with the 125. With almost identical top end, it was the greater mid-range power that gave the YZ the advantage over the RM, but it was really close. The suspension and steering on both machines was very good making the two almost inseparable, except for the $35 higher price of the YZ. Machine performance wouldn't be able to make the one a best seller over the other; that would have to be left to the advertising people.

Development of the 250 model was carefully restricted to correcting the deficiencies of the 1975 model. The engine was left largely untouched except for a new exhaust which flattened out the powerband a little and straight-cut primary gearing for maximum mechanical efficiency. Two extra bolts were used to secure the cylinder and head of both the 250 and 400 machines. Most changes were made to the chassis with new air forks, a tubular section upper fork on the swinging-arm, plastic drive chain tensioner, caged needle roller bearings for the lower swinging-arm pivot and what would appear to have been thicker mild-steel frame tubes. Apart from the slightly longer wheelbase caused by the longer forks, frame geometry remained identical, but the weight of the machine increased by 9 kg. This could only be accounted for by a sturdier frame which would correspond with some reports of broken frames in 1975.

Whereas little changed on the 250, little remained of the MX400B in the YZ400C engine. Additional piston support was provided not only by the redesigned inlet skirts found on all the C models, but also by a bridge in the rear cylinder wall between the boost port and the inlet port.

This was a direct reaction to the MX400B problems experienced by desert racers, who were forced to replace pistons after every race to maintain reliability. Detonation and seizures had also occurred on the old 400, and Yamaha's reaction to the seizure problem was to move to a two-ring piston. Their expectation was that the two rings would provide a better gas seal and reduce the chance of blow-by passing the rings, heating the piston wall and breaking down the oil film between the piston and cylinder wall. The factory tackled the detonation problem by replacing the CDI system and modifying the 38 mm carburettor needle jet so that it, and the main jet housed within it, were held at a lower position in the float bowl, resulting in reduced surges in fuel delivery when running over rough terrain. The clutch and transmission were unchanged in design, although stronger gears were used in the gearbox. The chassis was common to that of the 250.

Both 250 and 400 proved to be very good machines, the front suspension now matching the efficiency of the monoshock. Even the most difficult terrain was soaked up efficiently by the new set-up. The chassis changes combined with the less pipey engine power made the 250C easier to ride than its predecessor, the main criticism, except for the inevitable rear brake, being the slowness with which it steered through corners, a typical Yamaha trait of the time. The excess weight also made itself felt on both machines when the rider was negotiating tight turns. The 400 baulked at clutchless gearchanges so important in close racing, a criticism that had been made of the YZ125 before. Aside from these comparatively minor criticisms, the YZ250C and 400C functioned well and were as good, if not better than the Japanese competition.

There couldn't have been a sharper contrast between the official factory efforts in Europe and the US. For 1976, Yamaha had withdrawn from the world championship competition to get a

The compression-release mechanism that had been provided since the 1973 MX360 was still present on the YZ400C

team properly organized after the increasing shambles of 1974 and 1975. In the US, Pete Schick, Yamaha's motocross team manager, signed up a batch of promising youngsters to form what was to be the kernel of the team for the next four years. You can say one thing for Schick, he certainly knew talent when he saw it. Signed for 1976 were Bob Hannah in the 125 class and Rick Burgett in the 250. Hannah was

After four years of production, the 1976 Open Class YZ400 was reaching towards the title of class champion

factory machine that had been used in 1975 in the Japanese championships, the OW27. A small radiator was located behind a wire gauze front number plate nestling between the front forks. A water pump was located in the space vacated by the Autolube equipment and drove the coolant to the heavily finned cylinder and head. Output was judged to be around 23 bhp at 10,500 rpm. With mechanic Bill Buchka, who seems to have been the man behind so many US and World champions, to look after the factory machine, Hannah easily defeated reigning champion Marty Smith for his and Yamaha's first 125 title. The only panic of the season came when a disgruntled privateer invoked the AMA's infamous claiming rule to gain possession of the machine for $2000. Hannah immediately issued a counter claim and had the luck to be picked out of the hat! Yamaha got such a fright that the machine was rushed out of the country, to be replaced by the 1975 US factory machines which Hannah was able to win on equally well. Burgett had a less successful year than Hannah, finishing 7th, two points behind his team-mate who had also come out in a few 250 races.

The same 5 models were available in 1977 as the D series. The C series had been a success in terms of both sales and results, so it must have been tempting for the factory to allow the models to mark time for a year. With one exception, the YZ machines were updated for the new model year, the factory realizing that in the fantastic pace of development in which the motocross world found itself, the best machines of one year can easily be the worst of the year following. The competition, primarily between the three Japanese companies, was fierce.

The YZ80C had been the undisputed king of the egg-cup racers in 1976, the four-stroke XR75 of Honda finally well and truly beaten. No complacency from Yamaha; word was out that a new RM from Suzuki would appear in 1977. New carburation involved the next size Mikuni at 26 mm. Wider ports could be found in the new

stolen from under Suzuki's nose as they hesitated to sign him up for a crack at the National title after a few months riding for them in southern California.

Hannah immediately showed how ready he was for National competition by winning the five-race Florida winter series for Yamaha. For the 1976 attempt on the 125 title, Yamaha gave Hannah all they had in the form of a water-cooled

Yamaha's first water-cooled YZ125 was run in the US during 1976, until a close-call with the infamous AMA claiming rule caused Yamaha to restrict its use to Europe

cylinder. The transfers and intake grew 2 mm, while the exhaust came out 1 mm wider and 0·5 mm higher. The engine modifications added a single bhp to the bike's output bringing it up to 13 bhp at 9500 rpm. The chassis was not forgotten, 25 mm extra wheel travel was found at the front and 13 mm at the rear. A slight change in steering geometry, reducing the rake and trail helped quicken the steering of the bike. Out on the track it had the edge over the Suzuki, but it was only an edge. The YZ had a wider powerband and better front suspension, the RM turned more easily and soaked the bumps at the rear end better. Probably the $36 price advantage of the YZ was all it needed to outsell the RM.

Nothing changed on the 100 model, except the use of the new transmission of the YZ125D and the paint job. Hopped-up RMs had given the YZ a hard time in 1976, but the company didn't have the time or resources to spend on the 100 and the class was handed to Suzuki for safekeeping for a year. A new model appeared to keep face but it was just not competitive with the RM100B.

The 125 was once again a monoshock reed-valve six-speed single, but that's where the similarity with the YX125X stopped. The bike had undergone a major redesign during the winter of 1976 to produce what was considered by everyone to be a Hannah replica. Engine cases were cast with water passages at the base of the cylinder, an indication of the way Yamaha were pushing the development. The right-hand crankcase sidecover was magnesium alloy, whereas plastic was used to cover the CDI magneto and drive sprocket on the left-hand side of the machine. The separate head-to-cylinder and cylinder-to-crankcase fastening technique was lifted from the larger MX machines, to prevent any cylinder distortion or head warp caused by the different expansion rate of the aluminium muff and the steel fastening bolts. Inlet and exhaust ports were narrowed slightly to flatten out the powerband while the compression ratio was raised a fraction to 7·8:1. Lighter full-circle flywheels were found in the crankshaft, as Yamaha raised the engine speed for peak power by 500 rpm. The new conrod had large slots milled in the big-end eye to improve the bearing lubrication. The piston was

The last of the dual-shock YZs was this 80D model of 1977

two models old, dating back to the YZ125C. The carburettor throat diameter came back a size to 32 mm which was considered more suitable to the new power characteristics than the old 34 mm Mikuni. With the carburettor offset slightly to the left of the bike it was possible, due to the revised frame design, to incorporate a single air filter box, replacing the double unit that had occasionally broken on earlier models.

Primary transmission was still via helically cut gears, the power loss this incurred probably being imperceptible, but the noise reduction not. Three less teeth on the transmission gear raised the gearing slightly. An extra pair of plates was added to the clutch and the clutch-release push-rod was actually bolted to the outer pressure plate instead of butting up against it. The gearing throughout the gearbox was higher than had been found on the X model. The engaging dogs on the gears were also undercut less to help shifting under power, something earlier 125s had not excelled in.

Complementing the engine changes was the first upgrade to the chassis since the introduction of the monoshock suspension. As always con-

structed in mild-steel, the main feature of the new chassis was the frame employing an enormous pressed-steel backbone member extending from the headstock to the rear subframe. A single front downtube extended down to a point just above the exhaust manifold. Here a dual-rail cradle started and looped down under the engine up to the rear subframe. Cross-bracing for the cradle could be found under and behind the engine and bracing with the central backbone above and behind the engine. Really massive gusseting was present at the backbone/headstock joint.

The frame backbone had been so designed that the new De Carbon-type rear shock absorber fitted inside the tube and was attached to the headstock by a bolt that passed through both the backbone and upper eye of the suspension unit. This design resulted in a lower centre of gravity, as the upper rails of the frame had previously passed over the monoshock unit. The new rear shock had discarded the awkward cannister containing the nitrogen under pressure and the diaphragm separating it from the oil in the shock. It looked much like a conventional shock absorber with a half-length external spring. Preload adjustment was possible but necessitated the removal of the unit from the bike. Damping, both compression and rebound, was more easily adjusted with the unit *in situ*. A knurled ring at the top of the unit was accessible via a hole in the frame backbone and could be turned by a screwdriver. As the ring was turned, a rod within the unit was screwed in or out and the tip of the rod restricted or eased an oil jet, giving infinite damping adjustment. The material of the rod was so designed that as the oil temperature rose, the expansion of the rod would compensate the reduced viscosity of the oil by its increasing restriction of the oil jet. Ingenious.

The front suspension remained air-charged, but this was no longer an eye-grabber, since the air cannisters at the fork top had disappeared. The sophistication of the C-model forks had proven too difficult for the average rider to set up properly, so Yamaha bought in Kayaba air forks with a leading-axle. The air pressure was used primarily to prevent mechanical bottoming of the front fork, and not as a replacement or enhancement to the coiled springs. Leading-axle forks were coming into vogue in the mid-1970s as the manufacturers worked on increased wheel travel and found that the wheel axle at the end of the fork was in the way and correct steering geometry was not possible on the long forks with the conventionally placed wheel axle. With the same braking power as the X model, the retaining rod for the rear brake plate was replaced by a tongue and groove arrangement fastening it to the swinging-arm and preventing it rotating as the brake was applied.

The finished article weighed in at 88·5 kg, the lightest 125 motocrosser available despite the mild-steel frame and swinging-arm. The D model steered like a dream, going exactly where pointed, and the low weight and centre of gravity making it easy to throw about. The suspension was extremely good at both ends, the compliance of the rear end seeming to have been improved considerably. There were some reports of swinging-arm flex but it was not noticed by all tests of the period. The wider powerband made the 125D a lot easier to ride. The price was a slightly lower top end making the machine less attractive to expert riders who were happy with 1000 rpm wide powerbands. The clutch was a little too sensitive making it difficult to get the bike cleanly away from the start line without stalling or lifting the front wheel.

The amount of detailing on the bike showed how important the ergonomics of the machines were becoming. Properly cleated footpegs, soft foam handlebar grips, large neck to the plastic petrol tank, a front mudguard that provided real protection to rider and machine, plastic drive chain tensioner were all small details that added up to an excellent functional motorcycle. When lined up with the competition, there were two that could run with the 125D, one surprising, the other not. Once again Suzuki were there with a touch more power throughout the mid-range and top end and a suspension to match the Yamaha. Surprisingly, both Japanese machines were bested by one of the last traditional and competitive European motocross machine manufacturers—Husqvarna. Expert riders found the sharper and significantly higher power output combined with an excellent chassis much to their liking; the extra $400 over the Suzuki and Yamaha was not.

The same chassis was to be found on both the 250 and 400 models, using the design found on the 125. A small change was the use of a thick aluminium plate to act as mounting point for the rear engine bolts and to provide further bracing to the frame behind the engine. The mill of the 250 changed nearly as much as had that of the 125. The new 250 cylinder contained taller transfer ports and a wider exhaust while the inlet was lowered a touch to give more support to the inlet side of the piston. The new cylinder head raised the compression ratio a fraction. As on the 125, the bore of the carburettor throat came down

Lucky recipient of the YZ kettle was Gerard Rond who put it to good use by finishing runner-up in the 1977 World Championships

a size from 38 mm to 36 mm, matching the shrinking of the inlet port. The single air filter element was located under the right-hand sidecover. All five speeds of the 250 were lowered significantly, but the spacing widened slightly to take advantage of the incredible increase in midrange power over the 250C, due to the new porting and exhaust pipe. The clutch, common to both 250 and 400, lost two plates without any noticeable problems and the gearshift drum gained an outer roller bearing on which to turn, to eliminate any stiffness in the gearchange. The 400 underwent less engine changes, being restricted to new cylinder and head, exhaust, clutch, gearshift drum and air filter.

Both 250 and 400 were right at the top of their class, the 400 undoubtedly the king of the open class. The 250 was a revelation in comparison with its peers, where engines were either peaky and powerful or flat and feeble. For the first time there was a quarter-litre with a respectable top end and a sensational mid-range output. With more than 240 mm of travel at both ends of the bike, excellent steering geometry, at long last two effective brakes and a really comfortable riding position, the 250 was a very good machine. The 400 was virtually unbeatable, with considerably more power than the competition, and all the good handling characteristics found on the 250. In 1977, Yamaha had a range of motocross machines to be proud of.

The year 1977 proved to be a good one for the factory teams on both continents. In Europe, the hard man of Grand Prix motocross had been bought in from Husqvarna, Heikki Mikkola. Mikkola was capable of doing astonishing things with uncompetitive machinery, so when he was handed the factory 400 for the 1977 World Championship, he was almost certain to take the title. Nor did he disappoint the company for with nine wins out of a total of 18 legs, he easily brought Yamaha their first 500 motocross world championship title. In the 125 class, Dutchman Gerard Rond gave the god of the 125 class, Gaston Rahier, and his Suzuki a run for his money which resulted in Rond taking second place and Rahier his third successive 125 world title. When Yamaha had hastily withdrawn their water-cooled 125 from US competition during 1976, they decided to make use of it in the world championships. Rising-star Rond was entrusted with the machine but received no financial support from the factory. The maintenance of the machines was left to the experienced hands of Lucien Tilkens and the bike was the fastest, if not the most reliable, in its class for 1977 and 1978.

In the US, Bob Hannah and newcomer to the team Broc Glover, gave the factory every reason to be pleased with the year's results. During the winter of 1976/77, Hannah added to the aura that was building round him by winning all eight races of the Florida winter-AMA 250 series on a bog-standard YZ250C. Even when the works YZ250D machines became available Hannah persisted in using the standard bike to total 12 unbeaten races. He went on to take the Supercross championship, winning six of the ten rounds. In the National 500 class he was pipped by Marty Smith on the works Honda but still won two of the six rounds. The 125 National championship turned into a real nail-biter that went all the way to the last moto. Seventeen-year-old Broc Glover joined the Yamaha team after a successful year riding his own Elsinore in 1976 and ending up 5th in the National standings. He joined National champion Hannah in the 125 class and it was immediately clear that he was not going to be guarding Hannah's back. A three-way battle developed between Danny La Porte on the Suzuki and the two Yamaha riders. La Porte won the Hangtown opener, then Hannah won twice, then Glover and then Hannah again. Going into the last meet at San Antonio La Porte had 200 points, Glover 190 and Hannah 183. The complete Yamaha US motocross team, Mike Bell, Pierre Karsmakers and Rick Burgett, was entered to cover whichever Yamaha rider needed help. Glover won the first moto, shrinking La Porte's lead to five points. In the second race, Hannah built up a 30-second lead until team orders were made clear and Glover was let through to win the moto, meeting and National title by virtue of the same number of points as La Porte, but two meeting wins to the Suzuki rider's one. You can't get much closer than that!

By September 1977, the 1978 models were already being assembled in Japan. Once again the complete line-up from 80 cc to 400 cc were updated, in the case of the 125 and 250 as significantly as the C to D transition. Yamaha were pursuing a philosophy of continuous evolution, characteristic of all Yamaha's machine development. In 1978, the dangers of such a system were clearly demonstrated as the factory slipped behind the competition in some of the classes.

The YZ80E minicrosser went monoshock. At last Yamaha's trademark in the motocross world had been extended to the complete range. A De

Bob Hannah at the peak of his career in 1977 when he effortlessly won the US Supercross title and was runner-up in the 500 and third in the 125 class

Carbon-type shock, much shorter than the one found on the larger YZs, was mounted under the seat, the lower end bolted to the apex of the upper swinging-arm fork, the upper to the bottom of the frame backbone tubing. The frame was similar to that used on the rest of the YZs, with a single large-diameter backbone tube and a double-cradle engine support. Rear wheel travel increased 35 mm and a larger chain and a chainguard were fitted, as well as a wider rim for the rear tyre. Front fork travel increased a fraction with the provision of leading-axle forks. Rake was one degree less steep than the D model, improving straight-line stability at the expense of sharpness of cornering although pulled-back handlebars offset some of the steering slowness.

In the engine, almost everything changed. Narrower crankcases held a new crankshaft, revised to enable the new CDI rotor to be keyed to its left half. A two-ring piston replaced the single Keystone item. In the cylinder two extra transfer ports were added to the two previously used, matching the layout that had been universal on the other YZ models from their inception. An extra pair of plates were added to the clutch and the transmission ratios closed up. Weighing-in 2 kg more that the D model, the YZ80E and RM80C of Suzuki were evenly matched in all the areas used to evaluate motocross machines, power, handling, suspension and brakes.

Having marked time for a year with the YZ100D, Yamaha had to make up their minds to either quit the class or perform a much-needed upgrade. They decided on the latter, not content to leave the class to Suzuki. Engine changes included radial cylinder head, base-mounted cylinder, peakier porting in the cylinder, a thinner flat ring in place of the Keystone ring, a shotpeened crankpin for extra reliability and a straighter exhaust helping peak revs. The chassis was updated along the lines of the large-diameter backbone found on the other YZs, except the pipes of the double cradle looped up to the base of the backbone pressing, instead of supporting the rear subframe. Travel on both

Above **Winner in a class of two was the YZ100E whose stronger engine made it a better machine than the Suzuki**

Right **Reliability considerations forced the adoption of both vertical and horizontal bridges on the YZ125E cylinder inlet port**

front and rear suspension dropped a little, presumably in the interests of reducing seat height for the youngsters expected to go for the 100 class. The front forks were not air-charged as other larger YZs but were equipped with leading-axle fittings. With a number of detail changes such as a plastic fuel tank and bonded transfers, the YZ100E was considerably better than the D model. When it came to the RM100C, it was the YZ every time, the RM offering a little more power in the mid-range but losing out at the top end, and the steering and handling competent on both machines. With a single dollar price difference in Yamaha's favour there was little need to choose between the two; the Yamaha was better.

The philosophy adopted by the factory for the YZ125E seems to have been one of correcting deficiencies reported for the D model rather than developing any major new ideas. Deficiencies covered both a number of items on riders' wish lists as well as some changes to improve reliability. The 125 followed the lead taken with the 400C in 1976 when the inlet port was bridged to provide better support for the piston skirt. At 45 mm, the width of the intake port represented 80 per cent of the bore of the cylinder, while the maximum acceptable percentage was considered to be 75 per cent. Above this value, support for the piston was insufficient and cracked skirts would be the result. With the bridge in place it would be possible to open up the intake even more, 85 per cent of the bore being the accepted maximum. There was a slight penalty to pay for the use of a bridge in that the bridged port can only flow about 85 per cent as well as an unbridged port of the same area. On the other side of the cylinder, the gaping 41 mm wide exhaust port was also at the limit as far as width was concerned since it represented 73 per cent of the cylinder bore. At anything over about 71 per cent, the chances that the rings would bulge into and catch on the upper edge of the port increased enormously. The single Keystone ring of earlier models was replaced by two plain rings as on the other YZ models, at least doubling up on the gas seal. The ports in the iron liner of the cylinder were covered with a very thin paint-like coating that produced a really smooth bore and reduced gas flow disturbance. Smooth bores of ports always help get the maximum power from the engine and in mass-produced castings the bore is anything but smooth. In order to provide the maximum space for the new ports, the long-reach studs passing through the cylinder casting were replaced by base-mounting studs.

The polyspheric combustion chamber of earlier 125s was replaced by a simple concentric squish band chamber. The shotpeened crankpin was shared with the YZ100E, but the rest of the crankshaft remained unaltered as did the transmission, clutch and ignition. An attempt was made to widen the powerband of the engine a little by the redesigned exhaust pipe, whose rear cone taper was very long, providing a less powerful positive stuffing wave at the exhaust port to return any charge lost from the cylinder, but effective over a wider engine speed.

The weight of the new 125 was down by 2·5 kg and the saving came mainly from the new chrome-molybdenum frame that replaced the mild-steel item of the past. Not only is chrome-molybdenum lighter than mild-steel, but also stronger, enabling the wall thickness of the frame tubes to be reduced. The rear swinging-arm was also fabricated from a new material, aluminium. After a small cottage industry had built up in the US offering aluminium box-section swinging-arms to YZ owners unhappy with the flex they found with the standard item, Yamaha took the logical step and introduced them on the 125, 250 and 400, saving themselves almost a kilogram in the process and adding 20 mm to the wheelbase for extra straight-line stability. Attached to the swinging-arm was a loop of aluminium to protect the chain and the tensioner, which had been moved closer to the rear wheel, thus providing better engagement between the rear wheel sprocket and the drive chain. Overall travel on the front fork did not increase, but the inner and outer tubes were lengthened to provide greater overlap support and consequently reduce fork flex. The rake was set one degree less at 30 degrees in an attempt to correct the age-old criticism of Yamahas, the slow steering.

So the Yamaha 125E had undergone some updates to make it a better machine than its predecessor. When tested alone it proved to be a good machine, with no apparent suspension flex at either end and a noticeably more powerful engine. The major criticism was that it would not change gear with the throttle fully open. This deterioration in shifting qualities could only have been due to the extra power of the engine as the transmission had not changed. When raced back to back with two other new 125s, the Kawasaki KX125 A4 and the Suzuki RM125C, the lack of mid-range power became apparent and the narrowness of the powerband. Kawasaki in particular were proponents of the leapfrog development process and after years of uncompetitive 125s were back with a vengeance with the best machine available. With both the RM and the KX spraying dirt over the YZ, Yamaha's record of excellence in this class had taken a sharp knock.

Although the D models had proven to be good machines, the 250 and 400 were updated for 1978. Both 250 and 400 underwent the same chassis changes that had been made to the 125, but whereas the engine of the 400 remained unaltered for the E series except for a shorter piston inlet skirt, that of the 250 was completely redesigned. The common frame changes involved the use of chrome-molybdenum for the tubing as well as the slightly longer aluminium swinging-arm. Also the front forks offered the same travel as the year before but were stiffer due to greater overlap of the inner and outer tubes. Although the rake of the 125 had been pulled back one degree, that of the 250 and 400 remained steady at 30·5 degrees.

The prime objective of the design team for the 250 engine seems to have been to get the weight down, and in that they were commendably successful. The engine unit lost a fantastic 7 kg, despite the addition of an extra speed in the gearbox, but in the process pushed the power output up the scale and made the 250 a touch peaky. All the main engine components were new. The crankcases were cast in aluminium, a compromise between the cheap and heavy alloy cases and the light but expensive magnesium alloy cases usually only found on works machines. The right-hand crankcase cover was, however, made of that precious alloy as well as the front and rear brake backing plates. Whereas the cylinder head of the 125 machine had changed from a polyspheric combustion chamber to one with squish band and centrally located spark plug, the 250 went the other way. The plug was moved 5 mm towards the rear cylinder wall, with its own small-radius pocket located within a large-radius pocket and a thin strip of squish band round the outer edge. Reasons for the move were probably a combination of worry about overheating of the exhaust side of the piston crown and redirected transfer ports that aimed the fresh charge towards the rear of the cylinder forcing the plug position to move too,

Above **Most striking change to the YZ series for 1978 was the use of an aluminium swinging-arm, illustrated here on the 125**

Above **The 1978 version of the factory water-cooled YZ125 which enabled Gerard Rond to once again mount a strong challenge to the all-conquering Suzuki team**

Above **The polyspherical combustion chamber found on the YZ250E**

if it was to benefit from the cooling the charge stream would perform.

The porting of the 250 changed a little in what would seem to be a quest for more power, which was found at the expense of powerband width. The exhaust port was opened up 2 mm bringing it into the danger zone for piston ring failure. The height of the transfers was reduced 2 mm to give the scavenging process longer to complete its task of cleaning out the exhaust gases. As on the other YZ machines, the ports were coated with a film to smooth the gas flow through them. A 38 mm Mikuni fed the inlet port via a 10 mm wider reed case assembly, helping to get more fresh charge into the crankcases and of course a new exhaust pipe was developed to match the new port dimensions of the engine. As well as getting the two-ring treatment, the piston also had small vertical grooves cut in the lower section of its skirt. This was intended to improve the oil retention of the piston surface and provide a lubricating cushion between the piston and cylinder wall when subjected to high loads. Hopefully seizures would be virtually eliminated.

All engine shafts were shorter to fit the narrower crankcases. The left-hand half of the crankshaft was shortened by having a much smaller taper for the CDI ignition rotor; the right-hand half remained unchanged. Thinner gears were used throughout the transmission, enabling an extra speed to be squeezed into the smaller width dictated by the narrower engine. The extra gear helped keep the engine within its peakier powerband but really treated the symptoms rather than the disease. Kickstarter and the gear selection mechanism were modified to work with the new six-speed gearbox and a 10 mm longer gearchange lever fitted to increase leverage and make shifting easier.

How did the 250 and 400 perform on the racetrack? The chassis changes alone made the E models better than the Ds. Rear swinging-arm flex was eliminated with the aluminium fork, and the frame and front forks seemed equally rigid.

While a large improvement over the D model, the 1978 YZ250 was still bettered by other Japanese machines, due mainly to a weight problem

Having lost a total of 4 kg the 250 was in the same class as its competition but the bike still felt a little heavy due to the position of the monoshock high in the frame. When matched against the other Japanese creations, the 250E's power characteristics let it down, since the others had more mid-range power making them easier to ride. For expert riders that wouldn't have been too much of a problem but for the other 90 per cent of motocross riders it would. The transmission seemed to have suffered as a result of redesign for it felt stiff and came up in neutral often enough to threaten the health of the engine. The problem lay in the close tolerances found in the ultra-compact gearbox. When riders used normal weight gearbox oil, the problem occurred, but with lighter oil everything was hunky-dory. The 400 remained king of the open class, despite the lack of engine development. With 40 + bhp on tap, it had plenty of power and with a frame that was better able to get it to the ground, it was almost unbeatable.

The most successful year of motocross competition in Yamaha's history was 1978. In the US, *all* the National titles were won by the Yamaha team, a feat never achieved by a manufacturer before or after. In the 125 class Broc Glover won

Above **Broc Glover was the undisputed king of 125 motocross in the US during 1978**

Left **The first sighting of a power valve on a motocross model occurred in 1978 when this works 250 appeared at the last race of the Japanese National Championships**

the title more conclusively than the last-moto decider of 1977. With a total of 13 moto wins out of a total of 20 races, he ended the series 110 points clear of second man Gaylon Mosier on the Kawasaki. Bob Hannah maintained his reputation as the hardest rider in US motocross by cakewalking the 250 championship, winning 14 out of the 20 motos, including eight overall wins. The Supercross title he had won in 1977 remained his as he beat Honda's Marty Tripes by 52 points in the final standings. At one point in the year Hannah had won 22 consecutive motos, recording the longest winning streak in US motocross history. Finally, in the 500 class, Rick Burgett came good after a poor year in 1977 and headed a Yamaha 1-2 in the class. Second man was Rex Staten, riding the first half of the year on his own YZ400E, but later getting the

Europeans never got much of an opportunity to see Bob Hannah in action. Once exception was the Motocross des Nations of 1978 held in Gaildorf in Germany, when he was only bested by Mikkola

loan of injured Mike Bell's works 400 to close the season. In total Yamaha machines had won 40 out of a total of 60 motos in the National series, an incredible achievement.

In Europe Heikki Mikkola retained his 500 title, winning 14 of the 24 motos along with two 2nd places, six 3rds, a 6th and a single DNF in Sweden when the drive chain broke. Without a contender in the 250 class, still very dominated by European machines, the 125 representative was Gerard Rond who was classified as third despite tying on points with second man Gaston Rahier. By virtue of his five overall wins to Rond's three,

Pierre Karsmakers flying high on his 1978 US works 250

Rahier was given 2nd place behind Suzuki teammate Akira Watanabe.

In 1979 the F series of machines were introduced and were likely to be in big demand in the US after the factory's domination of the US National series. The production machines had a lot to live up to. The YZ80 had been at the top of the class since the introduction of the B model in 1975. In 1979 it was to remain there, with a number of engine and chassis changes consolidating its position. A combination of new cylinder porting, head and exhaust served to increase the power output to 14 bhp at 11,000 rpm, without excessively narrowing the powerband. A sixth-speed overdrive was added to the gearbox, with the ratios for the first five gears remaining the same. The frame was extended into a full double-loop cradle of tubes as opposed to the pressed-steel rails under the engine on the E model. The change was prompted by frequent reports of

frame cracking on the E model, at the join between the front downtubes and the pressed-steel rails. The YZ was more powerful and steered as well as the Suzuki and Kawasaki opposition, and although its suspension gave second best to the Suzuki, it was these qualities that made it the winner.

The YZ100F was functionally identical to the E model, the only distinguishing mark being the factory's name in 50 mm high white lettering on the sidewall of the seat. The engine was still a killer, vastly more powerful than the new Suzuki, which in its turn was a vastly superior handler. In stock form, the engine of the YZ just about pulled the Yamaha through but with some money spent on the engine the Suzuki would prove to be the winner.

The 125 didn't get into 1979 without some

work, as always to raise power and improve handling. New cylinder, high-compression head, exhaust pipe and rejetted 32 mm Mikuni helped the YZ to a claimed 20 per cent improvement in power output that would have added another 4 bhp to the top end. This seemed a little wide of the mark although an improvement was noticed in mid-range power. Despite the increase in power, a pair of plates were removed from the clutch. The rake of the frame was pulled back 0·5 degrees to 29·5 degrees to help quicken up the steering. The frame design was not changed but extra gusseting was provided at the headstock/frame joint. Despite the use of a thermostatic valve in the De Carbon-type rear shock absorber, to regulate the size of the oil jets as the temperature of the oil increased, the E models had suffered from monoshock fade towards the end of 40-minute motos. The F-model rear shock had cooling fins along the length of the shock absorber body instead of the radial fins of the previous year, as well as a slightly stiffer spring. An extra 20 mm of front fork travel was added but the total of 250 mm was far less than that offered on competitor machines.

The track test of the YZ125E demonstrated 1979 not to be a vintage year for the Yamaha 125 model. Both Suzuki and Kawasaki had better, more compliant suspension and comparable power output. The shorter suspension travel of the YZ as well as the monoshock design did result in a lower seat height which combined with the steepish rake to enable the YZ to be easily flicked through fast S-bends. But by and large the YZ125F did not live up to the reputation set for it by Broc Glover's domination of the National 125 series.

The 1979 YZ250 appeared to be identical to the previous year's model except for the position of the number plates on the side panels. In fact the 250 had yet again undergone a major update. The engine changes were aimed at widening the peaky powerband of the E model that had made it a machine that only experts were able to get the best out of. The exhaust and transfer ports were lowered 3 mm and an exhaust pipe fitted with fatter mid-section and reverse cone all of which would contribute towards greater mid-range power at the expense of the top end. New gearbox ratios were selected to make better use of the wider powerband with a higher first gear, second and third unchanged, and slightly higher fourth, fifth and sixth. The better power at the low end made the YZ easily able to handle second gear starts. The RT1 crank-pin that had seen many years of service in YZ250 and 360/400 engines was finally replaced by a shotpeened equivalent as used on the smaller YZs. A double-thickness air cleaner element was fitted and the air flow to the carburettor improved by better venting through the side-cover.

Changes to the chassis were similar to those made on the 125. A one-degree steeper rake to quicken the steering, a 35 mm longer swinging-arm increasing the wheelbase and rear wheel travel, 20 mm increase in front wheel travel, aluminium body rear shock absorber with longitudinal cooling fins. Worthy of special mention was the adoption of a full-floating rear brake. A torque arm was bolted to the rear brake backing plate and to the bottom rail of the frame just behind the footpeg. The result was excellent chatter-free rear braking power. Also the engine was dropped 25 mm in the frame by the use of new mounting plates, which lowered the centre of gravity.

These changes brought the YZ250 right back into the ring with the best of the 250 machines. With an edge over the Honda and Suzuki in the engine department and steering characteristics as good as could be found on any bike, including the legendary Maico, it was only the stiffer rear suspension and 50 mm less travel that could be counted against the YZ.

The final bike in the YZ range for 1979 was, of course, the open class YZ400F. Once again deceptively little had changed externally, but the

The YZ250F laid bare and exposing the chassis design that dated back two model years to the 1977 D series

The engine of the YZ400F had a super-wide powerband providing plenty of gutsy torque

engine was a complete redesign. Having skipped a year with the E model's unchanged engine, the passing of another year without update would have been fatal in the YZ's battle with the Maicos, Suzukis and Husqvarnas in the open class. Primary design objectives were to narrow the engine to enable the weight thus saved to be better used elsewhere and as always to broaden the powerband. Rather than spending too much time juggling with port dimensions, the factory lengthened the stroke of the 400 from 70 mm to 75 mm with a corresponding reduction in bore from 85 mm to 82 mm to give a displacement of 396 cc. Long-stroke engines are usually torquier than their short-stroke brethren, which in their turn give higher peak power output. Without any changes to the inlet port dimensions, the new bore and stroke meant that it was open for 32 degrees more of the crankshaft rotation. The exhaust port height was raised 2 mm and the main transfer ports widened 7 mm. Thus more charge got into the crankcase through the inlet port, the transfers were widened to flow it into the combustion chamber and the exhaust opened earlier to give the charge slightly longer to scavenge the cylinder.

Complementing these cylinder changes were an exhaust pipe similar to that on the 250 with a very fat centre section and a 10 mm wider reed assembly, an update that had been made on the YZ250E. Although the volume of the hemispherical combustion chamber had been reduced slightly, the effective compression ratio dropped due to the higher exhaust port roof. Lower compression ratios are associated with torquier engines. Some of the weight saved by the narrower engine went into the crankshaft, as the F model had noticeably more flywheel effect.

The combined effects of these changes were to bring the peak power of the 400 down 4 bhp, without a decrease in maximum torque but with a healthy fat 3000 rpm powerband. Power delivery from 4000 rpm was smooth, constant and meaty right up to the peak at 7500 rpm before signing off 500 revs later. The engine was as strong as anyone at the time could want or imagine. With the need to produce a new, more compact gearbox to match the narrower crankcases, the opportunity was taken to cut slightly lower overall ratios, although the difference was not significant. The 400 and 250 used the same chassis and the larger bike benefited just as much as its smaller brother. Steering was precise and quick enough to enable the rider to steer

Right **The 1979 YZ400 was generally accepted as being the best open class machine on the market**

Below **In 1979, Bob Hannah was still the best motocross rider in the US**

round tight corners or go for the berm shot whichever he preferred. The suspension was spot on at front and back, although the monoshock still tended to fade after about 20 minutes when given a workout by an expert rider. The 1979 YZ400F had gutsy power, precise steering, competent suspension, powerful brakes, light weight, good looks and a low price. In the words of *Cycle Guide*, it was: 'So close to the best that only the best will ever know the difference'.

The US Yamaha factory team were once again the dominant force in the AMA National series in 1979. Broc Glover walked off with his third 125 title after only slightly more pressure from Suzuki's Mark Barnett than in 1978, when Barnett's challenge had ended with a bad mid-season crash. Bob Hannah had equally little difficulty sewing up the 250 and Supercross titles, bringing his tally to a record of six National titles. The only blot on the perfect copy book was the three-point defeat of Mike Bell by Suzuki's Danny La Porte in the 500 championship. In Europe the factory did less well. Gaston Rahier took over Gerard Rond's place in the 125 team but his chances of making a serious run for the title were badly dented in the first GP in Austria where he crashed heavily in the second moto and dislocated a shoulder. Missing the next round and taking it easy in the following two, by the time he was fit again, the Suzuki duo of Harry Everts and Akira Watanabe had built up an unassailable lead, the title going to Everts. The 250 class was not contested by the factory team and Mikkola was hunting for his 500 title hat trick. Unfortunately for him, 1979 proved to be an injury-plagued year which started with a pre-season training injury to a knee. After missing the Austrian round he was getting back into his stride again by the Canadian GP where he crashed very hard and badly bruised his ribs

causing breathing problems in racing conditions. By not scoring in either the Canadian or subsequent German rounds, Mikkola's chances of retaining the crown disappeared and he ended the season a disappointed 5th place in the championship. At the end of the year Mikkola announced his retirement from the sport after nearly ten years at the top and with three World Championships to show for all the battering his body had taken. His name could be added to the list of great Scandinavian motocrossers who had come, seen, conquered and sadly departed.

By the end of the 1970s the Japanese domination of the motocross sport was almost complete. Certainly the greatest percentage of motocross machines sold came from the Big Four, with Yamaha and Suzuki making the front running. Yamaha's success in the US had been devastating, the combination of good machines with enormously talented riders had led to their total domination of the sport by the end of the decade. But the pressure was really on. Yamaha were at the pinnacle of their motocross success, and when you're at the top there's only one way to go.

The factory team's success had led to Yamaha's position at the top of the sales charts for off-road machinery in the US, the factory's corporate philosophy of sales through racing successes completely endorsed. By and large, the YZs were very good machines, benefiting from the factory's direct link with the sport, through a careful, considered annual update of the design. This philosophy of continuous evolution seemed to have worked well enough in the first years of the YZ series. Would it continue to be satisfactory in the eighties?

Heikki Mikkola—one of the great men of motocross sport

6 | The IT blues

One of the IT400s at the 1976 Austrian ISDT. He seems to be having a little trouble steering the bike with a broken right fork leg

Back in 1966 as the prototype models of the DT1 were being developed in the desert of southern California, the concept that was driving the development was of a motorcycle that would perform as well, if not better, on rough terrain as on the street. The developers, with their experience riding and competing in the desert, had attempted to produce a motorcycle that was functionally suited to the peculiarities of rough riding. They had been only partially successful as production-line deadlines had forced the use of intermediate test results and the resulting stock DT1 was not a serious dirtbike. Fortunately, this was not important. The T series appealed to the thousands of Americans who wanted to buy into the concept of getting back to nature and to be seen to be buying in. That the machines gave the impression of being able to take their owners into places where no man had passed before, was sufficient for 90 per cent of the owners. Only ten per cent actually wanted to go there.

For these people, the DT1 was barely adequate. It did, however, form the base from which more serious off-road machines were to develop, in the direction of both motocross and enduro riding. As far as the enduro riders were concerned, there were once again two types of riders, those wishing to get back to nature and those wishing to conquer it. Those wishing to get away from it all, needed strong reliable motorcycles that would get them to their destination, sooner or later, without any hurry, taking their time to see, feel, smell, hear this new world that was opened up to them. DTs would be good enough for them, if there was nothing else available. Those who saw nature as a challenge would not be happy with anything short of the sharpest weapon with which to triumph over everything nature placed in their way. They were the competition riders whose contest between each other was to show who was best able to overcome Mother Nature.

The enduro competition riders were such a small minority that they were not initially catered for by any of the Japanese manufacturers. Their requirements were not fully understood and it was left to them to produce what they needed based on whatever was available. In addition, there were two different types of enduro terrain, the deserts typical of the southern states of California, Arizona, Nevada, Texas, etc., and the tighter wooded terrain of the north. Machines suitable for one were not suitable for the other. In the desert, power and stability are of prime importance, whereas in the woodlands, quick steering and agility are necessary. So it was that riders developed their own machines, often based around motocross machines which came the closest to meeting their needs. European enduro machines were available, but the high price counted heavily against them.

As the YZ and MX series of motocross machines were developed at Yamaha, many of them began finding their way into places they had never expected to see. In southern California, MX400s began to dominate the desert racing, for, with their beefy engine and good straight-line stability, they met some of the basic requirements of the enduro rider. In woodland they would have been less successful, being too bulky and cumbersome in the tighter sections. Yamaha noticed the numbers of MX machines being bought for use off the motocross track and decided that there might just be a large enough market for them to exploit, since the machines

they would offer as genuine enduro would borrow heavily from other models in the company's range of off-road machinery. The stage was set for the introduction of the IT series at the end of 1975.

Once again influenced by the California-type of enduro run in wide open spaces, a single IT model was offered for sale in 1976, the IT400C. A casual inspection would have suggested to the insider that the new enduro model was little more than a YZ400C with lights and a new paint job. That was exactly what it was. Of the 790 components that together formed the IT400, only 61 of them were unique to the model. Yamaha had produced an enduro model for the cost of developing 61 components, essentially meaning that development costs were zero. This was absolutely the best way to test unknown waters, since a failure to penetrate the market would be disappointing but little more. The chances of failure were very real, since Honda's MR enduro series had had a troubled couple of years since their introduction in 1974. Kawasaki had had a nasty experience in the 1973 International Six Day Trial (ISDT) held in the US, when all five of their prototype enduro machines had given up the ghost leading to the cancellation of the whole prototype development. With 90 per cent of the IT borrowed from other models, Yamaha could fail and not get their fingers burned.

But where their fellow countrymen had faltered Yamaha scored a resounding success. In the 1976 Austrian ISDT, three IT400s with carefully prepared engines and modified chassis, won gold medals, the most coveted of prizes in the enduro world. While the ISDT machines had been extensively modified, the IT400 was a sound basis for further development work. The few differences between the IT and the YZ resulted both from the need to make the machine socially acceptable in the off-circuit environment and to adapt it to its slight functional change. Changes that fell in the first category were primarily the need for extra silencing of the YZ400C pipe, which knocked off a couple of horsepower and in so doing made the 400 slightly tamer. Also the lighting consisted of the head and tail-lights from the TY250.

The transition from motocrosser to enduro mount was accompanied by slightly higher gearing accomplished by new ratios for first and fifth gear and an altered final drive ratio. First gear was now slightly too high, but could not be compensated by lowering the final drive ratios since the high gearing was suitable for the other ratios. The IT was prevented from drowning by the use of a snorkel type of cover fitting over the air filter and feeding the engine from under the seat. The recently introduced air-assisted front forks of the YZ series were not adopted but their replacements were very good, although a rather soft spring allowed the IT to bottom out occasionally.

The first generation of monoshock suspension was in use at the back end, with the damper fitted with a nitrogen-charged chamber at its base. The spring rate and damping properties had been matched to the slightly heavier IT. The damper, mounted high in the frame, contributed to the rather poor handling in tight sections, and at low speeds, by keeping the centre of gravity high and combining with the slow steering to give the bike a tendency to flop over in turns. The brakes were standard YZ items and consequently excellent up front and remarkably insensitive at the back. An incredible thirst forced the use of a large 12-litre tank giving the bike an effective range of 50 to 70 miles.

Reflecting the great blue beyond beckoning to the truly adventurous motorcycle owner and the weather every enduro rider hopes for, the IT was painted in a striking sky blue colour. The colour scheme was to stay with the IT series and result in some of the most visually striking and exciting of all off-road motorcycles.

So the IT400C was a good baseline from which to build serious enduro machines. If it sold well, the new models would need to undergo some

development to improve the handling, reduce the weight and get the brakes sorted. When brought up to the standard of the excellent engine power and competent suspension, the IT series would not be simply proficient but truly outstanding. Perhaps the last domain of the European off-road machines would be conquered.

Sure enough, 1977 saw the expansion of the IT series, with a 175 and 250 joining the 400. The 175 class was still a very active one in the world of enduro competition in contrast to motocross racing where it had largely disappeared. In 1976, Yamaha had produced a one-off YZ175 and it had been a decent machine, but without a future as a motocrosser. Many had been used in enduro races with only a few concessions to the change of environment in which it was being raced. Once the decision had been made to introduce an IT with a capacity of 175 cc, it was necessary to choose a design process to be adopted. Either the IT175D could be a modified YZ175C or it could be a totally new model making use of the latest YZ technology. Having learnt from their experience with the IT400, that an enduro-equipped YZ was only partially successful, Yamaha decided on the second option.

As on the YZ, the 175 was basically a bored-out 125 with short-stroke dimensions of 66 mm by 50 mm, giving a displacement of 171 cc. The traditional YZ porting was used, with two main transfers, two auxillary transfers, an inlet and exhaust port and the boost port above the inlet port. The two-ring piston had a bridged window in the inlet skirt, through which charge passed from the crankcase to the boost port on the downstroke and fresh charge from the carburettor on the upstroke. The four-petal reed valve was fed by the same 34 mm carburettor that had been used on the YZ, and the new exhaust exited the manifold and dropped down several inches before sweeping up left to thread through the frame rails and exit in a sizeable stinger that brought the noise down to an acceptable 90

Above **A peek inside the cylinder of the IT175D revealed standard YZ/DT port layout**

Top left **The IT400C as it went into production in 1976— 95 per cent of the bike came from the YZ series**

Left **A year later came the first version of the most successful model in Yamaha's enduro line-up, the IT175**

decibels. The airbox was mounted under the right-hand sidecover and drew in air from under the seat. The position of the airbox forced the inlet manifold to bend to the left, considered at the time to be a sure way to ruin an engine's performance. This did not occur with the 175 and later experience with the YZs proved this to be incorrect.

An 11-plate clutch passed the power on to the six-speed gearbox, with a new set of ratios. First gear was incredibly low, intended for the slow plodding in the tighter rocky sections. This was fine, except second gear which although quite low was a mile higher than first. The gap should have been a little smaller. All other ratios were spot on, culminating in a high top gear for blasting along fireroads and open desert. CDI ignition

was fitted with an external flywheel, which helped increase the inertia of the crankshaft and improve traction.

The frame on the IT175 was of the latest YZ design with the new De Carbon-type Kayaba monoshock damper located within the fabricated backbone. The rake of the IT was slightly higher than that of the YZs, to ensure straight-line stability. Less travel was present on the front and rear suspension than on the YZs, but the operation was good. The springs in the front forks tended to sag after a couple of hundred miles, and they were a little too soft for some riders. Both ends absorbed bumps very well, providing a really cushy ride. Handling was extremely good, with rocksteady straight-line stability and yet, despite the slow 32-degree rake, surprisingly

agile on tight trails. True to tradition, the front brake was excellent and, breaking with tradition, so was the rear.

A great deal of thought had gone into the ergonomics of the machine as witnessed by some of the small details found on the IT. A clear plastic bubble protected the front headlamp—much more effective than the coarse wire grids used by most machines. A pukka quickly detachable (QD) rear wheel was provided, with open axle slots in the swinging-arm allowing the wheel to be slipped out after the axle locking nut had been loosened. A small hook was welded to the upper fork of the swinging-arm to retain the rear brake activation rod while the wheel was being installed or removed. A tool bag was mounted on the rear subframe behind the seat, and filled with a good selection of tools that unfortunately were of the usual poor-quality steel and therefore useless.

The IT175 was really an outstanding little bike that would rev like a motocrosser, handle very confidently, brake well and prove absolutely reliable. There were more powerful 175 enduros available, but their advantage would only be significant in the WFO desert races. The only strong criticisms levied against the bike were an inaccurate odometer, an absolutely essential requirement for the serious enduro rider, and a seat whose foam stuffing packed down too quickly, making the ride unnecessarily uncomfortable. Furthermore, the ground clearance left something to be desired, and although the substantial bash plate did a good job protecting the engine, some obstacles could not be easily cleared. But there was one thing that made the IT175 quite simply the most attractive machine in its class. Priced at $998, it was between $600 and $880 cheaper than the European competition. The remarkable low price guaranteed the success of

The agility and reliability of the IT175D, combined with a good power delivery and incredibly low price, guaranteed its success

what was anyway an extremely good enduro mount for beginners through to experts.

The IT250D was developed in a similar fashion to the 175 and had all the enduro features included. Although the same engine dimensions, the porting and pipe design were such as to rub off the sharp edges of the YZ power delivery. In fact the engine of the YZ250D had not been peaky and had delivered bags of mid-range torque, very suitable for enduro applications. The gearing was raised crazily high by a combination of transmission and final drive ratios, and it was necessary to drop a tooth on the drive shaft sprocket to match the engine characteristics. Since the design was functionally so similar to that of the 175, most of the good and the bad points applied to the 250 as well. Weight was a rather high 115 kg, which along with the slightly detuned engine meant that the IT was definitely not the fastest enduro machine in its class. The excess weight also made the lofting of the front wheel more difficult than it should have been. Priced at $1348, the IT was an attractive alternative to the expensive European models, although the experts paid for the improved steering and extra speed. Suzuki's PE250 was also available for the same approximate price and had a slight edge over the IT in terms of handling qualities although the suspension was too soft. Whereas the IT175 was really unchallenged in its class, the 250 was not the clear-cut choice.

The IT400C had served its purpose in testing the waters of the enduro market and for 1977, the hastily assembled bitza was replaced by a totally new motorcycle designed from scratch to be an enduro motorcycle. Although almost all engine components were new, the 400D adhered to the same broad design concepts as its predecessor. Engine dimensions were not altered, compression ratio, carburettor and transmission all bore the same values as the C model, but the new cylinder porting and exhaust, combined with revised jetting and ignition to

Below **By 1977, the IT400 was no longer a modified YZ, but purpose-built for enduro riding and consequently a better machine than the 400C**

Below **The polyspherical dual spark plug head of the IT250E**

produce a far tamer open class enduro machine. Narrower crankcases necessitated new crank and transmission shafts and smaller gears were also cut. The new engine fitted into the Mark 2 monoshock chassis common to IT250D models. The only significant difference for the rider was the lower centre of gravity the new design gave, making the 400 a little more manoeuvrable. No other attempt was made to improve the 400's chassis and it remained a slow steerer with only adequate suspension travel.

Despite being far from perfect, the 175 and 400 ITs remained unaltered in 1978. Although they had been by and large good packages, their flaws, if left unattended, would quickly develop into glaring deficiencies. In 1978, the slow steering and inadequate ground clearance began to be seen as serious problems. Fortunately for

Yamaha, the enduro market was not especially cut-throat, with only Suzuki offering comparable machines at a comparable price. Consequently the loss of a year would not necessarily prove fatal as it might in the motocross world. Inevitably, one thing did change for 1978, and that was the price. With the 175 increasing by $140 and the 400 by only $70, it was clear the 175D had been underpriced. What was not clear was if this had been a clever marketing ploy to guarantee good sales or a mess-up by someone in the pricing team. But the negligence of the two IT models was good business for the after-sales accessory manufacturers, with anything from new suspensions to replacement air filters being offered.

Not the complete IT series stagnated in 1978. The IT250E was an update on the D model, with a number of small but important changes. In the engine, the port timing was not altered but the direction of the transfer ports was changed to aim the fresh charge at the crown of the piston rather than towards the cylinder head. This could be attributed to the age-old argument of whether the exhaust gases are best scavenged directly by the streams of charge issuing from the transfers, or by a rising column of gas. The latter was achieved by directing the transfer ports towards each other so that the charge would collide above the piston, ramming itself to a halt and rise as a wedge, drawn by the exhaust suction wave. The rising column school of thought seemed to have prevailed. Also the location of the spark plug in the cylinder head was altered. It was moved towards the inlet side of the engine, a move that was claimed to improve thermal loads on the cylinder and especially the piston. Pipe and carburettor were unaltered.

Perhaps the single most noticeable improvement for the rider was the six-speed gearbox. It was now possible to define a set of gears where the lowest speed was slow enough to plonk through tight sections whilst the top gear would pull 85 to 90 mph when riding WFO. The rideability of the IT was improved enormously, with a gear available for every situation.

Unfortunately, the updates were restricted to the engine, when it was clearly the chassis that needed the most work. The same complaints were still valid, with well-matched suspension, but not enough travel, clumsy slow-speed steering, inadequate clearance for the footpegs and levers and a rather heavy feel to the bike in general. Suzuki had cured the suspension problem on their PEs and were consequently gunning for the IT. In fact the 1978 PE was probably a better machine than the IT due to its superior handling but there was not that much in it. They were both excellent value for money.

Thankfully, in 1979 Yamaha took the necessary steps to cure the sole major problem on the ITs. Whereas on the YZ-line it had taken incremental changes through three model years to bring the rake down to a figure needed for the quick steering so essential on the track, a single frame update for 1979 put the ITs into the right ballpark. The frame change, common to all three models, was to bring the rake back from 31·5 degrees to 29·5 degrees. This simple modification seemed to be the panacea for all the handling ills of the ITs, for the clumsy slow steering on tight trails was replaced by a sensitivity

The IT250E was given an extra transmission gear and reworked porting to produce a good engine compromised by a poor chassis

that allowed body language to do as much of the steering as the handlebars. The steeper rake seemed to have been taken as far as it could without affecting stability, for by and large the ITs performed as well as ever. Slight deterioration could be found (the 175 would shake its head a little in deep sand above 50 mph, 90 mph WFO runs along fireroads on the 400 would find the front end fluttering a little), but the price was a reasonable one.

Another update that was common to all the ITs was the use of a chrome-molybdenum frame and swinging-arm in place of the previous mild-steel items. This enabled the weight of the chassis to be pared down in the case of the 250 and 400, and by so doing bring the machines closer to that of the competition. The ITs were still a touch overweight but the couple of kilos difference was not enough to cause any problems. On the 175, the frame was toughened up rather than reduced in weight for it already had a healthy power-to-weight ratio. The suspension travel was increased somewhat on all three models, although only the rear wheel benefited on the 175. Since this bike was considerably lighter than the other two, it could be argued that the resulting 195 mm front wheel travel and 210 mm rear wheel travel was adequate, especially as greater travel might result in increased seat height. Out on the trail it was only just adequate, another 20–30 mm at both ends would have been perfect. On the 250 and 400, the figures were 230 mm up front and 205 at the rear end and were plainly too low.

None of the engines changed significantly in the transition from E to F models. For the 175, the inlet and exhaust port were lowered 1 mm, giving the engine a touch more mid-range. The lower plain piston ring was replaced by a Keystone design which is claimed to keep the ring grooves cleaner and prevent the rings from sticking. The gearbox and clutch were not touched since gearchanges had always been smooth and precise and the ratios well chosen.

Both the 250 and 400 followed in the footsteps of the YZ design of 1978 when narrower, lighter crankcases had been introduced. The drive shaft in the new design was moved closer to the swinging-arm pivot, helping to reduce the variation in tension that the drive chain would be subjected to as the wheel passed through its arc of travel. On the 250, the exhaust port was lowered 2 mm, in the search for more mid-range power. Carburation and pipe changes complemented the cylinder change. The clutch lost a friction plate and drive plate and all the gear ratios were new, matching the engine characteristics perfectly.

The 400 underwent slightly more extensive updates, with new longer stroke dimensions of 82 × 75 mm, in keeping with Yamaha's goal of increased mid-range. The flywheels of the crankshaft were heavier, intending to provide the extra inertia that is so useful when picking a path through a slow section. Carburation of the 38 mm Mikuni was modified for the 400F and the reed cage was widened 10 mm to try to flow a little more charge into the engine. The clutch was not altered, but top gear was lowered and all the others raised, to match the new engine. The engine of the 400F was a vast improvement on its predecessors, being almost perfect for enduro riders, with excellent power available from 4000 rpm up to the peak of 6000 rpm. Even under this range of engine speed, there was enough power available to pull itself back into the meatier section of the powerband without the need to change gear. The basic functional competence of the machine, combined with the numerous small details such as snail-cam chain tensioners, drainage hole for the bash plate, tommy-bar release mechanism for the front axle, Volcanduro tyres with built-in rim protectors, etc., made the 400, and indeed the 250 and 175, front-liners in their class in 1979.

Yamaha celebrated the turn of the decade by introducing a fourth model into the IT line-up, a 125. This was largely uncharted territory as far

as commercial enduro machines were concerned, the 125 class in both international trials and enduro events being composed mostly of modified motocross machines. The engine was based on that of the YZ125F, with the engine detuned to produce a wider, lower powerband. The piston used two thicker rings than those found in the YZ, where thinner more expensive rings were necessary to ensure no flutter developed at the higher engine speeds of the motocross model. The skirt of the piston was windowed in traditional IT form and the engine fed by a 30 mm Mikuni replacing the YZ's 32 mm item. Thicker reed-valve petals were fitted to match the intended top engine speed of around 9500 rpm in contrast to the 11,000 rpm of the YZ. The ratios in the gearbox were borrowed from the IT175 and matched to the smaller engine output by lowering the primary transmission ratio and final reduction. The frame was of the contemporary monoshock encasing spine variety, with a tight 28·5-degree rake and shortish wheelbase.

The light weight and quick steering geometry combined as could be expected to make the little machine very easy to steer at low speeds and rather lively at the high speeds the powerful motor was capable of producing. The 32 mm diameter front fork stanchions seemed a little wimpy, but fork flex was not the most serious of the suspension problems. Both ends were too soft for average-weight adult riders, especially under race conditions. Almost continuous bone-shaking bottom-outs were to be encountered when travelling at speed over rough ground. Heavier duty springs were available and offered an improvement, but the real culprit was the lack of wheel travel, especially at the rear end. All the other goodies associated with the IT series were

Top left **For 1979, the IT series was cosmetically almost identical and also sharing a much-needed chassis update**

Left **The ITs could take you where no man had been before**

present, although the tools were substituted for a single multi-function wrench that attached to the front downtube of the frame. As a playbike, the IT125G was quite adequate in stock form, although more fun could have been found with one of its larger brothers. For racing, some serious suspension upgrades were necessary before the powerful little engine could do its stuff properly.

It is clear from the updates made to the existing models in the IT line-up, that Yamaha already considered the 175 to be the most important machine. This must have been a reflection of the sales figures for a purely objective judgement would probably choose the 250 as being the class offering the best compromise between the scaled-down motorcycle impression of the 175 and the rather gross 400. However, it was the 175 that underwent the most radical changes, and they would have been of greatest benefit to competition riders. Rather than wait around for a model year for a motocross-proven chassis, the IT175G shared the same design as the YZ G models. The monoshock came out of its hiding place within the frame backbone and bolted to lugs welded to the top of the backbone, which now passed under the damper assembly. In addition, a single large-diameter front downtube tied the headstock to the duplex cradle supporting the engine. The main advantage of the new design was the lowering of the centre of gravity it achieved by pulling the upper frame tubes under the rear damper. In point of fact, it was the monoshock itself that was the main source of the high slung weight of all the single shock Yamahas, so the improvement was only marginal.

As on the YZs, this change was accompanied by the provision of a box-section aluminium swinging-arm and an aluminium rear damper with an external reservoir that bolted on the front downtube. Both preload and rebound damping could be adjusted without removing either machine equipment or the unit itself. As a final concession to the state-of-the-art chassis design, 36 mm forks with air caps were fitted, with the recommendation of running them at 0 psi. The total suspension package was therefore the most tunable ever presented on an enduro machine, reflecting the expertise the company were expecting 175 owners to have.

A totally new engine was also part of the IT175G package. It was based very closely on the YZ125G, including the mirror-image swap of component location so that the drive chain was now on the bike's right-hand side. One unusual feature found in the engine that had been given the customary detuning to produce characteristics more suitable for an enduro machine, was the 32 mm power-jet carburettor, previously only seen on the Yamaha TZ350F road-racer. An extra jet was tapped into the inlet tract of the carburettor which flowed more charge from a pipe fed directly from the float bowl when the intake velocity exceeded a certain value, i.e. at high engine speeds. It was therefore possible to enrich the engine in its upper range of engine speed without giving it the blubbers at the low end. Gearbox ratios were new on the 175, with first gear lower and sixth higher, and the ratios between spread to cover the gap.

So the IT175G was a new machine, with a lot going for it on paper. The chassis was a noticeable improvement, as good as anything in the class, although ground clearance was still insufficient. The engine on the other hand was a bit of a failure. Both the low and top ends seemed to have suffered, since it could not lug up steep inclines the F had managed to conquer and it was almost 1 bhp down on maximum power output. In addition the opposition in the form of Suzuki, now joined by Kawasaki, had engines that produced 2–3 bhp more and that's noticeable on a 175. So the IT had to make do with its good handling and hope that someone would breathe on its engine for 1981.

On the other hand, the 250 and 425 seemed to have been almost neglected. Changes were

Above **For 1980, the IT175 received the same chassis upgrade as was applied to the YZ models that year**

Below **Although updated for 1980, the IT250G and 425G lagged behind the 175 with its state-of-the-art chassis**

Left **The engine of the IT250G produced too little low-end power, with too rapid transition into a generous mid-range**

Right **This stripped-down IT465H shows the updated chassis that was at last provided to all the IT bikes**

made but they seemed just small detail changes in comparison. Engine updates for the 250 were restricted to a new cylinder, pipe, rejetted carburettor and revised CDI ignition. The product was a slight increase in mid-range power. However, this increase did seem to be, as on the 175, at the cost of low-end power. This became evident in situations when the frightening WFO speeds that could be reached by the 250 could not be used and it was necessary to use the slogging power of the engine to climb a muddy hill. It couldn't be done, as the rear tyre would either break away or the engine would stall. On the 425, this wasn't a problem. It had bags of power throughout the range. Apart from the increase in bore by 3 mm, requiring a new cylinder and piston, nothing in the engine was touched. The extra few ccs displacement confirmed the big IT's place as the combined rocketship and tractor of the wastelands. Both models shared the same chassis and both frame and suspension were revised. Although not getting the new G-series frame as found on the 175, it did receive some attention in the form of the quickening of the

rake another 0·5 degrees. The 38 mm front forks were fitted with air caps to allow the pumped-up air pressure to be bled off, or to provide a very small amount of air pressure to assist the coil springs. The forks were good, soaking up the rough stuff without any problems. Finally, steel-bodied monoshocks dating from the YZ E series were utilized, which increased rear wheel travel by a welcome 45 mm. Anyone used to the accessibility of the new G-series dampers, would have found the need to remove the petrol tank to alter the rebound damping and the complete monoshock for the preload an unacceptable chore. The chassis of the IT250G and 425G was an improvement over the F version, but enduro riders had seen the way the road was heading on the 175 and couldn't wait to see it happen on the other IT machines.

Their wish came true on the 250 and 465 models for 1981, and it was the turn of the 175 to mark time for a year, with the sole distinguishing feature between model years being the new all-white cosmetics of the IT line-up. Not too much activity took place around the 125 either.

Sales had been a little disappointing in 1980, and Yamaha were already wondering if it was worth keeping the 125 in the range. It survived 1981 in slightly modified form over the G model. A revised CDI ignition added a touch more power to the mid-range of the engine, making the little IT's best feature better. The 32 mm front forks were replaced by 35 mm items with 20 mm more travel. The new units were flex free, but the travel at either end was still inadequate. Hand guards were added to protect the rider's hands from sticks and stones while on the trail. This equipment had been provided a year before on the other IT machines. Those were the changes for 1981, not enough to turn a good bike into a fantastic one or to avoid its discontinuation at the end of the model year.

The main improvement undergone by the 250 and new 465 cc displacement top-of-the-range model, was the use of the YZ G-series chassis as found on the IT175G. On the 250, steering geometry was left untouched, but the wheelbase grew by 20 mm, reflecting a change the YZs had undergone during the same transition. On the

465, the rake was also reduced another 1 degree, bringing it down to 28·5 degrees. Front fork stanchions of 38 mm diameter were very rigid, with the provision of air caps for those who wished to disregard Yamaha's recommendation that they be used with 0 psi air pressure. The rear damper was now aluminium-bodied, with the external reservoir and preload and rebound damping adjustments at its base. The aluminium swinging-arm was also conspicuous in contrast to the matt black of the engine. The massive aluminium bash plate of old was discarded as too much dirt-collecting weight. Instead, an additional rail was added under the engine welded at one end to the main downtube/engine cradle join and supported at the other end by two heavy-duty brackets welded to the cradle frame tubes. The 465 got the benefit of a twin-leading-shoe front brake to haul its bulk down from high speed. It was the best front brake fitted to any enduro machine at the time.

Some engine changes were also made. The mid-range-based engine of the 250 got more, and a little assistance was given to the low end in the form of YEIS, also making its début on the motocross machines. The 36 mm Mikuni needed rejetting as a consequence. The resulting engine power curve was smooth and straight from right off the throttle stop to WFO, making the bike a lot easier to ride. Overall gearing was raised a little by adding two teeth to the rear wheel sprocket, but internal ratios remained the same. Although hardly in need of more low-end grunt, the 425 had followed the line taken in the YZ series and grown a 7 mm longer stroke to displace the 465 ccs. Narrower crankcases were used, a heavier crankshaft to add some flywheel inertia, a slight lowering in primary gearing and a massive increase in final gearing took place. The rest of the transmission remained intact, so overall the ratios were slightly higher, which gave the more powerful 465 mill absolutely no problems. It had a clear edge over the 425 in power.

Both 250 and 465 responded well to the engine and chassis updates. The characteristics of the bikes that were the responsibility of the chassis could hardly be faulted, and as a package, the 465H was very close to being as good as the enduro-dominating Husqvarna. The 250 was perhaps a little weak in the engine area and really in need of some tune-up tips to extract more power. Yamaha's newly introduced wrench report series remained unmercifully silent and it was left to the backstreet tuning wizards that seem to abound in the US to come up with the goods.

With the J-series ITs appearing at the end of 1981, it seemed to be a case of *déjà vu*, with the 175 undergoing a major upgrade whilst the 250 and 465 marked time. Once again the IT175 got the benefit of the same changes to the chassis as the YZ series, namely rising-rate suspension. Most noticeable feature of the 1982 175, except for the return to the sky blue cosmetics for all the ITs, was the massive extruded aluminium swinging-arm. This was now just a single fork, in place of the lower and upper forks used on the traditional monoshock set-up, with a set of three

pivot and rocker arms in front of the rear wheel attaching the arm to the rear damper. The rear shock had been retained in more or less the same position and attitude as previously so that the monoshock concept was not seen as discarded after nearly ten years' assertion that the system was the best there was. There was a mild rising rate of resistance to further compression achieved through the geometry of the rocker arm linkage and this worked well with some of the YZs and poorly with others. On the IT, it worked just fine. Whereas the YZ linkage components were aluminium, those on the IT were mild-steel sprayed with aluminium paint.

Front forks were beefed up with the 38 mm units that had been based on the 250 and 465 of 1981. The sliders in the forks were Teflon coated to reduce friction. In the engine, new cylinder, head and pipe combined to produce a stronger yet better balanced engine. The inlet port of the cylinder was opened up to gaping proportions, and was provided with a double vertical bridge to support the piston skirt. The power-jet 32 mm carburettor was replaced by a plain 34 mm unit and an YEIS bottle tapped into the inlet tract. This seemed to work well, since the 175 had the most low end ever, providing plenty of torque for the tighter sections. The gearbox ratios were brought closer together by raising first and second, and lowering fourth through to sixth. The new ratios matched the engine well, with its super-strong mid-range and top end.

At last, Yamaha had produced an enduro bike everyone could enthuse about. With a loss of 5 kg the weight had come down handily and the extra-low end helped the slow situations enormously. The suspension was good, with generous travel at both ends almost on a par with the motocross machines. Inevitably it was too soft as delivered, but higher rate springs were available as replacements. For 1982, it was probably the best in class, its closest competitor being the bitza CanAm Qualifier, with its Rotax disc-valved

engine, Öhlin shocks and Marzocchi forks.

Only a few very minor chassis changes were made to the 250 and 465. These were a wider and longer front mudguard, Teflon-coated fork seals were supplied, a stronger front wheel hub, polyurethane rollers replaced the spring-loaded drive chain tensioner and a new, straighter shift lever. These new parts had to be enough to tide the two bikes over to the next model year when no doubt they would be decked out in the trick parts that had been used on the 175 in 1982.

And sure enough, as the wraps came off the

By 1981, the IT465 rivalled Husqvarna for the title of best open class enduro machine

1983 IT K-series line-up, the 250 and 490 models were the YZ lookalikes, while the 175 lagged behind with its year-old design. Apart from a new set of decals and a new paint job, the 175 was not altered. The 250 and 465 stretched to 490 received updates to both engine and chassis. The highlight of the chassis changes was the adop-

Above **Once again the IT175 was treated to a simultaneous upgrade with the YZ series, when the J version received rising-rate rear suspension in 1982**

Right **The bulbous exhaust pipe of the IT175J did its work well as the engine produced excellent well-balanced power**

tion of the 'mark two' version of the rising-rate rear suspension. The initial version as used on the IT175J had worked well with the smaller bikes but the YZ250J and YZ490J had been disappointing. The new design featured a rear damper placed considerably lower in the frame and a new aluminium linkage system. On the YZ, the new lightweight rear damper had provision for setting both compression and rebound damping. The compression-damping adjustment was not present on the ITs. On the front end were state-of-the-art 43 mm Kayaba forks with an internal blow-off valve that was intended to open under the high pressure build-up caused by a sudden suspension jolt. The opening of the valve would allow fork oil to pass through a larger orifice than when it was closed and hence allowed the fork to respond better to a sudden sharp movement. The new frames found on the 250 and 490 were also modified to improve the steering sensitivity of the machines. The 250 frame had steepened a full degree, whilst that of the 490 made do with a 0·5-degree steeper rake. This was compensated by a 35 mm longer wheelbase for both machines. The 250 joined its big brother in the use of twin leading-shoe front brakes.

The engine dimensions of the 250 followed the lead taken by the YZ series with a move to a square 68 mm bore and stroke. New head, cylinder and exhaust pipe were the result of this, along with a 38 mm carburettor as used on the YZs. All the internal ratios of the gearbox were raised as well as the overall gearing which lost two teeth on the rear wheel sprocket. As with its predecessors, there was really insufficient low-end power in the 250K mill. Once the revs were up a bit it pulled well and the top end was very strong. But an enduro machine needs a good low end and the IT250K didn't have it.

A 2 mm increase in bore brought the largest IT up to a displacement of 487 cc. This increase in displacement added to the power output throughout the low to mid-range, and an extra punch was added to the low end by the addition

The 1983 IT250K was the last 250 in the IT range and was less proficient than its brothers, with too little low-end power

of the YEIS bottle. A number of other minor changes were implemented. A straight-cut primary transmission gear was used for the first time. The kickstart mechanism was given some attention, with a thinner shaft, wider gears and a larger securing bolt fitted. The shifting of the large IT should have been a little smoother than before due to a slight change in the profile of the gears. The gear ratios themselves remained the same. The engine retained its reputation as being both a lugger and fireroad flyer, as required. Plenty of power was available at both low and top end. The suspension was very good allowing the rough stuff to be taken at speed, although it did bottom out fairly regularly but thankfully quite softly. It was left to the rider to decide on a relatively cushy run with occasional bottoming or to stiffen up the rear end with some more preload and eliminate the bottoming at the cost of a harsher ride.

A summary of the situation of 1983 shows that the IT175 was selling well and of a comparable ability to its green competitor, the KDX. In the US, the 250 was less successful, eclipsed rather by both the KDX and the KTM and Husqvarna mounts. It was the best IT250 Yamaha had made

Above **Despite being the best of the under-200 cc ITs, the 200L was bettered by the Kawasaki, with its superb rear suspension**

Above left **Always an attractive bike to look at, the performance of the IT250 never quite lived up to its image**

but the gap between it and the class-leading Husky was still too large. Finally in the open class, it was again IT against Husky and they were really very close, the Swedish machine getting the nod by virtue of its superior low-speed handling. By 1983 Yamaha had realized that their corporate economic situation was not a healthy one. Cutbacks were announced in both machine production and in the company offices throughout the world. The IT250, with its rather average performance was one of the victims and disappeared from the US enduro line-up, although it remained available in Europe and Australia in unchanged form for another year. This left two sole survivors—the IT175, Yamaha's enduro blue-eyed boy, and the IT490.

The IT490 got two new items in the transition from K to L, a new set of decals and a new voltage regulator to prevent a rash of blown bulbs that the 490K had suffered. It was still the only opposition to the outrageously expensive Husqvarna and KTM 500s and it was almost as good. The 175 underwent a serious update and grew 25 cc in the process, to remain competitive with the full-capacity bikes of the 200 cc class. The extra displacement was achieved by increasing the stroke by 7 mm, to give an actual displacement of 195 cc. The 34 mm Mikuni and YEIS were retained, but some pretty radical porting

changes, similar to those on the motocross machines, were used. The extra inlet sub-port feeding directly into the crankcase was common to the 125 and 250 YZs of 1984. Both big- and small-ends of the conrod were beefed up to handle the extra power the engine produced. The primary transmission was raised slightly as were the top two gears in the transmission.

Naturally enough, the 200 benefited from the latest chassis and suspension components. The same linkage for the rear suspension was fitted as had been used on the other models in 1983, although the dimensions were slightly different. At the front end the 38 mm Kayabas were replaced by the superb 43 mm units common to all the 125, 250 and 490s of the YZ range. These forks had a built-in compression-damping adjustment capability that varied the size of the orifices through which the fork oil passed. Air caps were provided but as always it was recommended that the bike be run without any air pressure. More weight was pushed on to the front end by pulling

Above **The last of the big-bore ITs, and more than a match for any European enduro bike. The IT490K was almost unchanged for 1984 and was then discontinued**

Below **The IT490K engine displaying its YEIS boost bottle that helped it produce the stump-pulling torque it was capable of**

back the steering head 20 mm, although the overall wheelbase remained the same thanks to a longer swinging-arm. Weight was lost in a big way, so that the IT came on to the scales a fighting 93 kg.

The IT200L was a marked improvement over the 175. Its engine was excellent, being able to lug at slow speeds up steep hills or rev out when given the chance. Since it was still strongest on the mid-range, the best technique for going places fast was to short shift slightly, to keep the engine in the meatiest part of the powerband. The gap between the first three gears was perhaps a bit too large, but the tough clutch could be slipped to keep the revs up without any problem. The front suspension was perfect, period. As tradition seems to dictate, the rear end was too soft, requiring considerable preload to stiffen it up. If the preload and rebound-damping adjustments were juggled enough, a satisfactory set-up could be achieved. Steering was quick enough but not very precise. This

seemed to originate from the need to get even more weight up on the front wheel, and the ergonomics of the machine prevented this. When pitted against arch rival the KDX200, there was not a lot to choose between them, but the mediocre rear suspension and steering inaccuracy counted against the IT and gave the KDX the nod.

For 1985, the IT200N found itself alone in the Yamaha enduro line-up. Most unfortunately, Yamaha had decided to axe the IT490 from the series, despite the quality of the machine. A few 490s and 250s were still available in Europe during 1985, but no more machines were assembled in Japan. For once the European manufacturers had won a battle and the Japanese had retreated to the markets they already owned. After the massive revision in 1984, it was hardly surprising that the 200N model was virtually identical. The sole change was a swap to a six-petal fibre reed in place of the previous steel items. A slight increase in low-end power output could be dis-

Whatever else they may have been, the ITs have always been fun to ride

cerned but it was not significant.

After ten years of building enduro machines, only a single model is offered just as at the start. During the wildly optimistic days at the end of the 1970s, there was a time when it was thought that a four-bike range could be supported. With the drop in interest in off-road riding in general at the end of the 1980s this was not practical. The sole survivor, the IT200, has a pedigree built from the experience of some 27 IT machines and many, many more YZs. So it might be only a 200, and it might be the only Yamaha enduro machine available, but its bloodline stretches back to the first IT400s splattered with the mud of the Austrian Alps and even further to the monoshock YZ Hakan Andersson first rode to victory that Sunday in May 1973. The IT200 is a fully qualified survivor.

7 | Class warfare

The YZ125G was the perfect all-rounder, only the soft rear suspension coming in for criticism

Back in the 1950s as the sun was slowly rising on an unsuspecting motorcycle world, the base was laid for a rivalry between two emerging Japanese motorcycle manufacturers that would be as intense 30 years later in the eighties. Both companies saw the medium of sport as the means of humiliating their rival, and this led to the legendary era of European road-racing during the 1960s when the technological skills of both companies were harnessed in the life and death struggle to win. Each company had chosen a combustion process and placed their complete faith in its superiority over the other, for both competition and road use. Both were proven to have misplaced their faith, as the one process proved more acceptable for street use and the other essential for competitive racing machinery. So the companies went their separate ways, the one to build up a reputation as being the unconquerable king of the road-race track in the 1970s and the other to build a series of good, solid street machines that sold in their hundreds of thousands. Necessity forced both companies to dabble in the other's domain but it never seemed to be with a sense of commitment. As the 1970s drew to a close a change seemed to be in the air. Honda had decided to actively re-enter the National and World Championships and Yamaha was one of their targets.

Honda's range of road machines during the 1970s had consisted of large-capacity, four-cylinder four-strokes and small-capacity twins.

Yamaha in competition: no contest for the YZ worldbeaters

YZ125 Derived from the works machines that made Yamaha a legend in world-class motor-cross, the YZ125 incorporates all the features that took the sport by storm: monoshock suspension employing a light alloy sub-frame, air-cushion front forks with offset axle, Torque Induction for trac-tabiiity throughout the rev range, ultra-accurate CDI ignition, and a six-speed gearbox. This year's engine has been redesigned to further reduce weight and mass and the chassis restyled to provide additional strength and also to reduce weight. And to enhance the effectiveness of the long-travel rear-suspension system, an additional reservoir has been located in the front down-tube. At Yamaha, development never stands still. The 1980 YZ125 is faster, lighter, stronger—and handles still better.

YZ250 One of the fastest, most forceful production motocrossers ever made, the YZ250 now incorporates a new chassis, designed to provide ad-ditional rigidity at an even lower weight. The 1980 engine is also both lighter and faster and, to take advantage of increased performance, the monoshock suspension system has been equipped with an additional reser-voir (located in the front down-tube).

The three most important YZs in Yamaha's 1980 line-up, all three the best in their class

All rather plain motorcycles that did their job well but hardly set the pulse racing in either appearance or performance. Then in 1978 the Honda CBX was announced, one of the most visually stunning motorcycles man has ever pro-duced, with a super sports tag. Honda were tak-ing the first step in rejuvenating their motorcycle line-up. During the 1970s Honda had produced two-stroke motocross machines, some quite good, but produced more from necessity than love. Their works team in the form of Gary Jones, Marty Smith and Marty Tripes had brought them five National titles, but the commitment from Japan had been missing. By 1979, this had changed. Graham Noyce had brought Honda the World 500 Championship crown in that year with a full works effort behind him, taking the title from Mikkola and Yamaha. Now it was

Yamaha's turn in the US.

To make matters even worse for Yamaha, Japanese motocross manufacturers were stand-ing at the edge of a technological breakthrough in rear suspension design. During the 1979 World Championship, Brad Lackey had the unenviable task of developing Kawasaki's new system, christened Uni-Track. If only the rear suspension had needed development it might not have been too bad, but in fact the complete motorcycle needed sorting and Brad ended up in 4th place in the world championship. But the design philos-ophy of the rear suspension was sound. A single shock absorber was mounted vertically behind the engine attached at one end to the frame rails and the other to the swinging-arm via a bell-crank. The design of the bellcrank was critical to the effectiveness of the suspension, for depending on the angles between it and the swinging-arm and the shock absorber, it was possible to produce a rising-rate suspension. This

Yamaha's sensational range leader, directly derived from the bike on which Heikki Mikkola won the 500cm³ world championship, has been updated and modified to include all the technological innovations developed in a hard season's racing. A larger capacity engine now produces 52bhp (an improvement of 7bhp). Both front and rear wheel travel have been substantially increased and the swinging arm lengthened to take advantage of the additional performance. Tank capacity has been increased, the front brake replaced by a new double leading shoe unit, and the monoshock suspension system equipped with an additional reservoir, located in the front down-tube. An outstanding competition motorcycle, refined by the rigours of world-class moto-cross, the YZ465 is designed single-mindedly for what it does best: winning races.

means that the more the suspension is compressed, the more it resists further compression. Some degree of rising rate is possible through the use of progressive rate springs but not the doubling of leverage rate (resistance to compression) that was possible with the bellcrank set-ups.

Yamaha were caught on the wrong foot as the competition started to bring out new motocross machines with rising-rate suspension. Progressively wound springs had been fitted to the De Carbon monoshock but the whole monoshock set-up was inferior to the new designs coming from the competition and Yamaha were slow to acknowledge that. One of the major problems had always been the position of the shock absorber high in the frame, upsetting the handling, rather inaccessible and prone to overheating in the poorly cooled confined space. In 1980, Yamaha took a step in the right direction and produced the third major frame design for the monoshock YZs.

The 80 cc and 100 cc egg-cup racers did not benefit from the new frame design. Instead, detail work was applied to the two models to improve them for the G series. The suspension travel on the YZ80G was considerably more than on the F, with a total of around 180 mm at both ends. Unfortunately some of this extra travel found its way to the saddle height which at 73 cm was a little tall for a typical minicycle rider. Engine changes added a touch more to the top end and also broadened the mid-range significantly enough to give the G a two-length advantage over an F at the end of a 100-metre straight. Gear ratios were not changed. The YZ80G was an improvement over the F model but unfortunately was overshadowed by Honda's return to the class with a fully trick CR80R. A powerful, peaky motor made it the experts' choice for the mini class, although less skilled riders could perform better on the YZ80G or RM80.

For 1980, it was the same story with the YZ100G as had been told for the D, E and F models before it; great engine but lousy steering. Both suspension travel and engine power had been increased a little, but the same flaw in the steering geometry that had caused the front end to wash out in the earlier models was still present. The YZ would get to the first turn of the track before its only competitor, the Suzuki, but the rider would have a hard time staying ahead.

The YZ125G really gave track testers a hard time when it was handed over for analysis. After being used to a long list of shortcomings that could be knocked up into a story, the new 125 must have come as a bit of a shock. There was almost nothing to complain about. It was now becoming standard practice to find a totally new motorcycle each model year and the Gs were no exception. Apart from changes to the power unit to increase maximum power slightly without sharpening up the already narrow powerband, all engine components were flipped to provide a rear wheel drive exiting on the right-hand side of the engine. Six-petal reed valves were also used, the natural resonance of the thinner petals more closely matching the engine speed of the 125. The piston returned to the old windowed skirt variety after yearly changes to the cut away skirt and inlet port had failed to solve the high piston-failure rate. The complete engine block was narrower and lighter. Other conspicuous changes included a new 'OW-style' cylinder head with different finning from the F model and attached to the cylinder by five bolts instead of four. With the change to a single front downtube frame, the exhaust port exited on the left side of the cylinder muff, enabling the pipe to clear the new frame.

It was the chassis, however, that was the star of the new machine. The large backbone tunnel for the monoshock disappeared. Instead the rear shock absorber was mounted in approximately the same attitude, but was upside down and attached to twin lugs welded to the top of the upper frame rails. The damper itself was also considerably shorter, with an external reservoir of oil that was mounted on the front downtube fully exposed to the cooling air flow. It was uncertain if this would significantly improve the overall cooling of the unit since only the hot oil in the damper body displaced by the damper piston would pass down the hose connecting reservoir and damper body. As the piston returned to its original position the same oil would be sucked back down the hose into the damper body. Maybe it would offer fractionally better cooling but it was no universal answer to the problem of cooling rear suspension. The reason for turning the damper upside down was twofold; firstly to reduce unsprung weight and secondly to improve access to the damping and preload adjustments.

The design of the frame had also changed quite considerably. Two large-diameter tubes supported the headstock, one running down in front of the engine and the other providing a short boomerang-shaped backbone above the engine. Under the engine two rails formed the cradle and swept up behind the engine to the lower end of the backbone tube. The twin-rail rear subframe joined the backbone just up from the cradle rails with two tubes running from the bottom of the cradle to support the other end of the subframe. Finally a single bracing tube ran from the front downtube to the point where the backbone tube angled up to the top headstock. The main advantage of this new design was the freedom it gave in the design of the rear suspension and consequent wheel travel, as well as lowering the centre of gravity of the bike. Wheel travel was extended to an amazing 290 mm, as much as anyone could ever need.

The YZ125G surprised everyone by its excellence. The only real complaint about the standard machine was the softness of the rear suspension, compromising the steering accuracy by allowing the rear end to break loose under acceleration. If the optional stiffer spring was fitted, this phenomenon disappeared, although the ride was not quite so cushy as with the softer spring. Everything else functioned extremely well and although not the fastest 125 available (the Honda was), it did have the most usable power. Unfortunately 50 per cent of the first batch of YZ125Gs to arrive in the US suffered persistent seizures, which were finally traced to the contact between a float bowl dowel pin support on the bottom of the carburettor float chamber and the engine cases. Under race conditions the two would knock together causing the fuel in the carburettor to foam, resulting in the engine running too lean, overheating and seizing. Shaving 3 mm off the dowel pin support fixed the problem and salvaged the YZs reputation as the best 125 available in 1980.

As well as undergoing the same chassis changes as the 125, the YZ250G was once again fitted out with a completely new engine. Narrower cases and a change in the number of teeth in the gearing without significantly changing the ratios, indicated a wish to save weight or use it to strengthen weak points. The compression ratio was raised a little and a head with both longitudinal and radial finning used. The cylinder was base-mounted to the crankcases to allow the complete cylinder casting to be used for the transfer ports without being restricted by the presence of long studs securing the cylinder. The porting was revamped with the intention of improving top-end power. First the exhaust port was bridged to ensure that piston ring life would be maintained. Only problem was, the port would need to be wider to be able to flow the same amount of exhaust gas. This was a little difficult since the main transfers were extremely close to the exhaust. The only possible solution was to 'eyebrow' the top of the port. This involved widening the top of the port in the cylinder wall above the transfer. If a pure T-form was used, the rings would suffer terribly from the sudden change of shape of the port. Instead, the roof of the port dropped gradually to the maximum width with the wall returning gradually to a normal port width. At its widest, the port was a gaping 68 mm wide with a 4 mm wide bridge, representing an amazing 97 per cent of the bore. It could scarcely be any wider! The other ports were also modified, the inlet being lower and wider, the transfers slightly higher. On the intake side the same 38 mm carburettor was used with different jetting, but the lift of the reeds was increased 3 mm to 12 mm. These changes, along with a larger volume exhaust pipe and an altered ignition curve, resulted in a gain of a total of 2 bhp from 7500 rpm to 9000 rpm with no loss of power at lower engine speeds.

Other engine changes included a bolt on the end of the kickstart shaft to hold the lever in place, instead of the pinch bolt on the splined boss. Some work was done on the shift mechanism to correct the stiffness and vagueness of earlier models. The same chassis changes were made as for the YZ125G with the added sophistication of progressively wound springs on the rear suspension. At the ends of the spring, both wire thickness and pitch between coils was reduced,

An air-cooled 250 factory engine of 1980 with a power valve

making the spring softer for small displacements but retaining the necessary stiffness for the serious stuff.

Just as the 125, the 250G proved to be almost faultless. The only deficiency of the bike as it was, was a chattering rear wheel on hard downhill braking over stutter bumps, but most testers considered it only a minor complaint. The front brake was described by some as the best fitted to any contemporary production motocross machine. That was until they got a taste of the double leading-shoe item fitted to works YZs. The engine could have produced a little more mid-range and low-end power, but that was a complaint that could be levelled at all 250 and 125 machines. The hot tip for YZ owners was to fit Boyeson dual-reeds that helped the mid-range significantly. But even left stock, the YZ250G was probably the best 250 motocrosser of 1980.

The open class bike in the YZ range was no longer a 400 but displaced 465 cc, with a larger bore and stroke than the YZ400F. A Yamaha tuning kit had been available for the YZ400F which consisted of a piston, rings and gaskets to match the 3 mm increased bore diameter that would result in an engine of 426 cc displacement. This bore was retained for the YZ465G, but the stroke increased 7 mm. Although the volume of the cylinder head was reduced, the new cylinder dimensions meant that the compression ratio actually dropped.

The same slimming exercise as the 250 had undergone was applied to the 465 which therefore had narrower crankcases and smaller gears throughout. In the transmission another attempt was made to improve the bike's poor reputation for gearchanges. The dogs on the engaging gears were no longer undercut, a technique to prevent the gears jumping out of engagement. Also for second, third and fourth gear, the number of engaging dogs was reduced from four to three, lowering the chances of missed gears at the expense of increased drivetrain snatch. The gearshift mechanism was also reworked with a ball bearing replacing the roller bearing on the outboard end of the gearshift drum.

Most of the chassis on the YZ465G was common to the YZ250G. There were, however, two noteworthy exceptions. Firstly, the front brake used a double leading-shoe to haul the 465 down from the frightening top speeds it was capable of. With a double leading-shoe system, there are two cam levers in the brake assembly that turn as the brake lever is squeezed. This results in the leading and trailing edge of both shoes being pushed into contact with the wall of the hub, thus providing far greater stopping power. At the beginning of the 1970s Yamaha's road-racing production machines had been equipped with *double* twin leading-shoes on the front wheel, so it was familiar territory for the company. The second chassis difference between the 250 and 465 was the 30 mm longer swinging-arm fitted to the larger bike to help keep the front wheel down under the ferocious acceleration it was capable of.

One thing about the YZ465G that guaranteed that it would be a best seller was that it was easily the fastest production motocross machine available. The only other machine that came any-

where near the Yamaha was the Maico 450, thanks mainly to its cornering agility. It was necessary to experiment with the position of the forks in the triple clamps to either sharpen up the steering a little by raising the forks or lower them for extra straight-line stability, whichever you preferred. The surfeit of power right off the low end, good steering, superb brakes and lengthy suspension combined to make the YZ465G the best open class bike of 1980.

Ironically, although Yamaha had produced its single best set of YZ racers in 1980, the works teams did not have a good year. In the 125 class Broc Glover was going for his fourth successive title but was finally beaten by the man who had been challenging him hardest for the two seasons before, Mark Barnett with his Suzuki. At the season's end there were only nine points between them but Barnett took four overall wins to Glover's two. An unfillable hole was blown in the Yamaha team when Bob Hannah broke a leg in a water-skiing accident before the start of the season and was sidelined the whole year. Mike Bell ended up second in the championship but was never a serious challenge to Kent Howerton riding superbly on his Suzuki. A consolation for Bell was the Supercross title, where he beat Howerton into 2nd place. The 500 class was a disaster with best Yamaha rider Rick Burgett finishing in 4th spot.

In Europe, Yamaha riders got off to a good start in the 125 and 500 classes. Marc Velkeneers was mounted on a water-cooled OW43 that was to appear a year later as the YZ125H. There were also occasional outings for him and team-mate Tetsumi Mitsuyasu, 1979 125 and 250 champion of Japan, on the OW47 equipped with power valve, not to appear on production machines until 1982. Unfortunately Velkeneers broke an ankle in the first moto of the mid-season German GP, at which point he was in 2nd place in the championship—a single point behind Harry Everts. Mitsuyasu ended 4th and Velkeneers 5th, a disappointing result after such a good start to

the year. In the 500 class, Andre Vromans and Yamaha's latest buy-in from Husqvarna, Hakan Carlquist, produced some good results, but were not consistent enough throughout the year to end higher than 4th and 3rd places respectively. Carlquist might have challenged Andre Malherbe on the Honda and Brad Lackey on the Kawasaki a little harder if he had not contracted

Left **One of the first Yamaha factory machines to undergo YEIS conversion was this 1980 125 of Mitsuyasu**

Below **Carlquist and Vromans spent a lot of the 1980 season racing against each other and were to end in third and fourth places in the world championships**

angina in the middle of the season, preventing him from starting in Finland and affecting his performance in Italy. He was clearly capable of winning on a Yamaha, but 1980 was not his year.

The Yamaha motocross line-up for 1981 totalled seven machines with the addition of the YZ60H, a sleeved-down version of the YZ80H which was unchanged since 1980. Another bike to mark time was the YZ100H, suggesting that Yamaha were about to forsake the 100 cc class and leave the tiny market to Suzuki. The serious machines in the series were the 80, 125, 250 and 465, and they were all significantly updated.

The YZ80H benefited enormously from the update, which was made to both the engine and chassis. The engine produced more power throughout the range and took over from Honda the title of holeshot king. The six speeds were changed to match the more powerful mill and a new compact shift drum running on ball bearings helped produce buttery-smooth changes. The clutch actuation mechanism also came from the 80's bigger brothers, the worm gear located in an engine sidecover being replaced by the vertically mounted cam rod. The frame design was the same but the steering had been quickened enormously by a tightening up of the rake to 27 degrees, causing the H model to shake its head a little down the straights. Suspension travel at both ends increased 35 mm, half of which was absorbed by other chassis changes resulting in an increased seat height of 20 mm. A chrome-molybdenum rear swinging-arm was fitted but painted aluminium to make it look tricker, although Yamaha claimed that equivalent aluminium aftermarket units were heavier and not so strong. With the era of rising-rate rear suspension dawning, the naming of the system used was becoming popular. Kawasaki had their *Uni-Track*, Suzuki their *Full-Floater* and Honda their *Pro-Link* so Yamaha's marketing boys got together and came up with *Mono-X* that was proudly emblazoned on the swinging-arm of all the YZ H series. The rear shock absor-

ber was also provided with an external oil reservoir that was clamped to the bracing rail between the backbone and front downtube. The weight of the YZ80H was two kilos lighter than the G, the use of a plastic instead of a steel fuel tank contributing. Faster, lighter and quicker steering than its predecessor, the YZ80H was the choice of the class experts in 1981.

For the YZ125H it at last happened. Yamaha had been running works liquid-cooled 125s on and off for five years and now at last the fruits of their experience was available over the counter. The machine that finally went into production bore a very close resemblance to the OW43 Velkeneers and Mitsuyasu had raced in GPs during 1980. In fact 1981 was the year that liquid-cooling entered motocross in a big way, with all of the Big Four except Kawasaki offering liquid-cooled 125s.

The YZ had a suprisingly intricate design that placed the radiator up above the front mudguard and used the frame to transport the coolant to the engine. It was a puzzling choice of location, since not only did it complicate the plumbing required, but the extra weight of the coolant along with the highish rear suspension could cause a return to top-heaviness experienced in the bad old days of the first monoshock-equipped YZs. The only real advantage was its relative invulnerability to crash damage in comparison to the side-radiators as used on the Honda and was in a better air-stream than a radiator directly in front of the engine but behind the front mudguard as on the Suzuki. The path of the water to the engine was from the bottom of the radiator via a short hose to the bottom of the hollow steering stem. From the steering stem the water passed into the frame, along the front downtube, exiting at the bottom, into a hose taking the coolant to the water pump on the left-hand end of the crankshaft. A pipe was bolted between the cylinder muff and the water pump. Exiting the cylinder head, the coolant passed via rubber hose up to the top

The 1980 YZ80G was good, but not as good as the CR80 from Honda

Water-cooling arrived on the YZ125H of 1981, but the works machines kept one step ahead by adopting power valves

of the headstock and into the top of the steering stem that was partitioned from the lower section that contained the cycled coolant, and into the top of the aluminium radiator. An intricate but ingenious design.

Apart from the changes required for the liquid-cooling, other modifications helped make the YZ125H a better bike than the best of 1980, the YZ125G. Porting, pipe and a 34 mm carburettor combined to give the H a touch more mid-range than before. There was no longer a copper gasket sealing the cylinder/cylinder head join. The two surfaces were carefully machined to give a good seal and two O-rings used to ensure no coolant found its way into the engine or out of the cylinder casting. With the cylinder well cooled, the designers felt it safe to return to the single ring first used on the YZ series and benefit from the reduced friction this would give. Primary gearing was reduced slightly and, since the transmission was unaltered, the overall gearing dropped as well. At last a functional shift lever with a spring-loaded tip was fitted to the YZ series.

The biggest change to the chassis became apparent as soon as the rider took his first tight corner. Just as on the YZ80, the steering rake had been pulled in 1·5 degrees to the extremely quick 27 degrees. The consequent instability could be felt on bumpy ground, aggravated by the weight of the coolant in front of the bars. But it sure could turn well. The stanchions from the YZ250G were used, with a flex-free 38 mm diameter. A new rear swinging-arm produced a 20 mm longer wheelbase for the machine, while minor changes in the rear suspension added 10 mm to the rear wheel travel. The progressively wound springs used on the 250 and 465 G models were now fitted to the 125, although the standard spring was still too soft to get the rear end to hook up well. No changes were made or needed for the excellent brakes.

The YZ125 had noticeably improved in the transition from G to H, but unfortunately the competition improved more. At least as far as Yamaha's arch rival in the smaller classes, Suzuki, was concerned. There was really only one thing that counted against Yamaha when backed up against the Suzuki, and that was the low and mid-range power differences. With its case reeds, the Suzuki had a far more useful powerband than the YZ, while steering and handling on both machines was excellent. Yamaha had slipped slightly from its two-year-old position as manufacturer of the best 125 motocross machine, but it hadn't slipped far.

After the drastic design changes the YZ250 had undergone each of the last few model years, the H model seemed to have hardly changed from the G. This was not entirely true, since the H was different in two important areas. Firstly another acronym came with the new bike and that was YEIS or Yamaha Energy Induction System. In the US this had been known as a boost bottle and had been available for a couple of years from aftermarket accessory manufacturers for any reed-valve-equipped machines. YEIS consisted of a small plastic bottle and a length of hose that attached to the rubber carburettor/reed-valve joint.

In a reed-valve engine, as the reeds closed, the inertia of the gas would carry it on towards the closed inlet port, where it would be reflected back into the carburettor and disturb the gas flow. With the bottle tapped into the inlet tract, the gas would flow up into the bottle rather than the closed port and not be reflected into the carburettor body. As the inlet port reopened, the gas in the bottle would join the main stream from the carburettor and flow into the crankcase. The time required for the charge to fill the bottle was such that the process was only effective for engine speeds below about 6000 rpm. But it was exactly these engine speeds where the YZ250G had been deficient and the mid-range power definitely picked up on the YZ250H.

Other engine changes were few. The width of the exhaust port 'eyebrow' was substantially reduced. Hot tip on cylinder mods was the raising of the tallest section of the exhaust port by 2 mm and widening it by 1 mm on either side of the bridge. Sixth gear was removed from the transmission, allowing the other gears to be widened, Yamaha claiming that the narrower gears on the G model had not been strong enough. The clutch-release mechanism cam rod now doubled as vent for the gearbox with a hose attached to the hollow shaft. An extra pair of plates was added to the clutch making a total of fourteen.

The other major change made to the YZ250H was the steepening of the rake by one degree to 28·5 degrees. At last it seems that Yamaha R & D had picked up on the gripe YZ riders had been making since the inception of the YZ series. The new steering head angle seemed perfect for motocross use, with no loss of stability noticeable but far quicker turning possible. The travel on the front fork was not increased, but 43 mm diameter Kayabas were fitted to eliminate all trace of front-end flex. The new forks were also equipped with phosphor-bronze bushes to reduce stiction. As on the 125, the wheelbase was lengthened with a swinging-arm 25 mm longer than the G model and the rear damper had a total of 30 damping adjustment positions. After a year with a smaller diameter rear hub, the 250 shared the same hub with the YZ465H, being stronger and more powerful. Cosmetic changes smacked of works trickery, as the alloy wheel rims were gold-anodized and the reservoir for the rear damper was painted the same colour.

The YZ250G had been the best motocrosser of its class in 1980 and consequently only detail changes were made to the H model. The suspension upgrade had unfortunately added 2 kg to the weight of the YZ, but this did not make itself felt. For one group, cross-country riders, the H model was a huge disappointment. The loss of sixth gear and the lower rake meant that they would stick to the G. For the red-blooded motocrosser it was a better machine, but the rising-rate suspension war was beginning to get off the ground and all the other Japanese manufacturers were offering machines equipped with the progressive suspension. In their first year

The 1981 YZ465H differed little from the previous model and was caught up by the competition

there were bugs to be sorted, allowing Yamaha to still hold a fine edge over the others. But Yamaha needed to join the revolution if they were to maintain their philosophy of continuous evolution.

Much the same story was true for the YZ465. Having been the best open class bike of 1980, only detail changes were made to transform it into the YZ465H. The new cylinder had a higher, wider inlet port and exhaust port and these coupled with the rejetted 38 mm carburettor and a new exhaust pipe were responsible for an extra bhp at the top end. Apart from the same transmission venting on the clutch release as the YZ250H and a new ignition coil to assist firing up the bike, the 465 engine remained unaltered. The power unit fitted into the same frame as used on the YZ250H and benefited or suffered from the rework in the same way.

The chassis changes alone were enough to guarantee that the YZ465H was a good bike, but it was no longer the best. Suddenly everyone was building large-capacity open class machines,

with the Maico 490 the clear horsepower king. Of the Japanese competition, Suzuki was the closest also with a 465 that produced similar peak power with the mill wrapped in a rising-rate suspension package. Ironically, the Suzuki lost out to the big YZ in exactly the same area that the Suzuki had defeated the YZs in the smaller classes—low-end power. The YZ had real low-end grunt and no discernible powerband, just tractor-like power right off the throttle stop. So for the moment the YZ465 was still close to the top but a major update would be needed in 1982 to keep it there.

The 1981 race season was not one of Yamaha's best. In the US, the 125 class was a disaster, with the highest placed Yamaha rider, Ricky Johnson, ending up seventh. The 250 turned into a two-man battle between a recovered Bob Hannah and the man who had stolen his crown during his recuperation, Kent Howerton, riding Suzuki. In fact the Howerton/Suzuki combination was clearly superior, winning 13 of the 16 motos in a wild battle throughout the season and taking the title from Hannah by 44 points. The 500 was Yamaha's sole championship title with Broc Glover, having grown too big for the 125s, leading team-mate Mike Bell to an easy 1–2 over Honda's Chuck Sun. After four years in the hands of Yamaha, the Supercross title passed to Suzuki's Mark Barnett, making 1981 the factory's best year in US motocross competition.

It looked like it would be Suzuki's year in the World Championship GPs and true to form they took the 125 title with little trouble. Marc Velkeneers once again put in some good rides but was not consistent enough to finish higher than fourth in the final standings. In the 250 Georges Jobé seemed to be running away with the championship for Suzuki until he broke a leg in the USSR and consistent second-place man Neil Hudson found himself with a chance of the championship. By winning both races in the USSR and riding to safe 4th and 6th places in the Netherlands, he took the title by two points

Far left **The début in France of the 1981 factory water-cooled 250 ridden by Neil Hudson and maintained by Bill Buchka ended in clouds of steam as mud clogged the radiator and the bike overheated**

Left **A month later in Austria, Hudson was on a totally different bike, with the 1980 power-valve air-cooled engine in a prototype rising-rate suspension chassis. He won**

Bottom **Despite the new chassis for 1981, Carlquist was unable to improve on his previous season's third place in the world championships**

and gave Yamaha their first 250 title since Hakan Andersson back in 1973. Carlquist and Vromans were once again pitted against the duo of Noyce and Malherbe in the 500 class but were not able to break the Honda stranglehold on the class and again ended up 3rd and 4th respectively. Only the 500 title in the US had been a clear-cut victory for Yamaha; their days of total domination seemed to have passed.

Having been displaced from their position as most successful motocross manufacturer, it could safely be assumed that Yamaha would wage total war on Suzuki in 1982. To do this it was vitally important to introduce a new rising-rate rear suspension. Suzuki's Full-Floater rear end had been instrumental in the success of both their factory racers and also their production machines. Yamaha had to come up with a comparable system not only due to the superior rear-end grip it produced, but to be seen not to be technologically stagnating. Well, Yamaha R & D came up with all the new technology the advertising guys could wish for. Two new liquid-cooled models, rising-rate suspension on four of the six-model range, power valves on two of the models and major changes to every bike in Yamaha's 1982 motocross line-up. Could so many changes all be effective?

The micro-cycles were given as much attention as the larger bikes. Even though there was no racing class for the 60 cc machines, the manufacturers considered them important since brand loyalty played a significant role in the move up the classes. The YZ60J got the benefit of the YEIS system used on the YZ250H, in a (largely unsuccessful) attempt at increasing low and mid-range power. Suspension travel increased 50 mm making it 170 mm at both ends. A cosmetically striking change that was made to all the 1982 YZs was the provision of a seat that extended up over the rear half of the petrol tank allowing the rider to move more easily over the bike without doing himself a mischief! A number of other small changes combined to make the YZ60J a powerful, light, well-suspended dirtbike, far superior to its only serious rival, the RM60 of Suzuki.

The YZ80J was almost totally new. Most striking development was the application of liquid-cooling, following the lines adopted on the YZ125H, with radiator above the front wheel and coolant passing through the frame to the engine. Two further engine changes were aimed at broadening the 80's powerband. The YEIS system was added as on the YZ60 and the exhaust port roof was 2 mm lower than the H model. Fed by a 26 mm carburettor, the YZ was far and away the most powerful 80 ccer and the liquid-cooling gave it the stamina to stay out front. Apart from the necessary frame changes for the radiator plumbing, the rake of the YZ80 was again steepened to an exceptionally acute 26 degrees, yet the bike maintained surprisingly good high-speed stability, helped perhaps by the 30 mm longer wheelbase. The only negative development on the YZ80J was the 7 kg weight increase caused by the conversion to liquid-cooling. Despite this the YZ80 was once again the best 80 cc dirtbike in 1982. For those expert riders who are never happy with stock engines, an improved performance was achieved by raising the roof of the exhaust port 2 mm, widening it 1·5 mm, the boost port by 2 mm and the inlet port by 4 mm.

In 1982, the two-marque battle for the US 100 cc class between Suzuki and Yamaha was finally decided in Yamaha's favour as Suzuki dropped the RM100 from their line-up. In retrospect it is interesting to consider if Yamaha would have made the bike they did in the YZ100J if they had known of Suzuki's intended withdrawal. Probably not, for in a class of one it's not too difficult to come out on top. So Yamaha produced a new machine for 1982 and it turned out, ironically, to be their best of the year. To maintain as low development costs as possible, the company used a combination of old and new technology. In 1980, the YZ125G had been the best 125 dirtbike money could buy, mainly because of its powerful engine. Without the complexities of liquid-cooling, this was a good starting point for the YZ100J. Sleeved down to 100 cc with a bore and stroke of 50 mm, the old transmission of the YZ100H was retained, since the ratios had been well chosen. Mid-range was boosted with the provision of the YEIS equipment. The mill slotted into a new frame that was built round Yamaha's new Mono-X rising-rate suspension. The general design of the frame was unaltered, but the rake had been steepened to 27 degrees and the mounting points for the rear shock had been repositioned.

The Mono-X rear suspension had the markings of a committee development about it. Yamaha were in a tricky position. After eight years of stating that the monoshock suspension was the best in the world, they would lose serious face by introducing a year after the other Japanese manufacturers, a vertical shock with rising-rate geometry. The loss of face is the worst thing that can happen to the Japanese so a compromise was needed. They had to produce rising-rate suspension without seeming to change the geometry of the rear suspension significantly. The damper would have to maintain its traditional sloping attitude under the seat and fuel tank. Unfortunately, if the design requirements are a compromise there is a good chance that the efficacy of the design will also be compromised. This was true for the Mono-X suspension.

The most conspicuous change to the rear end was the disappearance of the upper fork of the swinging-arm. Now a single, massive extruded-aluminium box-section fork held the rear wheel. Two lugs were welded to the swinging-arm just in front of the pivot point. A short push lever was mounted vertically between the lugs and turned on phosphor-bronze bushes. The top of the push lever was attached to an aluminium pivot arm. The arm was L-shaped but with the longer arm horizontal as if the L had been rotated 90 degrees anti-clockwise. The end of the longer arm bolted to the frame turning on roller bearings, the end of the shorter arm to the bottom of the rear damper, and the right-angle of the two arms to the top of the push lever. Phosphor-bronze bushes were also used at the damper mounting.

The rising rate of suspension resistance to compression came about as follows. As the rear wheel moved upwards, the angle between the push lever and the pivot arm attached to the frame would become more acute. The more acute it became the less rotation of the pivot arm took place for a given movement of the push lever, hence the suspension compression decreases. The disadvantage of the design in comparison to those of the other Japanese manufacturers was the position of the heavy damper high in the frame. This combined with the high-placed radiators on the liquid-cooled models, to produce a centre of gravity that had a detrimental effect on the handling of the machine.

On the YZ100J this was not the case and the Mono-X suspension worked well. Even with only 250 mm of travel, the evilest of bumps was competently absorbed. As was to be expected, the steering of the YZ100J was very quick yet, as on the YZ80J, there was no evidence of instability at high speed. So with an engine that could be revved or plonked and a chassis capable of taking everything thrown at it, the YZ100J was an excellent machine. The magazine *Motocross*

The chassis update that was common to the big three of Yamaha's YZ range, exemplified by this YZ250J, was unfortunately not a success

Action even went so far as to say that had they had such an award, the YZ100J would have been their Bike of the Year for 1982. Praise indeed.

Unfortunately, the YZ125J was not so well received. It was not a bad bike, but the competition was better, at least as they came out of the crate. The YZ125J was one of the two most innovative motocross motorcyles on the market in 1982, the other being the YZ250J. But despite what the ads imply, innovation doesn't necessarily mean superiority. The new 125 was decked out with liquid-cooling, rising-rate rear suspension and YPVS (Yamaha Power Valve System) to vary the height of the exhaust port with engine speed.

While most of Yamaha's 'technological tricks', such as reed valve, monoshock etc., had originated in the dirtbike world only to pass on to other types of machine, the reverse was true of the power valve. Originally developed to help Kenny Roberts win his first 500 cc World Championship in 1978, it had appeared on a production-line machine in 1981, when the TZ250H was announced equipped with a mechanically controlled power valve.

It was this design that was adopted for the YZ125J and YZ250J. The theory behind the

power valve was quite simple. At low engine speeds, a high exhaust port roof must not be used since if the port opens early, it will be open so long that the fresh charge squirting from the transfers will not only drive the exhaust gases out of the combustion chamber, but disappear down the exhaust pipe themselves and be only partially returned to the cylinder by the reflected exhaust pressure waves. However, if a low roof is chosen for the low engine speeds, at high engine speeds, the exhaust port will not be open long enough for thorough scavenging to take place. By increasing the height as the engine speed increases, the compromise of a fixed port roof height is avoided.

The cylindrical valve was located in the manifold close to the exhaust port, cutaway flush with the manifold roof. The mechanical governor was driven off the primary gear on the left-hand end of the crankshaft and splined to a short ball bearing-supported shaft. Pinned to the other end of the shaft was a cup with four radial slots, in which steel balls ran. Between the gear and the cup was a spring pushing up against two sets of thrust bearings sandwiching a grooved collar and a retainer covering the open end of the cup. As the engine speed increased, the centrifugal force caused by the spinning cup would cause the balls to move along their slots and push against the retainer covering them. This would in turn cause the retainer to move along the shaft and take a fork that engaged with the grooved collar with it. This lateral movement was translated into rotation of the valve via a bellcrank assembly running up the left-hand side of the cylinder. Claimed to be maintenance-free, some owners experienced problems of the steel balls sticking in the cup and jamming the power valve in a fixed position.

But the new engine as a whole worked well. Going for a mid-range and top-end increase without hitting the low end any more, the increased power was clearly felt and the YZ proved, once again, to be the most powerful 125 of the year. The power valve could not claim sole credit for this improvement, since piston, cylinder, head, ignition, carburettor and pipe were all new. The inlet port was widened to 56 mm, i.e. 100 per cent of the bore! It was of course necessary to provide some extra support for the piston skirt, or the engine would have self-destructed within five minutes of running. Two vertical bridges were used at the width of the boost port above the inlet port, ensuring adequate support for the piston, although reducing the amount of charge the port could flow. Gearbox ratios were not changed, but Yamaha claimed that the new gears were stronger than their predecessors. The number of fingers on the clutch basket was increased to reduce their wear. The final drive rear wheel sprocket lost two teeth, raising the overall gearing, which in fact proved to be too high.

On the 125, the Mono-X suspension did not perform as well as it should have. It seemed to be rather harsh and particularly poor when running over stutter bumps. The rear damper fitted to the 125, 250 and 490 now had a 20-position compression damping adjuster that worked by restricting the flow of oil between the main body of the damper and the external reservoir. With the ability to dial in both compression and rebound damping as well as preload the spring, the YZ suspension was undoubtedly the most adjustable available. The only problem was that with so many combinations possible and the varying degree of expertise in setting up suspension to be expected from YZ owners, the stock settings needed to be good for the majority of

riders. This was seldom the case, and while the suspension could be made to work well, it was beyond the capability of many of the owners.

So, with the most powerful engine and potentially good suspension and despite the 1 kg weight increase due mainly to strengthening of the frame around the rear suspension pivot point, the YZ125J could run with the Suzuki and Kawasaki opposition. But without considerable expert attention to the rear suspension it could not and was marked down by testers as an inferior machine. Despite this the J was once again a vast improvement over the H and not far off the best of the 1982 125s. For those who found the top end disappointing, the removal of 15 mm from the exhaust pipe at the header/diffuser junction would go some way to please them.

The YZ250J was purely the big brother of the 125J. With liquid-cooling, YPVS and Mono-X suspension, it, like the 125, was the trickest machine in its class. But just like the smaller bike it was not the best. The design of the 250 was identical to that of the 125 except, due to the mirror engine layout, the power-valve governing mechanism was located on the right-hand side of the engine. The exhaust manifold was centrally located, forcing a change to the frame design used on the 125, with a short downtube and the two rails of the cradle starting halfway up the front of the engine. The fully open exhaust port had a 2·5 mm higher roof than the H model, indicating how much the H model had been oriented towards the maximum power at high engine speeds. The port was oval shaped without the eyebrowing or bridge, the width having come down to a more reasonable 48 mm. The inlet port was not bridged on the J but a small lip in the centre of the port provided a fraction more support for the battered piston. The primary transmission was via straight-cut gears instead of helical, ostensibly due to the fact that the right-hand end of the crankshaft was now driving three gears, the water pump, power-valve governor and the transmission, and power loss had become more significant. The clutch basket was strengthened in the same way as the 125 and gearing was unaltered except for the use of a rear wheel sprocket with three extra teeth. As on the 125, this was a mistake and the 45-tooth sprocket listed as an alternative part needed to be fitted.

Left and far left **The difference an open and closed power valve made to the exhaust port height can be clearly seen from these photographs**

Right **Rear suspension problems sealed the fate of the YZ125J**

Chassis changes included the new frame modified for the Mono-X and the central exhaust manifold, as well as a steeper headstock at 27·5 degrees. As usual on the YZ series, the steeper rake was accompanied by a modest 10 mm increase in wheelbase. No change was made in the dimensions of the front forks, but the damping characteristics were altered to reduce compression and increase rebound damping. The tie rod for the full-floating rear brake was now an aluminium item. The twin-leading-shoe drum brake first seen on the YZ465H was fitted to the 250 to improve the stopping power that was needed to bring the 5 kg heavier machine down from speed. In fact it was this excess weight that was the most serious complaint levied against the 250, it being at least 5 kg heavier than the Japanese competitors. Once the gearing had been sorted out, the power was good, particularly in the mid-range. The general opinion of the Mono-X was that the principle seemed all right, but the progression it produced would have to be reworked. It seemed too soft in the first half of travel and too firm in the second, yet still managing to bottom out on occasion. As with the 125, the J was an improvement over the H, and it was a competent machine, but it was surpassed by all the other Japanese companies in this cut-throat class. A power improvement throughout the range could be achieved by widening the exhaust port 2 mm, raising the roof 0·5 mm, widening the boost port 2·5 mm on the ignition side of the engine, cutting away the lip in the inlet port and lowering the floor of the inlet port by 3·5 mm. It was essential to remove the lower piston ring or it would catch in the widened boost port.

Changes to the open class machine were somewhat less radical. In the drive towards more powerful engines, the YZ bore grew 2 mm giving it a displacement of 487 cc. The YEIS system, discarded on the power-valve models, was used on the 490 to clear the low-end blubbering the 465s had experienced. The inlet side of the cylinder

was altered slightly, with the port opening earlier and the boost port above the inlet port bridged. The same clutch mod was made as for the 125 and 250, and straight-cut primary gears were fitted. Only four speeds were provided in the gearbox, the old first gear being removed and the remaining four moving up a place. The resulting extra space in the gearbox enabled wider, stronger gears to be provided. In the US, the rear drive sprocket lost two teeth, resulting in higher overall gearing that was as inappropriate on the 490 as it had been on the 125 and 250. In contrast, the European models had rear sprockets

Above **Even the earth-moving power of the increased capacity YZ490J couldn't make up for the poor rear end**

Left **At last the 250 went fully trick with both water-cooling and a power valve. The engine was a killer but excess weight and the chassis ruined it**

with 50 teeth, probably too low to be totally effective.

In contrast to the other YZs of 1982, the rake of the 490 was not steepened, the only frame modifications being to accommodate the Mono-X suspension. Changes common to the 250 were front forks with less compression and more rebound damping, a 20 mm longer wheelbase, an aluminium rear brake tie rod and a new rear damper with adjustable compression damping.

Predictably, the 490 also shared some of the bad traits of the 250. The weight of the top dis-placement machine rose 3 kg although many riders complained that it actually felt a lot heavier. Recalibration of the rear suspension was also required, with the same gripe that it felt too soft over the first half of the travel and too hard over the rest. The engine produced good smooth power, but the four-speed transmission effec-tively eliminated the 490 from use off the motocross track. A pity since the largest YZ had made a name for itself in desert racing. As on the 250, it had the potential of being one of the best open class machines available, but not out of the crate. Mods suggested by Yamaha to improve performance included an extra 20 mm added to the exhaust pipe at the header/diffuser pipe junction to improve low-to-mid-range power and a 1 mm wider exhaust port for the top end. Some tuners took another 1 mm off the exhaust port and also raised the exhaust roof 1 mm.

Just to make matters worse, the first batch of 490s had some quality-control problems. The rear end was a mess. On both 490s and 250s, the chain-guides were off-centre and the marks

on the swinging-arm for aligning the rear axle were not accurate. The combination of these two production errors caused persistent chain problems. On some bikes the YEIS hose was too long and kinked, making the engine pop and bang its way around the track. The removal of a 20 mm section solved the problem.

As far as competition went in 1982, it was again a bad year for Yamaha. Only the 250 class showed any promise with Danny La Porte travelling to Europe for the 250 GPs and retaining the title for the company with a very strong perform-

ance in the second half of the season. In the US it was also the 250 class that was Yamaha's strongest. Rick Johnson and Broc Glover riding what was claimed to be very near stock 250Js pushed Honda's Donnie Hansen very hard for the title, but Johnson ended three points behind Hansen with Glover another three behind Johnson.

Honda were very strong that year taking the Supercross, 500 and 250 titles in the US. Apart from the 250 class Yamaha were not in the same class in US competition. The 500 cc World

Championship was dominated by the Suzuki pair of Vromans and Lackey, the American finally getting the title. Neil Hudson, 250 World Championship winner in 1981, did well to end in 3rd spot on a standard YZ490J. Factory rider Carlquist was never in the running after breaking his wrist just before the season started and a finger at the West German round.

In the 125 class, Marc Velkeneers again made an excellent start, winning the first two rounds in the Netherlands and Belgium. However, a leg injury sustained at the French round meant that he dropped back to a final 4th place in the end standings.

Left **An unusual mount for Danny La Porte is this 1982 factory 490 complete with power valve**

Below **The engine number every motocross rider in 1982 would have sold his soul to own. La Porte's 1982 OW57 250**

After the glorious years at the end of the 1970s, Yamaha had been displaced from their position at the top of motocross sport and their production machines seemed to have followed suit. In many ways staying on the top of the pile is more difficult than getting there in the first place. The fact that they had stayed there for so long reflects the competence of the designers that had produced the machines and the abilities of the riders to get them to the chequered flag first. Such a combination is essential; one without the other will not win races. Since several of the US team members from the 1970s were still riding YZs, but not into first place, it would suggest that the bikes were letting them down. In order to maintain a healthy slice of the diminishing off-road market, Yamaha had to improve their machinery.

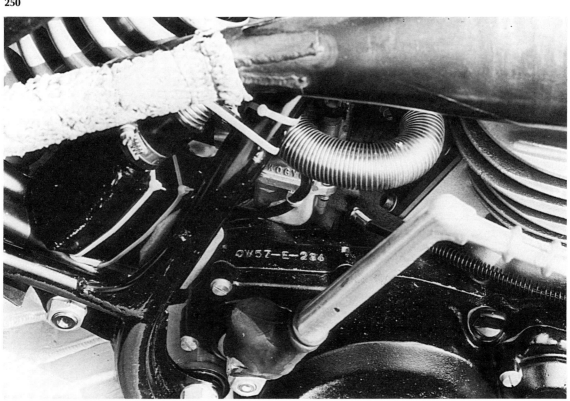

8 | The Stock Exchange

This revised version of the rising-rate monoshock suspension was introduced on the K series of YZs and remained unaltered through to 1986

After the disaster of the previous year, 1983 would be critical for Yamaha. The poor showing of both production and works machines had severely tarnished their image as top motocross manufacturer and a poor image hit the sales figures hard. This wouldn't have been so bad if off-road motorcycle sales were booming; a lower percentage of high sales can still turn out to be a lot of motorcycles. But there was no boom. In fact motorcycle sales had been declining since the peak at the end of the 1970s, and in 1982 the drop in sales had steepened. So, in order to maintain a steady income, every company was forced to go for a greater market share. The machines had to be good and the image one of success. Yamaha had neither in 1982. If this didn't change, the real possibility existed that the YZs would fall seriously behind their native competitors' models in terms of excellence. This would probably prove fatal for the company since its philosophy of continuous evolution would stifle the technological innovation that would be needed to bridge the ever-widening gap. The result could be the end of the company's involvement with motocross.

Yamaha had no intention of letting this scenario develop and thankfully there were some bright moments at the end of the 1982 season as the first 1983 production machines became available. In the US, Glover and Johnson took pre-production YZ250Ks to 1st and 2nd place at the last Supercross event at San Diego.

The bikes were 100 per cent stock and were handed over to a local radio station after the night, to be raffled. The winter-run five-event Trans-Cal series was also dominated by Yamaha, Glover taking the 250 title and Bell the 500. It seemed as if Yamaha had seen the danger and had produced machines that would get them back to the top. In fact this was not entirely true.

Two of Yamaha's six-machine K-series line-up were not changed significantly. The YZ60K got a new cylinder with wider inlet port and wider and higher exhaust port to boost power a little, but nothing else changed. The YZ60 had been unchallenged in 1982, but with the arrival of hi-tech Honda and Kawasaki machines in the class, it was no longer the undisputed king. In particular the Green Meanie with its powerful engine, long-travel suspension and rising-rate suspension challenged the YZ for the title of class champion.

Without another manufacturer in the 100 class to compete with, the YZ100K was unaltered, apart from decal changes, from its predecessor. All other models underwent a considerable upgrade in two main areas, the cooling system of the liquid-cooled bikes and the rear suspension for all of the series. It was these two areas that had caused so many problems for the J models and it was clear that Yamaha were responding directly to the criticisms that had been levied at the two designs. A redesign of the layout of the cooling system resulted in the repositioning of the radiator. The fork-mounted radiator had upset the front-end steering and also affected the performance of the front fork due to the hot air raising the internal air pressure by as much as 10 psi.

On the YZ80K, the single radiator was now mounted on the front downtube of the frame, offset to the right-hand side of the engine to reduce clogging from the front wheel and to place it squarely in the airstream. In addition a plastic shroud on the outside of the radiator helped protect it from dirt and debris and a crash-bar fitted to prevent destruction at the first slide-out. A simple two-hose arrangement carried the coolant from the base of the radiator to the pump mounted on the right-hand end of the crankshaft, returning via a hose from cylinder head to the top of the radiator. A safety vent in the radiator cap was piped to the rear of the bike out of harm's way.

The other major change adopted throughout the K series was a revised Mono-X suspension. After the criticism leveled at the J-series Mono-X by press and customers, fully supported by the opinions of their own factory riders, Yamaha redesigned the rear suspension. Of all the suspension systems produced by the competition, the new Mono-X was most like Honda's Pro-Link, in that the compression of the damper was imparted at the bottom of the spring rather than to the top via connecting rods as on the Uni-Track and Full-Floater systems. There was now a single aluminium pivot-arm with three mounting eyes. The front lower eye was attached, via a short connecting rod, to the frame. The rear lower eye was bolted to the forward face of the cross-bracing of the swinging-arm and the upper eye to the bottom of the damper. On the YZ80K all pivots turned on phosphor-bronze bearings, whereas the other models used roller bearings for the frame and swinging-arm pivots. Also grease nipples were fitted on the 125, 250 and 490 but surprisingly omitted on the 80. The upper end of the damper bolted to the end of the backbone rail of the frame and was therefore far shorter and, angled at about 45 degrees, closer to the vertical position of the other rising-rate systems.

One thing was certain about the new system, there was no way of estimating the change of leverage ratio over the wheel's arc of travel with the naked eye. There were too many pivot points to get a feel for the way the spring would be compressed, but Yamaha claimed that it was softer over the first third of travel, to take in the stutter bumps, and harder over the rest to prevent the

In the hands of an expert, the YZ250K was the fastest stock machine in its class

bottoming that occurred on the J. On the YZ80K it worked well, after the rebound damping and spring preload had been set up for the rider.

Other new items on the 80 included a new cylinder, head and pipe, giving the engine slightly more low end and a good top-end boost. All shafts in the engine were drilled to cut weight and this contributed significantly to the 5 kg reduction. The transmission was not touched otherwise but the carburation was modified for the new engine porting. Actually the first batch of YZ80Ks delivered to the US did not have rejetted carburation and needed to be called in for a dealer service to put them right. The repositioning of the radiator forced the use of a cutaway petrol tank, and the frame needed some extra lugs welded to accompany the revised rear suspension. The only other significant change was the upgrade of the front suspension to 33 mm diameter stanchions and an additional 15 mm of travel, to complement the 20 mm increase at the rear end. The total package of the YZ80K was a great improvement over the J but as so often happens, the others had improved more. The KX80 of Kawasaki had the most powerful engine, and the rest of the package was good enough to make it the best 80 cc motocross machine of

1983. Both the YZ and RM were close second-bests, the RM handling better and the YZ having a better engine.

Apart from the new Mono-X suspension and liquid-cooling system, the YZ125K underwent a serious weight-saving programme that succeeded in paring off 3·5 kg and bringing the figure down to the FIM minimum for the class. The sources of the saving varied from the thinner walled frame tubing and lighter alloy wheel rims to plastic water impeller instead of steel and a round slimline cylinder jacket. The weight saved was probably as useful as an extra pony from the engine. The 1982 YZ125 had been the fastest of the class, but with a very peaky delivery. Yamaha decided to mellow the power a little, concentrating on increasing the mid-range. The most conspicuous consequence of this decision was the new exhaust that exited straight out from the exhaust manifold and didn't bend up and over the engine until it almost fouled the front mudguard. The longer header pipe would knock a little off the top end but increase the low-to-mid-range torque.

Many engine components were replaced in the general weight-reduction exercise but their design was not altered. Although two radiators were used on the K, their total capacity was less than on the J and H models, so the water pump was geared up to circulate it faster. The sprocket on the rear wheel had been raised by two teeth to lower the gearing as had been standard practice on all Js, but another two teeth would have been better still.

The frame design was unaltered, although rake was raised slightly to just over 28 degrees, since the wheelbase had been brought back 15 mm. The front forks were of a new design with pressure-sensitive pop-off valves opening only under high loads caused by very sharp fork movement, and providing a dual-rate damping system, for gradual or sharp bumps. No increase was made in the already luxurious front wheel travel.

The YZ125K performed better in the company of its peers than had the YZ125J, but it was still bested by the Greens and the Red and Blues. The Kawasaki was a rocket ship, with a disc brake up front and excellent Uni-Track rear suspension, while the Honda's handling was superb. In the right hands and with the right mods, the YZ125K could be a winner, but the Honda and Kawasaki were awfully good motorcycles as stock. Performance mods for the YZ included narrowing each vertical bridge in the inlet port by 2 mm and lopping 5 mm out of the header of the exhaust pipe.

After Glover and Johnson's success at the end of 1982 with the pre-production YZ250K against full-factory machines, it appeared as if the new model would mark the company's return to the top of the pile. It transpired, however, that the new machines worked best in the hands of experts, especially Yamaha experts. As on the 125, Yamaha aimed to improve the mid-range power and the first step they took in achieving this was to change the engine dimensions to a square 68 mm. The lengthening of the stroke would lower the top engine speed a little and generally increase off-peak torque. The spring in the power-valve linkage was stiffened, delaying the rotation of the valve in the exhaust manifold and thus increasing the mid-range power. Maybe the spring was a little too stiff, for there tended to be a slight flat spot around the transition to mid-range that could perhaps have been caused by the exhaust port roof being too low. Although not as noticeable as on the 125, the new exhaust pipe was a few centimetres longer, helping the low end a little. On the inlet side, the six-petal reed was replaced by an eight-petal item, as the inlet port was opened out some more and the 38 mm Mikuni rejetted.

Aware of the complaints of the gearing for the J, all transmission ratios except first were lowered a little and the rear sprocket gained three teeth. As on the 125, still lower gearing would have been possible, since stock the 250 could pull 80 mph in fifth, not much use on a motocross track. A number of clutch failures in 1982, prompted the return to a steel pressure plate, dating back 15 years to Yamaha's R1 350 roadster, in place of the fragile aluminium plate of the J.

After mid-range fatigue, excess weight was declared enemy number two by the Yamaha designers as they fought to get the obese 107 kg 250J down to the 98 kg FIM minimum. Amazingly enough they succeeded, although it was possible that they might have been a little too fanatical in their efforts as the strength of a number of chassis components was barely adequate. The same items were lightened as on the 125, namely a thin-walled frame, lighter wheels and in addition thinner walled fork stanchions. Fork bending on landing from high jumps, although rare, did occur. The engine also delivered up a few grams, in the cylindrical cylinder muff, drilled shafts, narrower primary gears, an aluminium kickstart lever and a shorter gearchange pedal.

The resulting machine was an unqualified improvement over the previous model which had finished fourth in a field of four in most of the shoot-outs. Although the fastest 250 available, it was not as easy to ride fast as the Honda with a far smoother power delivery. The YZ required considerable concentration to be ridden hard, but the reward would be exceedingly fast lap times. There was no problem with getting the YZ to turn, despite the slight shortening of wheelbase and increase of rake caused by the new Mono-X suspension. There was a general agreement that the Mono-X was vastly improved but that it still had some way to go before measuring up to the competition from Japan. Some time spent setting it up for a track was essential and would produce a good ride, but not as plush as the others. Since Yamaha were the only company who still manufactured their own damper, a logical move would have seemed to be a switch to another company's product. In Europe, the company were developing close relations with Öhlins of Sweden, that were later to prove very profitable.

The same design criteria were applied to the YZ490 as had been applied to the 125 and 250. The weight came down by 9·5 kg, and the new power characteristics featured a very strong low- and mid-range power output. No power valve for the head of the family; without the need to tune for peak power, it was possible to port for off-peak power and take what there was at the top end. Similarly liquid-cooling was not deemed necessary since there was more power on tap than most people could use anyway, so if a couple of ponies disappeared during the course of a moto, it was no big deal. The header pipe of the 490K was longer than that of the J, but the overall length barely changed. No other significant changes were made to the engine, apart from the replacement of a few components for lighter items and the same clutch modification as the 250.

As on the 250, the majority of the weight saved came out of the chassis, with a lighter frame, wheels and suspension. The chassis geometry was not altered, despite the fact that the 490 had never been a very fast turner. In fact turning on the 490K through a tight corner was a real task, requiring a slightly open throttle and

weight on the front wheel, the latter being particularly difficult to achieve due to the width of the petrol tank. The suspension on both ends was too soft as usual, but worked reasonably well. It was the engine that really made the YZ competitive. Stump-pulling power right off the low end and a big fat mid-range powered it into the first corner well ahead of the competition. It was the holeshot king of 1983. But whereas the engine would have guaranteed the best of the class award a few years before, more finely balanced packages from Honda and Suzuki were given the nod over the YZ.

While not everyone liked the YZ490 in 1983, the two people most important to Yamaha did. Yamaha took both World Championship and US National titles in the 500 class and it was Carlquist and Glover that did the hard work in getting them. Glover pulverized the opposition with a mid-season series of wins that got him to the top of the table and kept him there. Kent Howerton's consistency brought him second place but a clear 33 points behind. In an injury-free year, Carlquist made a reasonable season start and got better as the summer progressed. From the fourth round in Sweden, he started reeling Malherbe in, taking over the number one spot with a win at Carlsbad in the USA. Apart from a DNF in France the next week, Carlquist kept a cool head and extended his lead week by week and clinched the title in the last round in the Netherlands.

These were the only two titles to go to Yamaha. Danny La Porte finished second to Georges Jobé on his Suzuki, but a long way behind. Jim Gibson had trekked to Europe to try for glory in the 125 class and Yamaha had produced a real factory special to make it worth his while. Jim Gibson, Pekka Vehkonen and Jack Vimond were provided with OW65 machines which were unusual in that the engine induction was controlled by a disc valve. Previously seen on the 1982 KTM factory 125, crankcase induction was provided via a disc valve mounted in

Broc Glover laps Dave Thorpe during the first race of the 1983 Motocross des Nations in Belgium

the position usually used for crankcase reed blocks. Driven by a train of gears from the crankshaft, the bike was initially down on power with respect to Rinaldi and Geboers' Suzukis but by mid-season it had an edge over them. Gibson could do no better than 3rd place in the final GP standings and 16-year-old Ron Lechien did well to finish 4th in the US 125 class on the same machine. In the US Scott Burnsworth was runner-up to Honda's Bailey in the 250 title, despite not winning a single event. The competition results of 1983 were better than those of 1982, but not a shadow on the halcyon days of 1979 and 1980.

So for 1984, Yamaha had at least some competition successes to boost sales of the new L models. Despite only being in the 500 class, where the sales of production bikes formed a fraction of total motocross sales, there was considerable prestige attached to the class. A mixture of awe and admiration surrounded the riders who were able to tame the 50+ bhp monsters and hustle them round the track in anything close to the times of the lightweight 125s. If the bikes were also good, Yamaha might just scratch its way back to the top.

By and large, the engines of the K models had been good enough to be used as a base on which to build improved blocks, correcting the weaknesses exposed when running with the competition during the year. The chassis was fine, except for the unending saga of the rear suspension, which, after ten years of YZs, should

131

have been sorted. The YZs had got within sniffing distance of the leadership of several classes. A careful upgrade and they might just be there.

Firstly, the YZ100L was there looking neat and tidy with its L-series decals on a YZ100J. With 100 cc classes still being run in the US and miscellaneous other countries around the world and zero development costs being incurred, every bike sold delivered a pretty decent profit margin. Being a single manufacturer in a class can be quite lucrative.

The Kawasaki had ended up as best 80 ccer due to its rocket of an engine. If Yamaha could get close to the Kawasaki in terms of engine output, the superior chassis would ensure its choice as class best. A touch of the 'eyebrowing' first seen on the YZ250G was decided upon to preserve piston life and yet allow the exhaust port to be opened up. With slightly wider transfers and a lower inlet port floor, the 26 mm Mikuni needed rejetting and of course a new pipe was fitted. Complementing the higher compression ratio was a drop in spark advance of the ignition, to reduce the chance of detonation setting in. Both primary and final gearing was changed as well as the upper three gearbox ratios. The overall effect was to raise the gearing to take advantage of the extra low- and mid-range power. The combination of radiator dimensions and pumping capacity were juggled to provide a smaller radiator able to dissipate more heat.

On the chassis side, the new frame of the same design was lighter and suspension travel increased at both ends to approach the stroke found on the larger YZs. The design of the Monocross suspension, as it was now called, was not changed but the dimensions of the linkages produced a slightly different suspension rate. The usual annual cosmetic changes took place, emphasized this time by a fire-red frame that all 1984 competition models received.

Yamaha did well with the YZ80L, but the KX80 was still a little more powerful than the YZ and thus the choice of experts. Low end was better

on the YZ and the mid-range present on the K was as strong as ever, but the engine signed off before delivering much on the top end. Handling and front and rear suspension categories were all YZ strong points and only the disc brake of the KX at last bested the traditionally good Yamaha brakes.

For 1984, Yamaha produced the best handling and suspended motocross 125. At last they got it right after ten years of criticism of the rear-end inadequacies and, in the early days, slow steering. The engine hadn't been a problem for a good five years so the YZ125L had to be a winner, right? Wrong. As unbelievable as it might seem, the designers turned a delight of a motorcycle into an out-and-out loser by fitting a dog of an engine. In their obsession for improving mid-range power, they completely sacrificed the top end, producing a mill that pulled well but ran out of steam at a woefully low engine speed.

A lot of attention had been paid to the engine as witnessed by the cylinder casting. There were two unusual features in the porting arrangement, neither of which had appeared on production machines before, but had been adopted by some enterprising tuners. On the exhaust side, the oval-shape port, with a significantly wider top than bottom, found on the K was exchanged for a symmetrical rounded rectangle, giving the piston ring an easy time. To effectively increase the width of the port without compromising ring longevity, 10 mm circular sub-ports were cut on either side of the main exhaust, and they exited into the power-valve chamber and only opened as the roof of the main port was raised. This was essentially the same as 'eyebrowing' without the increased loading of the piston ring.

On the opposite side of the cylinder, the inlet manifold was modified to include an oblong sub-port on the right-hand side of the inlet port. The port did not exit on the wall of the cylinder but extended down into the crankcase, joining up with the base of the transfer passage of the right-hand auxiliary passage. The use of a single sub-

port was puzzling but the intention was clear and linked to a rethink that was taking place in the world of two-stroke engine design.

The goal of every high-performance two-stroke engine is to scavenge the engine as thoroughly as possible of the exhaust gases. Even the most powerful engines of recent times have not achieved scavenging efficiency greater than 75 per cent, leaving the residual exhaust gases mixed with, and thus diluting, the fresh charge. The more charge flowed through the engine from the crankcase, the greater the purity of the ignited charge in the combustion chamber. This flow has always been achieved by pressure changes originating from two engine components, the exhaust pipe and the crankcase. In the early days of serious two-stroke engineering at the start of the 1960s, most credit for the transfer of the charge from the crankcase to the combustion chamber was given to the primary compression in the crankcase. In order to increase this pressure, small crankcase volumes were designed, resulting in primary compression ratios of 1·5 or higher. However, it was realized during the 1970s that correct exhaust design could achieve as effective a transfer of charge as a high primary compression ratio, which would then allow larger crankcase volumes to be used. The greater volumes would provide more charge to flow through the engine and improve the purity of the charge trapped and ignited.

Top **The 1984 YZ80L almost put Yamaha back at the top of the minicrossers, but the Kawasaki still had the edge in power and handling**

Centre **Despite a fully-trick engine, the YZ125L was disappointingly uncompetitive**

Left **In the hands of Ricky Johnson, a standard YZ250L defeated the might of the Honda factory effort to take the 1984 US National title**

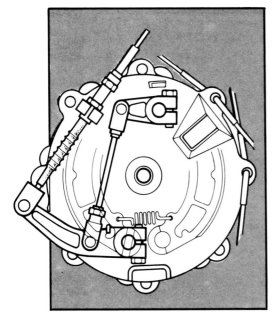

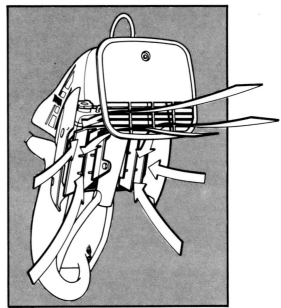

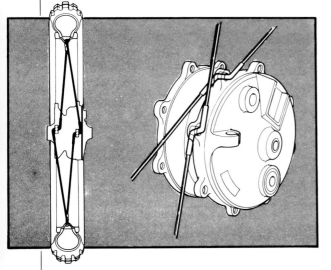

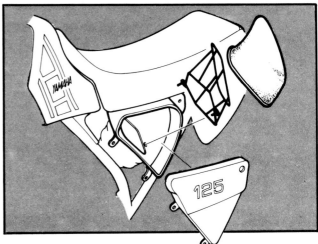

The larger crankcase volume now had to be filled, requiring larger carburettors, bolted to inlet manifolds that could flow so much charge. The problem of the motocross machines was the reed valve sitting in the inlet tract and obstructing air flow. The only way to flow more charge was to make the complete reed cage wider,

Some of the goodies available on the 1984 YZ range

hence the move to eight-petal reed valves on some machines. This in turn caused problems with the reed-petal dimensions, since the reed needs to be supple enough to open under the low crankcase pressure at low engine speeds, but stiff enough to close quickly at high engine speeds. This contradictory set of requirements had led to the famous dual-reed developed by Eyvind Boyeson, and so beloved by motocross riders from the end of the 1970s for the bolt-on power they seemed to provide. A relatively soft petal was clamped on the back of a stiffer petal which was cut away underneath the softer one. It turned out to be a smart application of a number of laws of physics that ensured that the petals would open and close, when they should, throughout the range of engine speed.

With the adoption of eight petals, individual thickness could not be reduced since this was determined by the need to match the natural frequency of the reed with the speed of the engine in its powerband. Consequently, the extra petals were pure extra weight that had to be opened by the same combination of crankcase vacuum and positive pressure in the resonant inlet tract comprising the manifold and carburettor. One way this could be helped was by exposing the inlet manifold downstream of the reed valve to crankcase pressure changes as early as possible and get the reeds thinking about opening again before the inlet port opens. This is what the sub-port found on the YZ125L achieved and it also helped fill the crankcase, without compromising piston life by reducing its support on the inlet face of the cylinder. The intended result was better scavenging and hence better power across the board.

As is so often the case, theory and practice, are not always in agreement and the 125L engine had a surfeit of mid-range power but not enough top end to make it competitive. No changes were made to the transmission, but a new pipe and a 36 mm Mikuni accompanied the cylinder changes. The frame design remained the same but the dimensions did not. The engine was moved forward 30 mm, helping get weight on the front wheel. The bulky radiators were lowered 50 mm and other changes resulted in a slightly steeper rake and 40 mm longer

wheelbase. The resultant handling was extremely good inspiring total rider confidence. Kayabas of 43 mm diameter found their way to the 125, with 16-position adjustment to the blow-off valves fitted to respond to sharp suspension jolts. Both wheels were fitted with Yamaha's new Z-spokes that were single rods that laced to opposite sides of the rim and zig-zagged through the hub, giving them their name. Despite Honda and Kawasaki supplying disc brakes on the front end, Yamaha retained their excellent twin leading-shoe set-up, although the disc brakes were better. A slight alteration of the rising rate of the rear suspension completed a significantly changed YZ125, that unfortunately was the least effective 125 motocrosser coming out of Japan in 1984, due solely to the engine.

A larger version of the 125 cylinder porting was found on the 250, also with a single inlet sub-port to the right-hand auxiliary transfer passage. One modification on the factory 250Ls in the US was to cut a second sub-port on the left-hand side of the inlet port, confirming the idea that the extra crankcase/inlet manifold link would assist getting the reeds open. The pistons of both the 125 and 250 were unusual in that the cutaway around the gudgeon pin boss was only present on the inlet half of the piston. Yamaha's reason for this move was that the cutaway had overlapped the exhaust port and on opening, the suction of the pipe had been strong enough to extract charge from under the piston crown, through the gap between pin and boss and away into the pipe. Also ring thickness was reduced to 1 mm from the previous 1·2 mm, reducing the chances of ring flutter at high engine speeds. Transmission changes involved lowering the top three gears as an answer to the two-year-old criticism of too high gearing. The impeller shaft of the water pump was lengthened and supported by bushes in both the crankcase and crankcase cover in an attempt to cure the leakage that had occurred on some bikes the year before.

There had been a number of occurrences of frames cracking at the headstock of the 250K models and so extra gusseting was added in this area. All the major chassis dimensions remained the same, and the only change to the 43 mm Kayabas up front was the addition of the 16-click blow-off valve adjustment also found on the 125. At the rear end, the Mono-cross suspension was recalibrated with a slight change to the pivot-arm linkage dimensions. As a result, the rear damper was slightly shorter. To make the adjustment of the compression damping a ten-second job instead of a ten-minute job, the knob was moved from the top of the damper hidden under the petrol tank, to the fully exposed base of the reservoir. On the wheels, the Z-spokes were new but the drum brakes were not. Once again Yamaha were leaving it a bit late in adopting new chassis technology, although it must be said, the YZ brakes were very good.

Despite a similar shortage of top-end power as experienced on the 125L, the 250 was a very competent machine. With a better engine the YZ would undoubtedly have been the top 250 of 1984. Yamaha racing support were quickly aware of this shortcoming and determined that 15 mm out of the header pipe really helped get the bike to rev. With this change it was more than a match for the Honda that was generally considered to be the best stock 250 of that year.

In comparison to its kid brothers, the YZ490L was beginning to look downright antique, both inside and outside the engine. Air-cooled and still using a boost bottle, instead of the YPVS-equipped liquid-cooled engines of the 125 and 250, were the external signs of antiquity, while the inside of the engine looked remarkably conventional without the use of sub-ports. The truth of the matter was that it was the best 500 production machine Yamaha or anyone had ever manufactured. All that was needed to turn the flawed package of 1983 into the winner of 1984 was careful refinement in the areas that had proven deficient. After the praise heaped on the

engine the previous year, one would have expected the development work to have been concentrated on the chassis. This was not entirely the case.

There were not so many changes made to the engine, but there was a noticeable improvement over the K, with a broader, more manageable powerband, that was still mid-range-based but extended into the top range enough to let the 490 rev out. On the exhaust side, this was achieved by centring the port and making it narrower! On first thoughts a pretty strange thing to do, but greater consideration reveals some logic to the move. The strength of the suction pulse in the exhaust pipe is dependent on the temperature of the exhaust gases. The higher the temperature the stronger the pulse. Road-racers found that a few hundred revs extra could be found from their highly tuned engines, if the header pipe of the exhaust was wrapped in asbestos cloth to insulate, and thus raise, the exhaust gas temperature. The same effect can be achieved by preventing the gas from expanding too quickly by limiting the width of the exhaust port. This was the step Yamaha had

Left **The design of the 490 engine had remained essentially unchanged since 1982, but was still the best around two years later**

Right **Although the only air-cooled motocross machine in production, the YZ490L was the best 500 available**

taken on the 490L.

On the inlet side, an even greater width reduction took place, with 10 mm narrower inlet port, and an eight-petal reed valve. Again a seeming contradiction, since the reed valve would be flowing more charge only to find a more restrictive port. However, although more restrictive, the air that does get flowed will pass through the port with a greater velocity and at the carburettor will produce strong vacuum to draw in the required fuel. The expected result was increased charge flow as witnessed by the 4 mm extra width of the main transfer ports and the move to a 40 mm Mikuni. As the Mikuni was set up in the factory, the 490 coughed and spluttered round the track. Slide cutaway, needle jet and pilot jet all needed to be exchanged and the cost of correcting the factory's mistake came to around $50. This should of course have been a warranty replacement, since it fell outside the realms of 'setting up the carb'. The four-speed transmission was left unaltered.

Since the exhaust now exited in the centre of the cylinder, the frame needed modification to the wishbone downtube that had been fitted to the YZ125J and YZ250J, when they had adopted power valves. A slight change in the geometry of the frame was made in order to place more weight on the front wheel, something riders themselves had needed to do on the K model, by moving around the bike. The wheelbase grew 25 mm, without a change in the rake and the already stable 490 tracked as straight as a die. The same suspension changes were made as on the 250 and once set up correctly, including stiffer springs on the front and heavier oil, worked very well. The combination of killer engine and razor-sharp chassis made the YZ490L the best 500 machine available, with only the Honda in the same class. The CR's tendency to shake its head at awkward moments and rather harsh suspension relegated it to second place behind the YZ. At last the company were back on top and it felt great.

The 125 excepted, Yamaha had produced a range of production motocross machines for 1984 that were the best or close to it. So confident were they of the quality of their 250 and 490 that Ricky Johnson and Broc Glover rode machines that were production items with modi-

137

Left **Ricky Johnson astounded the US motocross world by winning the 250 National title on a virtually stock machine**

Right **1984 was not to be Broc Glover's year on either his open class machine or the stadium bike shown here**

fications that could be performed quite easily by any YZ owner. Honda's approach was different, with fully fledged factory specials and a battalion of helpers to guarantee success. In the face of the all-conquering Honda steamroller, Yamaha's only title, gained by Ricky Johnson in the 250 class, is all the more remarkable. Glover finished second to David Bailey in the 500, but it was Bailey's year with eight straight wins out of ten events. The 125 US title was denied Honda by Jeff Ward and Kawasaki, with Honda's O'Mara second and Mike Beier third on a YZ. Beier's effort was essentially a private one, with some technical assistance from the company, and is consequently especially commendable, although there was a 150-point gap between him and O'Mara. In Europe, Carlquist attempted to defend his title, but a pre-season broken thumb and mid-season broken finger meant he never ran with the leaders and ended tenth. In the 250, Jacky Vimond was supported by sport-conscious Sonauto of France and rode inconsistently well,

to finish second behind Heinz Kinigadner with the KTM. Vimond, fresh from the 125 class, had difficulty completing both motos in each race, only managing it in four of the 12 GPs. More finishes could well have brought him the title.

Whatever the R & D guys were doing back in Japan during the 1984 season, it was not designing new motocross models. When the N series appeared at the end of the year, it was clear that only the absolute minimum of work had gone into the new series. Two of the new models received very few updates, only the engine of the YZ80 and the chassis of the YZ490, while the others got some attention in both areas but nothing in comparison with other years. The steel petals of the reed valves were replaced on all the YZs by resin equivalents, which could open up further without risk of fracture. Apart from the cosmetic change to white and red in the US, departing from their traditional yellow, this was the only change made throughout the range.

The updates made to the YZ80 involved a higher compression ratio, higher exhaust port, lower inlet port, wider main transfer, revised jetting and a new exhaust. It had only been a slight lack of power that had forced the YZ into 2nd place behind the KX in 1984 and with the increase in power these modifications gave, Yamaha hoped that the stock YZ would match or surpass the stock KX. Their supposition was correct, since although the KX came into its powerband about 1000 rpm earlier, the slight top-end advantage of the YZ enabled the bike to pull back in most ground lost. It was the handling and suspension that gave the YZ the advantage over the Kawasaki. It was not much of an advantage and the CR80 was also pretty good, but the YZ engine could be tuned for a couple of bhp more with relative ease, while the CR and KX were close to the limit stock.

Something went wrong with the lines of communication between the designers and the people in the field getting flak from angry YZ125L owners with a bike that needed almost as much spent on it as it cost, to get it into the winner's circle. Although there were no official 125 teams in either Europe or the US in 1984, certainly Yamaha personnel in the US were very much in touch with the racing community via their excellent competition support programme. There is also little doubt that, although filtered, many of the angry complaints they received were passed back to Japan. The result though was only a token attempt at improving the power delivery of the YZ, although it seems clear that Japan assured the national organizations that the YZ125N would be a winner. It certainly was embarrassing when the first units arrived from Japan and were found to have the basic flaw of their predecessor—no top end.

The usual collection of engine components were replaced in the quest for more power, namely cylinder head, cylinder, piston, exhaust pipe and carburettor. The cylinder porting was a mixture of old and new, perhaps in an attempt at harnessing the best of both. The main exhaust port was identical to that of the K model of 1983, and the sub-exhaust ports were rectangular and of slightly greater cross-sectional area. The transfer ports were a fraction higher, but the main transfers were appreciably narrower. In contrast, the boost port was widened by 50 per cent, and was also fed by a passage leading straight back to the inlet manifold just downstream of the reed valve. It was clearly the intention to flow more charge through the boost port. The purpose of the sub-port above the inlet port, in addition to the retained sub-port on the right-hand side of the inlet port, was to enhance the charge flow from the crankcase with an extra shot directly from the inlet tract via the reed valve that had been opened fractionally by the exhaust suction wave. It was found that the carburation was better if a smaller 34 mm bore unit was used, probably due to the enormously wide inlet port that had remained of the same height but had grown 5 mm wider. This wide port would have altered the resonant frequency of the inlet tract that is so important for correct carburation. The exhaust pipe design changed from a three-section diffuser pipe to a five-section pipe that would keep the exhaust gas temperature high.

So a lot of changes were found in the cylinder and related components, but the designers seemed to have been on the wrong path for the result was an engine that was a little more powerful at all engine speeds than the L model, but still a mid-range mill with little on the top end. When lined up against the other three, the Yamaha's engine was the slowest, by far.

The basic geometry of the YZ was left untouched as it had been the best feature of the YZ125L. Showa forks replaced the Kayabas, but maintained the good operation of the old units. A detail improvement found on all the larger YZs was the use of tapped set screws to secure the ends of the swinging-arm, after some problems with the arm falling to bits on 1984 models. One obvious change was made to the chassis. The introduction of a front disc brake on the YZ125 and all large-capacity YZs was a welcome improvement and in-line with the general trend of development. A less conspicuous change, but one that Yamaha were especially proud of, was the introduction of a system of linking the operation of the rear brake with a reduction of compression damping in the rear damper. The theory was that the compression damping was reduced by about six per cent on application of the rear brake making the rear end track the bumps going into the corner and help stabilize the bike. In the early days of the monoshock, Yamaha had been plagued by a lively rear end and although considerably diminished there was still a trace of the 'Yamahop' as the phenomenon had been christened. A cable on the rear brake pedal activated a rod that closed the main oil passageway into the damper reservoir and opened a larger passage, thus reducing the compression damping. The system worked well when braking for corners, and it worked, of course, whenever the brake was applied, such as slowing for a jump, leading some to question its effectiveness. In any case Yamaha made a mistake by introducing it on a motocross machine that was generally considered to be a failure. An acronym was of course needed to join the YEIS, YPVS, Monocross and Torque Induction. BASS was chosen, standing for Brake Activated Suspension System, and the testers had a field day with their fish jokes.

Funny how the fish jokes were notably fewer in the reviews of the 125's larger brother, the YZ250N. Probably due to the fact it was the best 250 of 1985, despite suspension flaws and the questionable merit of the BASS equipment. It could be coincidence but the presence of direct factory involvement in the 250 and 500 classes of the US and the 500 class of the GPs, seemed to be reflected in better models for 1985. Nothing too drastic was done to the engine of the quarter-litre. The drooping roof of the inlet port, offering more piston skirt support, was flattened off for the N, although the rest of the inlet port dimensions were unchanged. On the exhaust side, only the exhaust sub-port position was lowered by 3·5 mm and the port was cast rather than drilled as had been the case on the L model. The transfers were unaltered, although the boost port was fed from the inlet tract as on the 125N. The usual head, pipe and carburation modifications accompanied the revised porting and produced a slight increase in power throughout the range and a slightly higher top end, much like that of the 125. The one difference between the

Below left **Broc Glover's 1985 stadium bike maintained Yamaha's tradition of campaigning near-stock machines**

Below **Handling and power delivery were so good on the YZ250N that they made up for the flawed rear suspension to offer the best package for 1985**

Left **Some decided to take over the YZ development from the company. Innovation Sports produced this YZ250 for Ricky Johnson with carbon-fibre tank and rear subframe**

Right **Johnson practising on the carbon-fibre YZ that could not be raced in 1986 after changes to the AMA rules allowing only stock machines**

two was that the 250 was already on the top of the pile and could maintain its position by this evolutionary approach. The 125 was in need of a quantum-jump improvement to become competitive. The new cylinder casting also contained extra passages around the exhaust port to improve the cooling. The rest of the engine block was left untouched apart from a tougher big-end bearing, an external flywheel CDI ignition, an improvement to the clutch release mechanism making the clutch lighter and a new kickstart shaft.

The frame was constructed from a lighter gauge tubing to compensate for the extra weight of the stronger rims and spokes, and the dual-piston floating caliper front disc brake common to all the larger YZs. The factory kept the weight down close to the FIM minimum for the class. The usual meticulous set-up procedure was essential for the suspension to get it to work properly, but once dialled-in and with stiffer springs up front, it worked well enough for the majority of riders. For those who were not satisfied, there was the expensive step over to an Öhlins rear shock, for improved sensitivity and race-length consistency. But the slightly flawed suspension was not bad enough to

prevent the YZ250N with its class-beating power and diamond-sharp handling being hailed by most as the class winner for 1985.

Not a lot was new in the engine department of the YZ490N. Everyone had expected Yamaha to follow suit and introduce a water-pumper, but the factory refused to join the club and produced the only serious air-cooled motocross machine in the market. All three changes made to the engine unit were effective. The starter jets of the 40 mm Mikuni were replaced and starting became a two- or three-kick affair, assisted also by the revised kickstart. Finally the clutch actuation was lightened. Frame and wheels were 490N items modified as on the 250 and the suspension and rear swinging-arm were borrowed from the 250. The King of 1984, was still close to the top in 1985, with ample power and good steering and suspension. A question hung over the stamina of the bike, in comparison with the liquid-cooled competition, and the vibration was still excessive but experts could live with that and its stamina was good enough for the 1985 US Open Class title.

With the exception of the mediocre 125, the N series was probably the best since the Gs of 1980, in terms of superiority over the competi-

tion. Just as well really, since all the factory riders in both the US and Europe were only supplied with stock machines for the 125 and 250 classes. In Europe the OW64 factory 490 was campaigned in the hands of Hakan Carlquist and fellow countryman Leif Perrson. Although air-cooled, the OW machine did have various goodies on display such as a power-valve and five-speed transmission. John van den Berk took a stock YZ125N to a solid 5th place in the GPs with some good rides throughout the season. In the US, privateer Keith Bowen had a tough time against the reds, greens and yellows and managed 7th place overall. Ricky Johnson was unable to pull off his superhuman feat of 1984 in beating pukka-works machines with his

breathed-on YZ250, but finished a strong 3rd despite an end-of-season broken finger.

It seemed as if the 250 World Championship was to return to the Yamaha camp after a year's loan to KTM, as Jacky Vimond took his YZ250N into a start-of-season title lead and held it right to the last GP. With a 12-point lead over KTM's Kinigadner, the title was almost safe. The pressure was too much for the friendly Frenchman, who struggled round the German circuit to finish 12th in the first moto and 7th in the second, letting Kinigadner through to a two-point title win. That must have hurt. Hakan Carlquist must be one of motocross's most unlucky riders, for his 1985 season was ruined by a succession of injuries, beginning with a broken thumb and

culminating in a broken shoulder. With Carlquist more often absent than present at the GPs, it fell to 21-year-old Leif Perrson to wave the Yamaha factory flag in his first full season of GP competition. An erratic season meant that he was never in contention for the title but a good end-of-season 2–2 in Switzerland showed that he was capable of running with the class veterans, and augured well for the future. In the US, Glover was anxious to redress the hurt done by Bailey's overwhelming victory in 1984. Seeming to have

picked up some of the fluid smooth style of riding that Bailey had exhibited the year before, Glover got up to steam early in the season and had already sewn up the title by the time a wrist injury put him out of action before the penultimate round in Minnesota. This was Glover's sixth National title, equalling Hannah's record as America's most successful motocross rider of all time, and every title they had won, was won on a Yamaha.

Below left **The YZ125N was one of the most disappointing YZs Yamaha had ever built**

Below **Yamaha advertisement at the start of 1986**

9 | Rolling thunder

The 1976 XT500C initiated the start of the four-stroke thumper revival

Until 1970, every one of the 172 motorcycles that Yamaha had produced had used a two-stroke engine. With the turn of the decade, Yamaha indicated the direction in which future developments would proceed by announcing their Triumph Bonneville clone, the XS1. There were two clear reasons for the company's move into the world of four-strokes. Firstly, they were anxious to get a slice of the large-capacity market that Honda were threatening to monopolize with the introduction of the four-cylinder CB750. There were few good reasons for using the two-stroke principle on large-capacity machines, the four-stroke multi being able to produce enough power and retain air-cooling. Secondly, the anti-pollution lobby in Europe and the US was becoming increasingly vocal in its plea for tighter restrictions on exhaust emissions. Once these were introduced, the two-stroke would be strangled to death. So in February 1970, the four-stroke 650 twin began production, the engine format resulting from Yamaha's decision to compete with the ailing British industry and not to be accused of copying Honda by the introduction of a four-cylinder machine. Within a couple of years, the range of four-stroke twins had extended to include a 750 and 500. Clearly the four-stroke would play an increasingly important role in Yamaha's product line.

During the last decade of its existence as a powerful force in the motorcycle industry, British manufacturers had attempted to produce a range of what could be considered dual-purpose motorcycles. BSA had introduced the trail version of the B25 in 1971, known in the US as the Starfire and in Europe as the Barracuda. It joined the 500 Victor enduro that had been available since 1966, initially with a 440 cc engine, with both scrambling and roadster variants being available. The enduro models had been conceptually similar to the DT/RT series Yamaha had introduced at the end of the 1960s, but unreliability and brain-scrambling vibration gave them, and indeed many of the British machines, a bad name. It was a pity, for the Victor, when it ran, was a competent machine with 34 bhp on tap at 6200 rpm. Another well-conceived British idea that was ruined on transfer from paper to metal.

Within two years of Yamaha's introduction of the DT1, both Kawasaki and Suzuki had equivalent machines in their model range. For some reason Honda held back and it was 1971 before the SL and later the XL series were offered for sale. For the XL series, initially 250 and 350 bikes were produced but the range soon expanded to include 175 and 125 capacities. These were the first four-stroke dual-purpose machines made in Japan, but the upper limit of 350 cc precluded a direct comparison with the recently expired British thumpers. Functionally, they were very similar to the DT series, with good engine performance, reasonable handling and barely adequate suspension. They sold well, well enough to make Yamaha sit up and take notice.

Yamaha were well aware of the danger facing their DT series. The way things were going, the EPA would have ensured that all roadgoing two-strokes would be outlawed by the end of the 1970s. With this US ban on them, the DT series would suffer a body blow it would be hard to sustain. Worse still, Yamaha would lose a major sales market. Clearly a move would have to be made towards four-stroke dual-purpose machines. The confrontation with Honda could not and would not be avoided.

Once the decision had been taken to build a four-stroke, the capacity of the bike that would form the advance guard of the new series was almost a foregone conclusion. Two factors made the choice a simple one. The new bike should not be a direct competitor to the existing DT models and if possible it should put one over on Honda. Honda's top of the range was a 350, lacking some of the aura of the old British 500 cc thumpers. Top of the DT range was the 400. A 500 would be a perfect choice. The letter 'X' had been chosen to represent a four-stroke model and since it was a 'Trail' machine just like the DTs, it would receive the designation XT. A number of prototypes were constructed during 1975 and at the US dealer convention in September 1975, the XT500C was unveiled to a startled world.

The bore and stroke of the big single were an almost square 87 × 84 mm in contrast to the longer stroke of the British bikes. One of the problems of the BSAs and Triumphs had been the height of the engine, which had compromised the amount of ground clearance possible. The shorter stroke, coupled with smaller crankshaft flywheels and a dry sump kept the height to a minimum. The overhead camshaft, running on ball bearings, was driven by a chain passing through a tunnel on the right-hand side of the engine. A two-valve head was used since the intention was to produce a mill with a pancake-flat torque curve and reasonable power and this could be achieved without the complexities of the four-valve head Honda were using on their XL series. Bearing in mind the infamous starting habits of British singles, a decompression device was fitted that pushed the exhaust valve from its seat when a lever on the left-hand handlebar was squeezed. The head was attached to the cylinder by four studs and the cylinder to the vertically split crankcases with four more studs.

A conventional slide-operated Mikuni carburettor of 34 mm diameter was used, although it looked rather like a constant velocity carburettor due to a push/pull mechanism that was required. This was necessary since the carburettor, situated high on top of the engine under the petrol tank, could not be operated by the usual centrally placed cable. Instead, the cable operated a pulley mounted on the side of the carburettor body that would raise or lower the slide as the cable throttle was turned. The air filter was located high and dry under the seat. On the exhaust side, the pipe was not upswept as would be expected, but ran down under the engine, to a larger box angled up behind the engine. The final section of the exhaust pipe with the silencer and spark arrester ran parallel to the seat. This set-up was reminiscent of that used on the BSA trail machines, but it was not a satisfactory arrangement. When riding in the dirt, the exhaust was the part of the bike that received the most punishment and was easily damaged. Apparently Japan had insisted that this form of exhaust was used despite criticism from US prototype riders. Later they were to listen more sympathetically to the same criticism from owners of the XT500C.

The pressed-up crankshaft used full-circle flywheels, with a roller bearing for the big-end and a plain copperized bearing for the gudgeon pin. The magneto was keyed to the left-hand end of the crankshaft, with the contact breaker assembly driven separately from the right-hand end of the crankshaft via an idler gear. The crankcase was fitted with a Positive Crankcase Ventilation (PCV) system which circulated oily fumes in the pressurized crankcase through a hose to the air cleaner, where the condensed oil seeped back down to the gearbox. A cleaner exhaust was the result. Rather than use a separate tank

Above right **A two-valve head was deemed sufficient for the XT500 to produce the gut-wrenching torque Yamaha were aiming for**

Right **The backbone of the frame acted as an oil reservoir for the XT**

to hold the oil that was pumped through the engine, it was stored in the large-diameter backbone and downtube of the frame. The filler/dipstick was located just behind the headstock in front of the petrol tank. Two Eaton-type trochoidal pumps driven by the same shaft were used to flow the oil, one returning circulated oil from the sump to the frame reservoir and the other delivering oil via a gauze filter to the crankshaft and via an external line to the camshaft.

Straight-cut gears were used to transmit the power to the gearbox via a 15-plate clutch spring loaded to the primary transmission gear in true DT fashion. The five-speed transmission was of conventional design with well-chosen ratios, although the gap between the first two gears was a little wide. The gearchange mechanism used the rotating drum common to all Yamaha's dirtbikes, with the three forks running along two rails. Primary kickstarting was used, although the advantage of being able to start in any gear was lost somewhat by the need to follow a well-defined procedure in order to get the XT to light up.

The frame of the XT was different from its contemporary Yamaha dirtbikes. The large-diameter backbone and single front downtube supported the headstock with the usual gusseting between the two. At the bottom of the engine, two frame rails joined the downtube to form a cradle for the engine and passed up to support the rear subframe. Behind the engine, two more tubes tied the cradle to the lower end of the backbone tube. Bracing was provided between the cradle rails under and behind the engine as well as for the rear subframe at the join with the cradle tubes. Since it was expected to spend most of its time on the street, stability was provided by a fairly slow 30·5-degree rake and a 1420 mm wheelbase. A bash plate was bolted under the engine to protect the crankcases from rocks when out on the trail, but it was too short, ending halfway along the engine. The circular section rear swinging-arm was mounted on roller bearings and had a grease nipple tapped into the pivot support to simplify regular lubrication. With the tall engine block, there was no way that the monoshock design of the time could have been used on the XT. Instead two Kayaba gas/oil rear shock absorbers were mounted at a laid-down angle of about 45 degrees. Only spring preload could be adjusted, with a choice of five positions available. The front forks were of the same design as those fitted to the MX models providing 195 mm of travel, but 2 mm thicker in diameter. Double pinch bolts on the steering stem held the forks in place.

Wheels and half-width brakes were very similar to those on other Yamaha dirtbikes. One improvement that was made was the use of thicker rims, which although heavier, and unsprung as well, were a lot stronger than the MX rims which were easily dented. The left-hand side panel was lockable with the battery box and a small waterproof pouch hidden behind it. Cleated footrests ensured optimum grip for even the muddiest boot and no passenger footrests came as standard equipment. Full street equipment was provided, including a headlight, taillight, traffic indicators, two mirrors and both speedometer and tachometer. Finished in the styling common to the XT, DT and MX series in 1976, the 500 had a white tank with red sidewalls and a wide black stripe passing over the tank from side to side. White lettering on the black stripe recorded the capacity and the marque name. On the side panels the XT series identification and enduro function of the bike was proclaimed.

The press and the public loved it. It represented everything the British thumpers should have been and weren't. The engine had bags of torque from 2500 rpm right up to its maximum engine output at 5500 rpm. Off-road it could climb almost anything as long as the tyres hooked up, the smooth power delivery making it very easy to ride. It was a little less happy at high speed, since the suspension was not quite

Left **Inevitably, wheelies were the XT500's forte, but the suspension was inadequate for any hard dirt riding**

Below **Yamaha were right about the legend**

The 1977 Yamaha TT500: The makings of a legend.

Few motorcycles deserve to be called legends. Fewer still manage to lay claim to that title after just a single year of production. But the Yamaha TT500 is unlike any other machine. It is, quite possibly, one of the most significant advances in dirt bike technology ever to appear.

New, improved Thumper.

The TT500 concept is based on the classic Thumper—the four-stroke single machines that dominated off-road riding in the 1950s. Like them, the Yamaha TT500 is a supremely simple motorcycle. It's reliable, easy to maintain, with tremendous low-end torque. But with the aid of modern engineering, the TT500 is also much more.

The TT500 Kick Indicator Window. To avoid fighting the tremendous compression of this engine, (1) merely depress the compression release lever on the handle bar. (2) slowly turn the engine over until the silver marker fills the window on the chart. Now the piston is past the compression stroke and (3) the engine is ready to be started.

Engine torque.

The engine is a work of art. No four-stroke single is more advanced. In place of old-style push rods, the TT500 uses an overhead cam. Some parts are made of lightweight magnesium, a practice usually reserved for racing bikes. A 32mm Mikuni carburetor and a 9.0:1 compression ratio help produce usable torque from idle up to 6000 rpm.

New kick indicator window for easier starting.

Kick starting an engine of this size and power is often difficult. But with the TT500's compression release and new kick indicator, it's not. (See insert.) A dry sump lubrication system

Torque (ft. lbs.) at 4000 rpm			

Hard off-road riding demands huge amounts of low-end torque. A TT500 develops more of it, up through 4000 rpm, than many large displacement motocross racers.

keeps the crankcase size to a minimum, so ground clearance is a healthy 9.2 inches.

For serious riding a new high pipe has been added, along with a new aluminum skid plate.

Last year, proof of the engine's ultimate winning capabilities was witnessed in tough race competition throughout the country.

Refined suspension.

Modern Cycle noted, "(The TT500) can just about out-drag a full-blown Open class MXer to the first turn." And the suspension is up to it. At the front, the forks have a generous 7.7 inches of travel. Shocks are the cantilevered nitrogen/oil type. The ability of these particular units to handle small irregularities as well as large bumps has been refined to a new level of excellence. In the interest of reducing unsprung weight, the leading/trailing shoe brakes have magnesium backing plates attached to lightweight conical hubs.

Yes, a legend.

The Yamaha TT500 is more than just another dirt bike. It represents an undisputed engineering breakthrough. It is a legend in its own time.

When you know how they're built, you'll buy a Yamaha.

CIRCLE NO. 35 ON READER SERVICE PAGE.

New high pipe with U.S. Forestry-approved spark arrestor.

Cantilevered nitrogen/oil shocks provide 5.7 inches of travel.

Massive clutch has over 100 sq. inches of surface area.

Full 9.2 inches of ground clearance.

New lightweight aluminum skid plate.

Aluminum alloy piston and cylinder for better heat dissipation.

Front forks offer 7.7 inches of travel.

so competent as the engine. The front end was too soft and the rear end too hard for high-speed dirt riding. Also the semi-knobbly tyres were not perfect for either dirt or street riding. When on the street, the suspension problems disappeared and the XT500 was simply the best dual-purpose bike available. Somehow Yamaha seemed to have ironed out all the vices with which the British thumpers had been cursed. Vibration was low, the engine was oiltight, it was easy to start, if the correct procedure was used, and above all, it was reliable. As far as the XLs were concerned, with 30 per cent more torque and 20 per cent more power than the 350, it would eat them for lunch. With the high gearing, it was possible to screw a maximum speed of 90 mph out of the engine and it had enough grunt at any speed to easily pass four-wheel traffic. The rear brake was a little too sensitive and in fact this contributed to the only real criticism of the power unit. The deliberate use of lighter flywheels meant that the engine revved easily, but it was possible, when using the toggle rear brake in the dirt, to stall the engine. A more progressive rear brake would have solved the problem, but it took some time in coming. Yamaha had produced a winner with the XT500C.

The XT was not alone in the Yamaha's range of four-stroke dirtbikes for 1976. A stripped-down XT was offered for pure off-road use and was known as the TT500C. Identical engine units were used, with a lower final drive bringing the ratios down to a more suitable figure for off-road use. The chassis was of the same design, but with as much weight trimmed as possible. This, coupled with the loss of roadgoing electrical equipment, resulted in a weight saving of 15 kg. Despite this, the TT500 was not a serious enduro mount in standard trim. Increased engine performance and revised suspension were necessary to make it fully competitive. It would be expensive but there were some prepared to pay in their commitment to four-strokes.

With such a successful first shot at the concept of the big thumper, it is not surprising that few changes were made to produce the D model. Clearly with their ear to the ground, it was the chassis that was given the most attention by the Yamaha development engineers. The same frame layout was used, but the rake was pulled back one degree to quicken the steering. This was only of real use for the off-road ventures into tight-track woods, where the heavy four-stroke could prove to be a bit of a handful at low speeds. The front forks were updated with many components from the IT series, including longer springs, and gaiters were added to protect the sliders. At the rear end, new Kayabas provided another 20 mm of rear wheel travel with revised damping characteristics. All the electrical equipment was mounted on flexible rubber stalks, to restrict the damage when dropping the bike in the dirt or riding a narrow trail. The aluminium engine skid plate was extended up and further behind the engine, protecting the sump completely.

Few changes were made to the engine. Most important for the rider was the provision of a small inspection window in the cylinder head. This was to assist with starting the XT. The compression-release lever was depressed and the engine carefully turned over until a silver disc appeared in the window. The piston was now in the optimum position for the engine to be started. A hefty kick would normally result in the bike firing up. If not, the procedure just had to be repeated. Rather ominously, the kickstart lever itself had been strengthened! A new exhaust was routed above the engine cases, inside the first frame tube, outside the second and up along the rear of the bike. The new exhaust and rejetted carburettor resulted in a slight top power gain, but this was unnoticeable when riding.

The TT500D and XT500D were as close as ever, although the frame of the TT had a 30-degree rake and the lighter front wheel and brake from the IT400C were fitted. Both bikes were improved

by the update and the XT in particular maintained its position at the top of the dual-purpose motorcycles.

1977 was also an important year for the XT/TT 500 on the GP racetracks of the world. Amazingly enough a four-stroke machine was once again a competitive force in the world of 500 cc GP racing and the irrepressible Torsten Hallman was responsible for getting it there. The story goes back to the ISDT in October 1975, held on the Isle of Man. American Gary Surdyke had brought

Above **The TT was really in its element out in the wide-open spaces of the desert, where the fantastic torque of the machine could be given full rein**

Top **The TT500D had changed a little from the previous model, with quicker steering and an IT front wheel**

Right **Gary Surdyke gave Europeans their first sight of the new XT500 at the Isle of Man ISDT of 1975, before selling the bike to Torsten Hallman, who turned it into the famous 'factory' HL500**

a prototype XT500 with him to compete in the event. Although attracting a lot of attention from the public, the XT was clearly not suited to the rigours of ISDT competition and expired on the third day. In Sweden at the beginning of 1975, Hallman had heard of the forthcoming arrival of the XT in the US and an idea had begun forming in his mind of producing a competition version. When he approached Japan, he had been told that the XT would initially not be available in Europe and he would not be given a model on which to develop his idea. On learning of the XT500 in the ISDT, Hallman located Surdyke and bought the machine off him. So in October 1975, Hallman had the only XT500 in Europe.

The project was adopted by Sten Lundin, then service manager with Hallman's Yamaha importation business. It was, however, treated more as a hobby than a serious development project and was worked on in the evening and at weekends. Initially, work concentrated on the chassis and the engine was slotted into a far lighter Husqvarna frame. This frame was used as a basis for designing an original frame which was drawn up by Lundin and manufactured by Pro-fab in California. A special aluminium swinging-arm was fabricated and US Fox shock absorbers were used in place of the unsophisticated Kayabas. Later these were themselves replaced by shock absorbers manufactured by a new Swedish company called Öhlin. With ready access to YZ spares many of the original items were replaced by the motocross equivalents. Hence the latest YZ forks were used on the front suspension. The total wheel travel at both ends was to become 250 mm. YZ wheels and hubs were also pressed into service and as it seemed likely that the bike would be entered into the GPs in 1977, engine plates, nuts and bolts were replaced by duraluminium items. In the end the HL500, as it was named, weighed in at 102 kg, 25 kg lighter than the TT500.

Work on the engine was left to four-stroke tuning expert Nils Hedlund. He restricted himself

to giving the engine a mild tune-up and reducing the weight as far as possible. A lighter YZ250A clutch replaced the massive 15-plate XT item. The ignition from the MX125 saved 1·5 kg alone. The crankshaft and gearbox were not touched, but the cylinder head and piston were altered to give an 11:1 compression ratio instead of the standard 9:1 of the TT. The carburettor grew from the 34 mm to a 36 mm Mikuni.

As the development slowly progressed during 1976, it became clear that what was emerging was not just a reworked TT, but a serious motocross machine. The excitement grew as Lundin and Hallman began to realize that it might just be competitive enough to do the GPs. Four-strokes had long been discarded as top-notch GP machines, despite the continued presence of the CCM of Alan Clews, that had grown out of the ashes of the BSA motocross machines of the 1960s. The CCM was never a front-runner in the world championship 500 class, only occasionally picking up points in the lower places. This would not be good enough for the Yamaha. If it was to compete, it must be capable of finishing well. Hallman and Lundin gradually became convinced that it could.

After Yamaha reconsidered their decision not to import the XT to Europe, it was obvious that an XT clone competing in European GPs would be an excellent way of publicizing the new four-stroke's arrival in Europe. With a carefully itemized budget, Hallman approached Yamaha

in Amsterdam with a request for backing to the tune of $15,000. After initial hesitation he got the green light to run a small team in 1977 with veteran Bengt Aberg, winner of the 500 cc title in 1969 and 1970, riding the bike. To get the agreement Hallman had made what he, at the time, considered a rather rash promise that the HL500 would finish in the first five places at least once during the season. His faith in the bike was to prove well founded.

In the first GP of 1977 in Austria, a puncture brought a DNF in the first moto but an encouraging eighth place was the result of the second race. There followed a string of engine failures at the next three GPs, in the Netherlands, Sweden and Finland, which left the team rather despondent. However, a superb race in Germany brought Aberg a 3rd place in the first race, but he was brought down by another rider in the second. Hallman's promise had been kept and it was still only mid-season. In the USA, the engine blew a head gasket in the first moto while Aberg was in 8th place with a single lap to go. The gasket could not be replaced in time for the start of the second race. A week later in Canada, Aberg's luck was out with DNFs in both races. Back in Europe Bengt repeated his German result in the UK, with a 3rd place in the first heat and a fall in the second. Ceriani front forks had replaced the YZ suspension by now. There followed a three-week break before the next race in Belgium, where a puncture put Aberg out of the first moto but he claimed 7th place in the second. Luck had not been on the team's side during 1977. Then on to the penultimate GP of the season in Ettlebruck, Luxembourg. In the first heat, Bengt went straight into the lead and after

an initial battle with Hakan Andersson on a works Montesa, which ended as the Montesa faded, remained unchallenged to the end. This was the first GP moto win by a four-stroke for eight years and probably the last ever. In the second race Aberg made a slow start but pulled up to third place to tie on points with Mikkola. Unfortunately Mikkola posted the better time and so took the overall victory, but the moral victory lay with the small Swedish team. They had achieved the impossible, turning the pages of history back eight years and given the supporters of the four-stroke something to cheer. It was a truly historical event.

Sadly factory development support was not forthcoming in 1978. However Hallman and Lundin were so encouraged by the result in Luxembourg that they decided to employ Hedlund to develop a three-valve head for the bike. Des-

pite the resulting power improvement, the four-stroke Indian summer of 1977 was not to extend to 1978 and after a year of disappointing results, Hallman decided that there was no future for a four-stroke in world championship motocross and the team was disbanded.

The success of the bike in 1977 had aroused sufficient interest for Tanaka, European Yamaha motocross team manager, to decide to produce a limited run of replicas to be sold in Europe. Aberg's spare machine was handed over to the remaining small Norton factory at Shenstone in the UK with the instructions to build 200 replicas. For the first year of production of the HL500, a lightly modified TT500E engine was fitted into a chassis identical to the one Aberg had used during 1977. Experience showed that it was underpowered and very difficult to start. For 1979, 200 more were built with a new camshaft, CDI igni-

155

Left **Ceriani forks were in use by the British GP mid-season 1977, where Aberg took third place in the first race**

Below **Aberg on the three-valve 1978 factory HL500 at the French GP where he finished ninth in both races**

The 1979 version of the production HL500 of which only 200 were produced.

tion from the SR street-going brother of the XT and a larger 38 mm carburettor. This, coupled with a new exhaust pipe, raised the power output significantly. The design of the swinging-arm changed slightly with the mounting for the external reservoir shock absorbers moved forwards to the pivot axle. Rear wheel travel increased to 260 mm. The front suspension was taken from the YZ250F of that year, which had a total of 270 mm of travel. A number of other parts from the YZ250 found their way on to the HL, including the rear brake and its tie rod. No more HLs were made after 1979. They were too much hassle to produce in quantity local to Europe and as the memory faded of Bengt's victory in Luxembourg, so too did the demand.

It was pretty difficult to find any differences between the XT500E and XT500D. There were a few but they were minor such as a stronger drive shaft in the transmission, revised damping for both front and rear suspension and of course new decals to ensure that the customers were aware that a 'new' model was available. It was even more difficult in the transition from E to F at the end of 1978, as there were no changes. The XT500E and XT500F were the same machine,

with once again a cosmetic update. Twin brother, the TT, marked time in the D to E transition but received a little badly needed attention for the F model.

The chassis was beginning to look and feel decidedly dated and for what was billed as a pure dirtbike was really rather poor. A new frame was produced which was claimed to be lighter and with a 0·5-degree steeper steering head. Leading-axle front forks were used for the front suspension and the handlebar mounted further back to allow the forks to be moved up and down the triple clamp to suit the rider. Strangely enough, suspension travel was not increased. At 195 mm it was inadequate for the heavy machine. And it was heavy, since the reduced weight of the new frame and aluminium rear swinging-arm, were exceeded by the extra weight of the front forks. The operation of the rear brake was improved by the use of a single rod between lever and brake as well as a repositioning of the brake cam lever. This had previously pointed down and was easily damaged on a rough trail. The new vertical position kept it out of harm's way. The brake tie rod was eliminated by the adoption of the tongue-in-groove brake backing plate that had been used on the motocross models for a couple of years. Dog-leg handlebar levers were provided and the tips of the gear and brake levers folded. Only engine change was the provision of a hot starting lever on the carburettor that when depressed, raised the slide a fraction and leaned out the mixture. It didn't seem to help much since starting a hot TT was as hit-and-miss an affair as it had always been.

Despite the improvements, the TT500F was not a good dirtbike. The chassis was just not able to match the power of the engine. Suspension was not supple enough to absorb stutter bumps and the front wheel had a tendency to washout. Whoop-de-doos would have the TT500 wallowing like a pregnant hippo and the excess weight made it very difficult and tiring to control. It was only on high-speed fireroads that the TT500

Above **By 1980, the XT500G was beginning to look like a dinosaur that technology had passed by**

Left **The completely new XT250G with its monoshock chassis promised greater things for the complete XT range, but they took some time coming**

excelled, where the fantastic engine could let rip and haul the bike along at exhilarating speeds. With big-bore four-strokes now available from Suzuki (DR370) and Honda (XL500), the Yamaha seemed to have lost some of its charm and many found the Honda a better machine. Yamaha needed to review the XT and TT very carefully and make some big improvements if they were to retain their title as King of the thumpers.

None of the hoped-for improvements manifested themselves on the 1980 G models. The TT500 was left unaltered and the XT received a few minor improvements. Some of the components of the street-only SR500 were used in the engine to raise the overall power output. The inlet valve was 47 mm in diameter—2 mm wider than the one previously used. In the US an accelerator pump was fitted to the 32 mm Mikuni to help the low end by enriching the mixture flowing into the engine. The US models also got the benefit of a CDI ignition to replace the old points-driven ignition. Only some of the chassis improvements made to the TT500F were carried through to the XT500G. The rake of the frame was again steepened, ending up now with a quick 29-degree steering head angle. This was, in fact, an attempt at improving the slow-speed handling in the dirt that was compromised in fact not so much by the steering geometry as by the weight of the bike. With the new frame, the rider got the worst of both worlds, with a front end that was as imprecise as ever and now twitchy to boot. Leading-axle forks were lifted from the TT, but the rear end remained unaltered. Despite these changes, the riding characteristics of the XT were not improved. The extra power could be noticed but had hardly been necessary while the chassis modifications reduced the XT's off-road suitability. The XT seemed to be heading down a blind alley that could only lead to extinction as better (read Honda) machines became available.

Fortunately there was one bright spot in the four-stroke series for 1980 and that was the new XT250G which everyone took to be an indication of the direction Yamaha would be taking with the XT development. Rather than produce a shrunk version of the 500, Yamaha started more or less from scratch and designed a new four-stroke engine and chassis. With a short stroke of 56·5 mm and a bore of 75 mm, the 250 would be able to rev quite well and indeed its redline was marked at 7500 rpm, although it would go up to 8000 rpm before the power signed off. A two-valve head was used with a plate on the left-hand side through which the camshaft and rocker arm could be loaded. The camshaft was driven by a chain on the left-hand side of the engine and a ball bearing was used to support the camshaft of the drive side while a roller bearing was considered adequate for the other end. A compression-release mechanism was fitted, but in contrast to the lever-operated version on the 500, this was connected to the kickstart lever and automatically operated as the bike was started. On the first batch of XT/TT 250s, the mechanism quickly failed, leaving the exhaust valve open and the engine thus inoperative. Fortunately the 250 was an easier starter than its big brother so the mechanism could be disconnected until Yamaha came up with a service update.

The bottom end was of conventional design with full-circle flywheels and, as on the 500, a plain copperized bearing at the little end. When the XT500 had been introduced in 1976, the lack of vibration had been welcomed by all. However, everything is relative and they were welcoming the lack of vibration in comparison with the mind-numbing vibration produced by BSA and Matchless machines of a bygone age. On the 500s the vibration level had become increasingly irritating as each new model arrived and no improvement was noticed. On the 250 a counterbalance weight was driven from the crankshaft to produce an almost vibration-free engine. The clutch was of the same design as that of the larger XT, although only 11 plates were

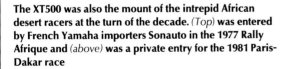

The XT500 was also the mount of the intrepid African desert racers at the turn of the decade. (Top) **was entered by French Yamaha importers Sonauto in the 1977 Rally Afrique and** (above) **was a private entry for the 1981 Paris-Dakar race**

Above right **At last 1982 brought a revision to the top of the XT range, with the introduction of the XT550**

considered necessary to transmit the lower power to the gearbox. Ball bearings were used to support both ends of both shafts in the five-speed transmission and as on all Yamaha dirtbikes, the XT250G could be started in all gears. A wet sump was used for the lubrication of the engine, since the new chassis design made it difficult to use the backbone of the frame as an oil reservoir and the highly placed weight of the oil would have a detrimental effect on the handling of the bike. A trochoidal pump on the right-hand side of the engine driven via an idler gear from the crankshaft ensured the lubrication of the engine through internal oil passages. An upswept exhaust pipe passed along the right-hand side of the bike and was capped by an enormous muffler that reduced the exhaust note to a whisper. The 28 mm Mikuni was also given an accelerator pump that was activated by the vacuum in the inlet tract. CDI ignition was used with the rotor keyed to the left-hand end of the crankshaft. Several of the engine covers were moulded plastic to keep the weight down as far as possible.

While the engine was of a completely new design there was little to see of this externally. The use of a monoshock chassis design was plain to see. At last the XTs were joining the trend set by the YZs, ITs and DTs. In order to position the engine low enough to make room for the monoshock damper, a new frame design was made. The single downtube was retained, but there was no frame cradle, the engine itself being used as a stressed member. A very short large-diameter backbone was used, from the end of which two rails dropped down behind the engine. Very thick engine-mounting lugs were welded to the inside of the rails and a rigid box structure held the front of the engine. A conventional rear subframe design was used with a rail loop attached to the main frame tubes just below the backbone joint and supported by two tubes running up from the back of the engine. Bracing was present between the backbone and front downtube as well as between the main frame and subframe tubes. Rake was set at a quickish 29 degrees.

A circular-section, double-fork swinging-arm was fitted according to the usual Yamaha design. The upper mounting point of the rear shock absorber was the lower end of the frame backbone. Only spring preload could be adjusted on the steel-bodied De Carbon damper and this required the removal of the petrol tank. Leading-axle forks were provided up front with 205 mm of travel and 35 mm diameter stanchions. The rear wheel was a 17-incher instead of the usual 18-incher, which combined with the monoshock design to give a very low seat height. The rear wheel was not QD but it did use snail-cam chain adjusters. Brakes were of the usual single leading-shoe drum type fitted to most of Yamaha's dirtbikes.

The XT250G was a big step in the right direction. It was very light, some 5 kg lighter than the class leader, the XL250 of Honda, and had a good powerful engine. The chassis itself was also a lot better than the old XT500 design, but a common Yamaha failing was also experienced on the quarter-litre machine. The suspension was much too soft as standard. Unfortunately no alternative springs were offered so it was left to the after-sales companies to sort out this problem. Gearing was just right for the dirt but a little too low for the street. In fact, the whole bike seemed to have been designed with the dirt in mind and consequently functioned there very well.

A TT250 was also offered with a few differences from the XT. A 30 mm Mikuni replaced the 28 mm item on the XT and the compression ratio was raised a little. Lower overall gearing was achieved by an extra four teeth on the rear wheel sprocket. An extra 25 mm of suspension was available at both ends and the stanchions on the front end were 1 mm thicker. Unfortunately the springs at both ends were unchanged and therefore too soft to enable the performance of the bike to be used to the full. Despite this the TT took the title of class leader over from the XL250R.

The appearance of the XT and TT 250s with a new chassis warmed the hearts of the XT and TT500 aficionados as it looked like at last their prayers for an improvement would be answered in 1981. There was even some delay in revealing the new range of four-stroke machines for that year and this fuelled the speculation that at last a major update would be made to the big machines. When at last the XT and TT H series was revealed, they could hardly believe their eyes. All models were unchanged. The XT500H and TT500H were identical to their G equivalents. Speculation now turned to a rumoured desertion of the big four-stroke class by Yamaha, since no one in their right mind would buy an H model with far better machines available. Sadly the vanguard of the thumper resurrection, so praised and admired in 1976, seemed little more than a bad joke five years later.

Exactly what went went wrong in 1981 is now difficult to determine, but it seems certain that production of new models was delayed by a hitch somewhere along the line. Thankfully, the mistake was rectified a year later as the J series was announced with an upgrade big enough to cause a flood of ex-Yamaha devotees rushing back to the fold. The range of XTs was even extended, with a 125 and 200 being introduced. This baby of the line-up was modelled very closely on the XT250, with the same engine configuration and frame design. With short-stroke engine dimensions of 57×48.8 mm, the 125 revved up to 9000 rpm to produce its maximum power of 12 bhp. A seven-plate clutch was felt adequate to transmit this power to the gearbox. One significant difference from the 250 was the use of a steel box-section swinging-arm painted silver to give the impression that it was a lightweight aluminium item. Even without the trick parts, the 125 was light with a dry weight of just 98 kg. This made it easy to flick about in the dirt and for once it was the engine that could have been a little better, the 12 bhp proving inadequate in some situations. The XT200 was simply a bored-out 125, sharing the same chassis and transmission.

Surprisingly the 250 did not share in the general update that took place for the J series. It didn't even get the new rear swinging-arm fitted to its smaller brothers. It would have to wait

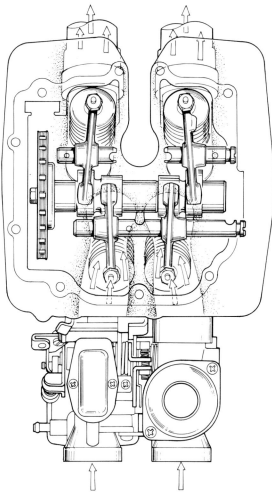

Top left **Four valves were introduced on the XT550 in the need to be seen to be employing the latest technology**

Bottom left **The YDIS dual-carburation system that was supplied on the XT550**

another year for the big change. This was not true of the 500, which grew 50 cc, two valves, another carburettor and a monoshock chassis. At last a complete redesign. Yamaha engineers might have been tempted to leave the engine alone when designing the new bike, since it had never been a real problem on the 500. But this was not to be. The company was anxious to shrug off the 'Stone Age technology' label many had hung on the big XT and a radical new engine design would certainly achieve this.

Only a few of the features of the XT250 were to be found on the new engine. One of these was the repositioning of the camshaft drive to the left-hand side of the engine and the use of a Hy-Vo chain in place of the normal linked chain. The camshaft turned on plain bearings in the aluminium head instead of the ball bearings used on the old 500. A single cam with four lobes drove the four-valve head, necessitating a rather unusual design, with the inlet valves very close to each other and the exhaust valves forced apart. Twin header pipes were fitted to receive the exhaust gases. Both intake valves were 36 mm in diameter and offered a 50 per cent increased flow area over the old single 47 mm XT500 valve.

Even more unusual was the fact that each valve was fed by its own carburettor. Known as YDIS (Yamaha Dual-Intake System), a slide carburettor fed the left-hand and a constant velocity carburettor the other, with fuel coming from a single float bowl on the slide carburettor. The two were linked in such a way that only the slide carburettor was operational up to half-throttle openings and then the CV carburettor kicked in to help. The theory behind this design was to provide an increased overall carburettor

intake diameter without the problems of low engine speed metering associated with single large carburettors. Each unit had a diameter of 26 mm, meaning at the small throttle openings the charge would be correctly metered in response to the lower intake air velocity. As the engine speeded up, the intake air velocity would increase and the second carb would open to provide the extra charge, linked through its CV operation to the intake manifold pressure. A rather complex but clever system.

The larger capacity of the engine had been obtained by boring out the XT cylinder to 92 mm and retaining the old 84 mm stroke. Compression ratio dropped a little, but both maximum torque and power were substantially increased. As on the 250, a balance weight was added to reduce vibration that had been excessive of the old XT500. The CDI ignition flywheel was keyed to the left-hand end of the crankshaft and the complete electrical system uprated to 12 volts. In contrast to the 250, a dry sump lubrication system was retained with the frame still doubling as oil reservoir. Although new components were used, the general design of the transmission was not altered. The primary drive was via helical gears and the overall ratios were altered very slightly. The same automatic compression-release device was fitted to the kickstart pedal, as had been perfected on the 250, resulting in the raising of the right-hand exhaust valve during the initial part of the kickstart lever's throw.

The frame design was essentially the same as that of the 250, but with a much larger backbone member to contain the oil for the engine. The rake of the frame was once again pulled in a degree bringing it down to 28 degrees but the wheelbase was essentially unchanged. Strong 38 mm forks were used for the front suspension and they gave a total of 205 mm of travel to complement the 190 mm possible at the rear end. Brakes and hubs were of the same design, but alloy rims were used to keep the unsprung weight down. In fact it was quite a success story as far as weight was concerned, since despite all the extra hardware, it dropped by 1·5 kg, although the XT was still no lightweight. Since Yamaha had decided not to introduce a TT550J, the possibility of the bike being used for more adventurous dirt riding was encouraged by the provision of QD street equipment. The complete instrument panel and front light assembly could be removed as a single unit.

As with the old XT500 series, the overriding virtue of the 550 was its power. Only the newly arrived and expensive Rotax-powered enduros were faster. The YDIS system seemed to work well, although some testers detected a mid-range glitch as the CV carburettor came into operation. Unfortunately, it looked like the XT550 would once again have to rely on its power for sales, as the chassis, while better than before, was not adequate for off-road riding. The lack of a TT model led many to consider the XT to be more than it was. When ranged against the more serious enduro four-strokes, its short-comings were obvious, as recorded in a *Dirt Bike* 'Shootout' dating from 1982. A few comments are such gems that they deserve recording for posterity. Referring to the ability of the XT to turn: 'It turns like a boat. A long boat dragging a net full of bowling balls'. How about high-speed stability? 'Several testers got religion as they grappled the XT down from speed. One tester commented, "It was a lot like mud wrestling a 300-pound carp".' Finally, ease of riding: 'It lumbered across the landscape like a giant crab and pounded the rider . . . even at trailriding speeds'. You had to give credit to these guys, they certainly knew how to put a bike down.

Not too much changed for 1983. The 125, 200, 250 and 550 were all identical to the previous year's machines, except for the odd decal. Good news for a lot of people was the reintroduction of the TT model and even better news was the extensive update it had undergone. The cylinder of the 550 was bored out to 95 mm and now displaced 595 cc. In fact the cylinder was of a new design using a chromed aluminium liner instead of the usual steel liner. With the lower chance of seizure in comparison with a two-stroke, the new surface could be safely employed, without the risk of having to junk the cylinder. At the top end, the exhaust valves were 1 mm wider and a new camshaft had longer duration. A total of 4 kg was saved from the new cylinder, the crankshaft assembly, the use of a magnesium clutch cover and an aluminium kick-start lever. The engine oil was no longer carried high up in the frame tubes, but in an oil tank located behind the engine.

The chassis was based around the fifth genera-tion of monoshock design. The same frame design was used as before with the engine acting as a stressed member, but the size of the back-bone and front downtube was reduced now they no longer had to store the engine oil. Steering head rake was identical to that of the XT at 28 degrees, but the wheelbase was 85 mm longer. The most significant difference between the two chassis was to be found in the suspension. Full 43 mm diameter Kayaba forks were lifted from the YZ series where they had been found to be totally flex-free. A massive 270 mm of travel was provided, comparable to motocross standards. Tuning of the front suspension was possible due to the provision of air caps on the forks. The rear end appeared to have been lifted directly off the IT490K, and as far as Yamaha was concerned it was state-of-the-art technology. In fact the extruded aluminium swinging-arm was 25 mm shorter and the rear suspension leverage ratio was more progressive than that found on the IT. Stopping power was improved up front by a twin-leading-shoe drum brake straight off the large capacity IT and YZ models. There was no doubt about it. This was the major change TT aficionados had been waiting for.

The improvement over the last TT model, the TT500H, was enormous. Here at last was a serious four-stroke dirtbike from Yamaha. An extremely powerful engine, in a rigid frame that gave the

Monoshock suspension and an aluminium swinging-arm improved the XT550 enormously but it was not enough to put it back at the top of the tree

The XT600 Ténéré was introduced in 1983, in a successful attempt at cashing in on the Paris-Dakar rage that was sweeping Europe

Yamaha the quickest steering in its class, and fantastic brakes that brought the heavy bike down from speed without fuss added up to an excellent all-round package. Inevitably there was one slight deficiency that spoiled the TTs score sheet. The suspension was too soft at both ends. This was a failing that was continually occurring on Yamaha dirtbikes at the start of the eighties. No matter how often it was reported, Yamaha turned a deaf ear. Despite this flaw, the TT600 was the best four-stroke dirtbike of 1983 and it was good to see it at the top after so long away.

In Europe in 1983, an XT600 special was offered for sale alongside the XT550J. It was known as the XT600 Ténéré and was produced at the request of the French importer Sonauto, as a replica of the XT500/600 machines that had been entered in the Paris-Dakar desert race since its inception in 1979. Yamaha had won the first two of the annual races and finished well in the following two, and the 10,000 km race over a two-week period had attracted enormous publicity in Europe and in particular France. The new XT600 turned out to be a cross between the

XT550J and the new TT, although the changes made to the TT to reduce engine weight were not included. In particular, the larger exhaust valve, exhaust pipe and higher primary transmission ratio were fitted as well as a lower first gear. A small oil cooler was clamped to the left frame member behind the engine. The same frame design was adopted but a compromise was made with the suspension by using 41 mm Kayabas up front with 250 mm of travel and a Mono-cross rear end with different linkage giving less progression as the TT600.

Two features of the chassis were particularly eye-catching. The first was the massive 30-litre petrol tank perched on the top of the machine, which would have done terrible things to the handling if the Ténéré had ever ventured on to the dirt with a full tank. Secondly a 225 mm diameter disc brake was mounted on the front wheel to stop the heavyweight monster. A so-called safety seat overlapping the seat/tank join was pinched from the motocross and IT series, where it was important to be able to move easily around the bike. It was a little superfluous on the big XT. Finished in white and red, or Gauloise blue, the XT600 Ténéré couldn't fail to make an impression and that is exactly what the thousands of boulevard posers wanted. The Ténéré was the street scrambler of the 1980s.

In the general shakeout that occurred during 1983 throughout Yamaha's dirtbike range, the 125 and 200 disappeared from most markets, although Australia continued to receive the XT200K. Some of the 600 design was fed back into the new 250 which received the dual-carburettor YDIS set-up with 22 mm diameter throats. Most significant engine change was, however, the move to a four-valve head with double overhead camshafts driving them. In place of the screw tappet adjusters previously used on the 250 came inverted buckets and shims, so maligned by the home mechanic for the complication they add to routine maintenance. The move to four valves turned the 250 into a revver, with a redline at 9000 rpm. In order to keep the 250 on the boil, meaning above 7000 rpm, a six-speed gearbox was added, closing down the gaps between gears in the process. No other changes were made in the engine design and the mill was slotted into a smaller version of the TT600K frame. Kayabas of 35 mm provided 250 mm of travel at the front and the single Kayaba damper at the rear, 220 mm. Both ends were too soft and under hard braking the 250 mm of fork travel shrank to almost 0 mm. Not only were the springs too soft, but the damping characteristics were way off. Yamaha really had problems setting up suspension. The engine was too peaky for a dirtbike, even a dual-purpose dirtbike, since the engine needed to be kept up at the top of the rev range to produce any reasonable acceleration. It was a nice try, but the Hondas were better.

Of the 600s, the Ténéré and the TT were left untouched for 1984. Logically, the 550 was replaced by a 600 version, having much in common with its two capacity brothers. Ninety-five per cent of the engine was borrowed from the TT600,

the only significant difference being a slightly milder cam profile. The design of the chassis was also very similar to the TTs, except 41 mm Kayabas were 2 mm smaller than those on the TT and a different damper was used on the rear end. Total suspension travel was lower than on the TT. In contrast to the TT, the XT wore a drilled disc on the front wheel, distinguishable from the slotted version fitted to the Ténéré. The move towards a cosmetic similarity with the YZ models was marked by the provision of air shrouds under both sides of the tank, ostensibly directing air towards the head to assist cooling. This was also used on the 250 and gave the false impression that the bikes were water-cooled. The XT600Ls performance could be described in exactly the same words used for the TT600Ks. Everything was fine except for the inevitable soft suspension. On the XT, with its street-riding priorities, Yamaha could partially be forgiven.

The winter's development time was not spent updating the existing XT models. The XT250N was unchanged and the 600s only got a few detail updates. Stiffer springs were welcome for the suspension and the TT600 gained a disc brake with a plastic cover to protect it from the worst of the dirt. The cover was also added to the other 600s. The CDI unit on the TT was moved into a cooling air flow by clamping it to the steering head. Yamaha figured that some of the starting problems experienced on the K and L models were caused by a hot CDI unit. That was about it as far as the existing bikes were concerned. The good news was the addition of another machine to the line-up, a 350 based on the 250 machine.

An uncharitable observer might have said that, after showing initial promise, the XT250 had turned out to be a dog. The peaky engine and soft suspension had ruined what could have been a well-balanced package. Yamaha's idea was to get some more power by enlarging the engine and slip it into the compact and light 250 chassis. Luckily the suspension was also on their

The XT600 was an enormous improvement over the 550 but too heavy to be used seriously in the dirt

list of improvements. There was more to the engine change than simply the fitting of a big-bore kit. Throughout the engine, components were strengthened to accommodate the increased power output. Extra plates were added to the clutch and new ratios used in the gearbox. The lubrication of the engine was given the once-over to ensure longevity. The crankshaft was increased in weight to provide greater flywheel effect. The chassis design was unchanged but the rake of the frame was steepened to 27·2 degrees. Although stiffer springs were fitted to the 36 mm Kayaba, they were still a little too soft as witnes-sed by the diving experienced under heavy brak-ing with the front disc brake. Air caps allowed the forks to be tuned in to the rider's require-ments. The new rear damper provided rebound damping adjustment supplementing the spring preload adjustment previously possible.

The XT350N was a very capable machine. With 24 bhp on tap it was 3 bhp more powerful than the XT350R, and coupled to the reasonable 132 kg weight it could put some mid-size street-bikes to shame on a twisty bumpy road. The sus-pension was a vast improvement over that of the 250 and its tunability enabled owners to get it to perform as well as could be expected from a dual-purpose machine. Thanks to the tight steering head, the 350 turned very easily, yet the straight-line stability didn't seem to be affected.

Many claimed that the XT350N was the best of all the Yamaha's XT series with its combination of light weight, and good power and handling

Its balanced package made it the best XT model of 1985.

Ten years after the introduction of the first XT and TT models, the four-stroke dirtbike series was alive and well, confirming the soundness of the original concept. There had been good bikes and bad bikes produced in the intervening years, but the basic irresistible appeal of a large-capacity four-stroke single had always been strong enough to ensure the success of the series. At the outset of the development, a unique design had been introduced with very little in common with other Yamaha dirtbikes.

Gradually, as the performance of the XTs in the dirt became more important, and the TT began being considered a serious off-road mount and not just a playbike, technology from the competition series was incorporated. Fittingly, therefore, the TT600N was more closely related to the IT and YZ models than ever before. By 1985, Yamaha, the most prolific manufacturer of dirtbikes in motorcycling history, had pulled the different series together as a clearly related family. And just as a thread could be traced between each of the bikes in the 1985 Yamaha off-road line-up, so that thread could be traced back 20 years to those prototypes being tested in the southern Californian desert. The DT1, the harbinger of the off-road revolution, was long gone but its spirit lived on.

Appendix

Evolution of monoshock suspension

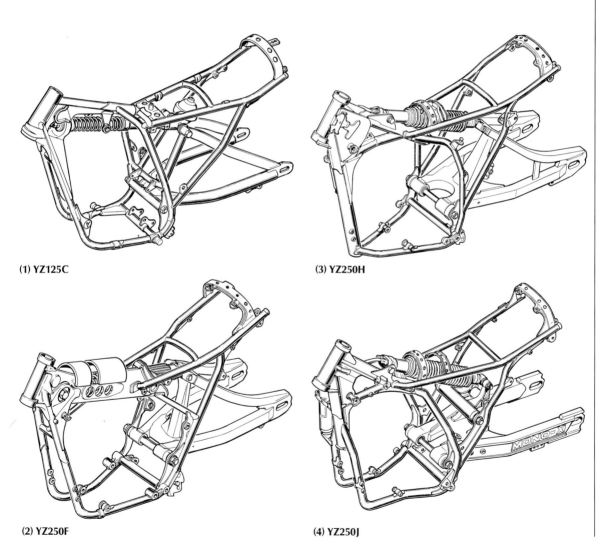

(1) YZ125C

(3) YZ250H

(2) YZ250F

(4) YZ250J

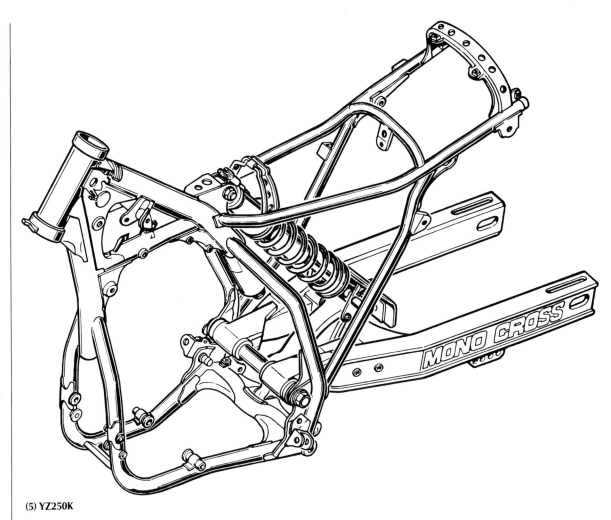

(5) **YZ250K**

Specifications

This specification appendix in fact covers both 'model recognition' and a model chart. There were just too many models to provide all the necessary information to recognize models, but the decisive information, frame and chassis numbers, I've included in the specifications. Unless otherwise stated, the number after the three

Model	DT1	DT1C/E	DT2/DT3	DT250	DT250
Year	1968	1970–1971	1972–1973	1975–1976	1977–1980
Chassis/engine id.	DT1	DT1/DT1-F	DT1F-160101/ DT1F-166101	450	1M2/1R7**
Bore (mm)	70	70	70	70	70
Stroke (mm)	64	64	64	64	64
Capacity (cc)	246	246	246	246	246
Compression ratio (to 1)	6·8 (8·2)*	6·4 (8·2)*	6·8 (7·13)*	6·8	6·7
bhp @ rpm	21@6000(30@7000)*	23@7000 (30@7000)*	24@7000 (31@8000)*	24 @ 7000	17 @ 6000
Torque (kgm) @ rpm	2·5 @ 5000 (3·1 @ 6500)*	2·4@6500 (3·1@6500)*	2·53 @ 6000 (2·86 @ 7000)*		2·12 @ 5000
Oil system	Autolube	Autolube	Autolube	Autolube	Autolube
Engine cooling	air	air	air	air	air
Carburettor (mm)	VM26SH (VM30SH)*	VM26SH (VM30SH)*	VM26SH (VM30SC)*	VM28SS	VM28SS
Ignition system	magneto	magneto	magneto	magneto	magneto (CDI)*
Ignition timing (mm)	3·2 (2·3)*	3·2 (2·3)*	3·2 (2·3)* (3·0)**	3·2	3·2
Primary drive gearing	3·1	3·1	3·1	2·83	2·83
Final drive gearing	44/15 (44/14)*	44/14	44/14	44/14 (47/14)*	47/14
Box gearing first	2·23	2·53 (2·25)*	2·53	2·53	2·54
Box gearing second	1·62	1·79 (1·65)*	1·79	1·68 (1·79)*	1·79
Box gearing third	1·21	1·30 (1·26)*	1·30	1·17 (1·30)*	1·30
Box gearing fourth	1·0	1·0 (1·0)*	1·0	1·0	1·0
Box gearing fifth	0·82	0·77 (0·77)*	0·77	0·86 (0·76)*	0·77
Box gearing sixth	—	—	—	—	—
Fuel (1)	9	9	9·5 (8)*	9	9
Engine oil (1)	1·6	1·6	1·6 (0·57)*	1·5	1·15
Transmission oil (1)	1·0	1·0	1·0	1·0	1·2
Front fork oil (cc/leg)	210	210 (175)***	175	175	190
Front tyre	3·25 × 19	3·25 × 19 (2·75 × 21)*	3·25 × 19 (3·00 × 21)***	3·00 × 21	3·00 × 21
Rear tyre	4·00 × 18	4·00 × 18	4·00 × 18	4·00 × 18	4·00 × 18
Front brake	sls drum	sls drum	sls drum	sls drum	sls drum
Rear brake	sls drum	sls drum	sls drum	sls drum	sls drum
Rear suspension	twin shock	twin shock	twin shock	twin shock	monoshock
Front suspension travel (mm)					195
Rear suspension travel (mm)					140 (150)*
Rake (°)				30·5	30 (28·5)*
Trail (mm)				135	135 (120)*
Width (mm)			910	870	870
Ground clearance (mm)	240	240 (255)**	240	220	255
Wheelbase (mm)	1366	1366 (1390)**	1330 (1340)***	1410 (1415)*	1420
Dry weight (kg)	105	104 (111)**	117 (102)*	123	122
	* = DT1-M	* = DT1C-M/DT1E-M	* = DT2-M	* = DT250C	* = DT250F, DT250G
		** = DT1E	** = DT3		** = Europe
		*** = DT1E/DT1E-M	*** = DT2-M & DT3		

alpha-numeric code is -000101. As far as models are concerned, Yamaha produced a new one each year, so a model chart would be meaningless. The year of sale of each model is also recorded in the specifications.

The one entry in the specifications that I hesitated about including were the power and torque values, since some are measured on a variety of dynamometers and others were claimed, so it is not possible to make any meaningful comparison between them. They have been included simply for the 'ballpark' values they indicate. The number following the 'monoshock' specification of the rear suspension refers to the 'Evolution of monoshock suspension' appendix.

Model	AT1	AT1-MX	AT2/AT3(M)	DT125	DT125
Year	**1969–1971**	**1969–1971**	**1972–1973**	**1973–1977**	**1978–1980**
Chassis/engine id.	AT1	AT1	AT1	452	2N0
Bore (mm)	56	56	56	56	56
Stroke (mm)	50	50	50	50	50
Capacity (cc)	123	123	123	123	123
Compression ratio (to 1)	7·1	8·0	7·1 (7·8)	7·1	7·2
bhp @ rpm	11·5 @ 7500	18 @ 8500	13 @ 7000 (20 @ 8500)*	13 @ 7000	9·4 @ 7000
Torque (kgm) @ rpm	1·17 @ 6000	1·57 @ 7500	1·38 @ 6000 (1·7 @ 8000)*	1·38 @ 6000	1·05 @ 6500
Oil system	Autolube	Autolube	Autolube	Autolube	Autolube
Engine cooling	air	air	air	air	air
Carburettor (mm)	VM24SH	VM26SH	VM24SH (VM26SC)*	VM24SH	VM24SS
Ignition system	magneto	magneto	magneto	starter dynamo	magneto
Ignition timing (mm)	1·8	2·0	1·8 (2·0)	1·8	1·45
Primary drive gearing	3·9	3·9	3·9	3·9	3·23
Final drive gearing	45/14	45/14 (45/15)*	45/15 (45/14)*	45/14 (45/15)*	49/15
Box gearing first	3·18	3·18 (2·83)*	3·18 (2·83)*	3·18	3·5
Box gearing second	2·0	2·0 (1·88)**	2·0 (1·86)*	2·0	2·21
Box gearing third	1·37	1·37 (1·37)**	1·37*	1·37	1·56
Box gearing fourth	1·0	1·0 (1·09)**	1·0 (1·1)*	1·0	1·19
Box gearing fifth	0·8	0·8 (0·96)**	0·8 (0·96)*	0·8	0·96
Box gearing sixth	—	—	—	—	0·8
Fuel (1)	7	7	7	7	7·2
Engine oil (1)	1·23	1·23	1·23	1·2	1·0
Transmission oil (1)	0·74 (0·76)**	0·74 (0·76)**	0·75	0·75	0·65
Front fork oil (cc/leg)	160 (150)*	160 (150)*	120	128	146
Front tyre	3·00 × 18	3·25 × 18	3·00 × 18 (2·75 × 21)*	3·00 × 19	2·75 × 21
Rear tyre	3·25 × 18	3·50 × 18	3·25 × 18 (3·50 × 18)*	3·25 × 18	3·50 × 18
Front brake	sls drum	sls drum	sls drum	sls drum	sls drum
Rear brake	sls drum	sls drum	sls drum	sls drum	sls drum
Rear suspension	twin shock	twin shock	twin shock	twin shock	monoshock (2)
Front suspension travel (mm)	145	145		145 (160)*	170
Rear suspension (mm)	110	110		90	100
Rake (°)	29·5	29·5		31 (32)*	30
Trail (mm)				124 (141)*	127
Width (mm)	909	909	910		826
Ground clearance (mm)	225	225	240		274
Wheelbase (mm)	1285	1285	1280 (1290)*		1350
Dry weight (kg)	94 (99)* (100)**	91	100 (92)*	105·5 (104·5)*	97·5
	* = AT1B	* = AT1–B	* = M model	* = DT125C	
	** = AT1C	** = AT1–C			

172

Model	CT1	CT2/CT3	DT175	DT175	HT1/HT2
Year	**1969–1971**	**1972–1973**	**1973–1977**	**1978–1980**	**1970–1971**
Chassis/engine id.	CT1		443 (559)*	2A7/2H5	HT1/HT2
Bore (mm)	66	66	66	66	50
Stroke (mm)	50	50	50	50	45·6
Capacity (cc)	171	171	171	171	89
Compression ratio (to 1)	6·8	6·8	6·1 (6·6)*	6·8	6·8
bhp @ rpm	15 @ 7000	16 @ 7500	16 @ 7500	12·2 @ 7000	8·5 @ 8000
Torque (kgm) @ rpm	1·64 @ 5500	1·64 @ 6000	1·65 @ 6000	1·32 @ 5500	0·9 @ 6500
Oil system	Autolube	Autolube	Autolube	Autolube	Autolube
Engine cooling	air	air	air	air	air
Carburettor (mm)	VM24SH	VM24SH	VM24SS	VM24SS	VM20SC
Ignition system	magneto	magneto	magneto	CDI	magneto
Ignition timing (mm)	1·8	1·8	1·8	1·8	1·8
Primary drive gearing	3·9	3·9	3·9	3·23	3·9
Final drive gearing	45/14	45/16	45/16	49/16	49/14
Box gearing first	3·18	2·53	3·18	3·5	3·18
Box gearing second	2·0	1·88	2·0	2·21	2·0
Box gearing third	1·37	1·37	1·37	1·56	1·37
Box gearing fourth	1·0	1·0	1·0	1·2	1·0
Box gearing fifth	0·8	0·8	0·8	0·96	0·8
Box gearing sixth	—	—	—	0·8	—
Fuel (1)	7	7	7	7	6·5
Engine oil (1)	1·23	1·23	1·2	1·0	1·2
Transmission oil (1)	0·74	0·75	0·65	0·65	0·75
Front fork oil (cc/leg)	160	120	130	146	140
Front tyre	3·25 × 18	3·25 × 18	3·00 × 19 (2·75 × 21)*	2·75 × 21	2·75 × 18
Rear tyre	3·50 × 18	3·50 × 18	3·50 × 18	3·50 × 18	3·00 × 18
Front brake	sls drum	sls drum	sls drum	sls drum	sls drum
Rear brake	sls drum	sls drum	sls drum	sls drum	sls drum
Rear suspension	twin shock	twin shock	twin shock	monoshock (2)	twin shock
Front suspension travel (mm)			145 (160)*	180	
Rear suspension travel (mm)			90	100	
Rake (°*)			31 (31·5)*	30	
Trail (mm)			122 (138)*	126	
Width (mm)	910			1016	900
Ground clearance (mm)	240			265	225
Wheelbase (mm)	1290			1350	1220
Dry weight (kg)	96	97	98·6	98	85

* = DT175C

Model	LT2/LT3	DT100 (A–G)	RT1	RT1-M	RT2/RT3
Year	**1971–1972**	**1973–1980**	**1970–1971**	**1970–1971**	**1972–1973**
Chassis/engine id.			RT1	RT1-070101	RT1-160101/ RT1-164101
Bore (mm)	52	52	80	80	80
Stroke (mm)	45·6	45·6	70	70	70
Capacity (cc)	97	97	351	351	351
Compression ratio (to 1)	6·9/7·8	6·8 (7·2)* (7·4)**	6·6 (6·3)*	7·5 (7·2)*	6·3 (7·13)*
bhp @ rpm	10@7500/16@10,500	10 @ 7500	30 @ 6000	36 @ 6500	32@6000(39@7500)*
Torque (kgm) @ rpm	0·97 @ 7000/ 1·12 @ 9500	0·97 @ 7000	3·6 @ 5500	3·96 @ 6500	3·82@5500 (3·82@7000)*
Oil system	Autolube	Autolube	Autolube	Autolube	Autolube
Engine cooling	air	air	air	air	air
Carburettor (mm)	VM20SH/VM26SH	VM22SS	VM32SH	VM34SH	VM32SH (VM34SC)*
Ignition system	magneto	magneto	magneto	magneto	magneto
Ignition timing (mm)	1·8/2·0	1·8	2·9	3·4	2·9 (2·5)*
Primary drive gearing	3·9	3·9	3·1	3·1	3·1
Final drive gearing	49/14 / 52/14	49/14	39/15	44/15	39/15 (51/15)*
Box gearing first	3·18/2·83	3·18	2·53	2·25	2·53 (2·25)*
Box gearing second	2·0/1·88	2·0	1·79	1·65	1·79 (1·65)*
Box gearing third	1·37	1·37	1·3	1·26	1·3 (1·21)*
Box gearing fourth	1·0/1·09	1·0	1·0	1·0	1·0 (1·0)*
Box gearing fifth	0·8/0·96	0·8	0·77	0·79	0·77 (0·79)*
Box gearing sixth	—	—	—	—	—
Fuel (1)	6	6·0 (7·0)* (4·5)**	9·5	9·5	9·5
Engine oil (1)	1·23	1·2 (1·0)**	1·6	1·6	1·6
Transmission oil (1)	0·70	0·65	1·0	1·0	1·0
Front fork oil (cc/leg)	136	160 (116)**	210	210 (175)*	175
Front tyre	2·75 × 18/2·75 × 19	2·75 × 19 (2·50 × 18)**	3·25 × 19	2·75 × 21	3·25 × 19 (3·00 × 21)**
Rear tyre	3·00 × 18	3·00 × 18 (3·00 × 16)**	4·00 × 18	4·00 × 18	4·00 × 18
Front brake	sls drum	sls drum	sls drum	sls drum	sls drum
Rear brake	sls drum	sls drum	sls drum	sls drum	sls drum
Rear suspension	twin shock	twin shock	twin shock	twin shock	twin shock
Front suspension travel (mm)		145			
Rear suspension travel (mm)		90			
Rake (°)		31 (30·5)**	29·5	29·5	
Trail (mm)		132 (130)*	137	137	
Width (mm)	800		890	890	950
Ground clearance (mm)	220		255	255	225
Wheelbase (mm)	1240/1255		1400	1400	1384 (1410)*
Dry weight (kg)	85	93	117 (108)*	108 (109)*	119 (103)*
		* = DT100C	* = RT1-B	* = RT1B-M	* = RT2–M
		** = DT100D, E, F, G			** = RT2-M & RT3

Model	DT360	DT400	DT400	MX360	MX400B
Year	**1974**	**1975–1976**	**1977–1978**	**1973–1974**	**1975**
Chassis/engine id.	446	501	1M2/1R6*	365	510
Bore (mm)	80	85	85	80	85
Stroke (mm)	70	70	70	70	70
Capacity (cc)	351	397	397	351	397
Compression ratio (to 1)	6·4	6·4	6·4	7·43	7·57
bhp @ rpm		27 @ 5000		39 @ 7500	38·76 @ 8000
Torque (kgm) @ rpm		3·8 @ 5000		3·86 @ 7000	3·92 @ 7000
Oil system	Autolube	Autolube	Autolube	Autolube	mix
Engine cooling	air	air	air	air	air
Carburettor (mm)	VM30SS	VM32SS	VM34SC	VM34SC	VM38SS
Ignition system	CDI	CDI	CDI	CDI	CDI
Ignition timing (mm)	2·9	2·9	2·9	2·5	2·7
Primary drive gearing	2·67	2·67	2·83	2·67	2·67
Final drive gearing	44/15 (44/16)*	40/14	45/16	51/14	50/14
Box gearing first	2·53	2·53	2·71	2·25	2·25
Box gearing second	1·79 (1·68)*	1·79	1·79	1·65	1·68
Box gearing third	1·30 (1·17)*	1·30	1·30	1·26	1·26
Box gearing fourth	1·0	1·0	1·0	1·0	1·0
Box gearing fifth	0·77 (0·86)*	0·77	0·77	0·79	0·79
Box gearing sixth	—	—	—		—
Fuel (1)	9	9	9	9	8
Engine oil (1)	1·5	1·5	1·2	0·56	—
Transmission oil (1)	1·2	1·0	1·2	1·2	1·0
Front fork oil (cc/leg)	175	175	190	175	190
Front tyre	3·00 × 21	3·00 × 21	3·00 × 21	3·00 × 21	3·00 × 21
Rear tyre	4·00 × 18	4·00 × 18	4·00 × 18	4·00 × 18	4·60 × 18
Front brake	sls drum	sls drum	sls drum	sls drum	sls drum
Rear brake	sls drum	sls drum	sls drum	sls drum	sls drum
Rear suspension	twin shock	twin shock	monoshock (2)		monoshock (1)
Front suspension travel (mm)					190
Rear suspension travel (mm)					90
Rake (°)	30·5	30·5	28·5		31
Trail (mm)	135	135	120		139
Width (mm)	870	870	870	950	985
Ground clearance (mm)	220	220	255	225	235
Wheelbase (mm)	1425 (1420)*	1410	1415	1420	1415
Dry weight (kg	125	124	125	106	103
	* = Europe only		* = Europe		

175

Model	MX100	MX125	MX250	MX250B	SC500
Year	1974–1980	1974–1976	1973–1974	1975	1973–1974
Chassis/engine id.		402/565	364	509	363
Bore (mm)	52	56	70	70	95
Stroke (mm)	45·6	50	64	64	70
Capacity (cc)	97	123	246	246	496
Compression ratio (to 1)	7·8	7·8 (7·5)*	7·05	7·54	7·1
bhp @ rpm	16 @ 10,500	20 @ 8500	31 @ 7500		44 @ 6500
Torque (kgm) @ rpm	1·12 @ 9500	1·7@8000(1·6@9500)*	3·03 @ 7000		5·12 @ 6000
Oil system	Autolube	Autolube (mix)*	Autolube	mix	Autolube
Engine cooling	air	air	air	air	air
Carburettor (mm)	VM26SC	VM26SC (VM30SC)*	VM30SC	VM38SS	VM38SC
Ignition system	magneto	magneto (CDI)*	CDI	CDI	CDI
Ignition timing (mm)	2·0	2·0	2·3	2·3	2·7
Primary drive gearing	3·9	3·9	2·83	2·7	2·66
Final drive gearing	52/14	45/14	51/14	50/13	51/14
Box gearing first	2·83	2·83	2·25	1·83	2·0
Box gearing second	1·88	1·88	1·65	1·41	1·35
Box gearing third	1·37	1·37	1·26	1·17	1·00
Box gearing fourth	1·09	1·09	1·0	1·0	0·80
Box gearing fifth	0·96	0·96	0·79	0·86	—
Box gearing sixth	—				
Fuel (1)	6	7	9	8	8
Engine oil (1)	1·2	1·2	0·5	—	0·56
Transmission oil (1)		0·75	1·0	1·0	1·2
Front fork oil (cc/leg)		120	175	190	194
Front tyre	2·75 × 19	2·75 × 21 (3·00 × 21)*	3·00 × 21	3·00 × 21	3·00 × 21
Rear tyre	3·00 × 18	3·50 × 18 (4·00 × 18)*	4·00 × 18	4·60 × 18	4·60 × 18
Front brake	sls drum	sls drum	sls drum	sls drum	sls drum
Rear brake	sls drum	sls drum	sls drum	sls drum	sls drum
Rear suspension	twin shock	twin shock	twin shock	monoshock (1)	twin shock
Front suspension travel (mm)				195	
Rear suspension travel (mm)				90	
Rake (°)	31	29·5		31	
Trail (mm)	135	137		139	
Width (mm)	865	910	950	985	950
Ground clearance (mm)	210	240 (274)*	225	235	225
Wheelbase (mm)	1260	1290 (1465)*	1420	1420	1420
Dry weight (kg)	84	92 (89)*	101	100	107

*= MX125C

Model	YZ80D	YZ80E	YZ80F/G	YZ80H	YZ80J/K
Year	**1977**	**1978**	**1979–1980**	**1981**	**1982–1983**
Chassis/engine id.	1T0	2J5	2X6/3R1	4V1	5X2/22W
Bore (mm)	49	49	49	49	47
Stroke (mm)	42	42	42	42	45·6
Capacity (cc)	79	79	79	79	79
Compression ratio (to 1)	7·3	7·2	7·0	7·1	7·5 (8·0)*
bhp @ rpm			14·3 @ 11,000		
Torque (kgm) @ rpm			0·94 @ 11,000		
Oil system	mix	mix	mix	mix	mix
Engine cooling	air	air	air	air	liquid
Carburettor (mm)	VM26SS	VM26SS	VM26SS	VM24SS	VM26SS
Ignition system	magneto	CDI	CDI	CDI	CDI
Ignition timing (mm)				0·8	0·8
Primary drive gearing	3·58	3·14	3·14	3·58	3·14 (3·58)*
Final drive gearing	48/13	51/14	51/14	44/13	44/13 (42/12)*
Box gearing first	3·25	2·40	2·40	2·77	2·77
Box gearing second	2·00	1·83	1·83	2·06	2·06
Box gearing third	1·43	1·48	1·48	1·63	1·63
Box gearing fourth	1·13	1·22	1·22	1·33	1·33
Box gearing fifth	0·96	1·04	1·04	1·15	1·15
Box gearing sixth	—	—	0·93	1·04	1·04
Fuel (1)	4·3	4·5	4·5	4·6	5·2 (5·0)*
Engine oil (1)	—	—		—	—
Transmission oil (1)			0·75	0·75	0·7 (0·65)*
Front fork oil (cc/leg)				188	188 (260)*
Front tyre	2·50 × 14	2·50 × 16	2·50 × 16 (2·75 × 17)*	2·75 × 17	2·75 × 17
Rear tyre	3·60 × 14	3·60 × 14	3·60 × 14	4·10 × 14	4·10 × 14
Front brake	sls drum	sls drum	sls drum	sls drum	sls drum
Rear brake	sls drum	sls drum	sls drum	sls drum	sls drum
Rear suspension	twin shock	monoshock (2)	monoshock (3)	monoshock (3)	monoshock (4/5)
Front suspension travel (mm)	132	140	165 (180)*	215	225 (240)*
Rear suspension travel (mm)	85	120	155 (170)*	205	205 (250)*
Rake (°)	27·5	28·5	28	27	26
Trail (mm)	80	84	80	84	80
Width (mm)	737	719	730	765	765
Ground clearance (mm)	201	195	200	255	270
Wheelbase (mm)	1171	1170	1180	1205	1230
Dry weight (kg)	65	67	62	60	67 (62)*
			* = YZ80G		* = YZ80K

Model	YZ80L/N	YZ100C	YZ100D/E	YZ100F	YZ100G/H
Year	**1984–1985**	**1976**	**1977–1978**	**1979**	**1980–1981**
Chassis/engine id.	39K/43K	1J4	1J4/2K5	2W5	3R2-000101/ 3R2-020101
Bore (mm)	47	50	50	50	50
Stroke (mm)	45·6	50	50	50	50
Capacity (cc)	79	98	98	98	98
Compression ratio (to 1)	9·2 (8·6)*	7·2	7·2	7·2	8·4
bhp @ rpm					
Torque (kgm) @ rpm					
Oil system	mix	mix	mix	mix	mix
Engine cooling	liquid	air	air	air	air
Carburettor (mm)	VM26SS	VM30SC	VM30SS	VM30SS	VM30SS
Ignition system	CDI	CDI	CDI	CDI	CDI
Ignition timing (mm)	0·6 (0·8)*				0·8
Primary drive gearing	3·15 (3·58)*	3·9	3·89		3·89
Final drive gearing	48/14 (46/15)*	40/12			45/12
Box gearing first	2·77	2·54	2·46	2·46	2·46
Box gearing second	2·06	1·93	1·88	1·88	1·88
Box gearing third	1·63	1·56	1·50	1·50	1·50
Box gearing fourth	1·38	1·30	1·25	1·25	1·25
Box gearing fifth	1·23	1·14	1·09	1·09	1·09
Box gearing sixth	1·13	1·05	1·00	1·00	1·00
Fuel (1)	5		5	5·2	5·6
Engine oil (1)	—		—		—
Transmission oil (1)	0·65			0·75	0·8
Front fork oil (cc/leg)	272			180	258
Front tyre	80/80 × 17	2·75 × 21	2·75 × 21		3·00 × 21
Rear tyre	110/80 × 14	3·50 × 18	3·50 × 18		4·10 × 18
Front brake	sls drum	sls drum	sls drum	sls drum	sls drum
Rear brake	sls drum	sls drum	sls drum	sls drum	sls drum
Rear suspension	monoshock (5)	monoshock (1)	monoshock(1/2)	monoshock (2)	monoshock (2)
Front suspension travel (mm)	255		180		200
Rear suspension travel (mm)	260		170		200
Rake (°)	26		29	29	29·5
Trail (mm)	80		117		130
Width (mm)	765				860
Ground clearance (mm)	290	275	260	280	310
Wheelbase (mm)	1235	1370	1365	1364	1375
Dry weight (kg)	60	91	91 (80)*	84	84
	*= YZ80N		*= YZ100E		

Model	YZ100J/K/L	YZ125A	YZ125C	YZ125X	YZ125D/E
Year	1982–1984	1974	1975	1976	1977–1978
Chassis/engine id.	5X3/5X3-060101/ 43L	453	537	1G8/1J8*	1W1/2K5
Bore (mm)	50	56	56	56	56
Stroke (mm)	50	50	50	50	50
Capacity (cc)	98	123	123	123	123
Compression ratio (to 1)	8·0	8·0	7·5	7·4	7·8 (7·4)*
bhp @ rpm		15·3 @ 9500	17 @ 11,000	20·67 @ 10,500	14·7 @ 11,000
Torque (kgm) @ rpm		1·27 @ 8000	1·39 @ 10,500	1·47 @ 10,000	1·01 @ 9500
Oil system	mix	mix	mix	mix	mix
Engine cooling	air	air	air	air	air
Carburettor (mm)	VM30SS	VM28SC	VM34SS	VM34SC	VM32SS
Ignition system	CDI	CDI	CDI	CDI	CDI
Ignition timing (mm)	0·8	2·0	1·2		
Primary drive gearing	3·44	3·89	3·23	3·23	3·23
Final drive gearing	50/12	47/14	53/14	46/12	51/12
Box gearing first	2·46	2·83	2·54	2·54	2·46
Box gearing second	1·86	2·07	1·93	1·93	1·87
Box gearing third	1·50	1·61	1·56	1·56	1·50
Box gearing fourth	1·25	1·32	1·30	1·30	1·25
Box gearing fifth	1·11	1·14	1·14	1·14	1·09
Box gearing sixth	1·00	—	1·05	1·05	1·00
Fuel (1)	8·2	5·5	5·5	5·5	6·5
Engine oil (1)	—	—	—		—
Transmission oil (1)	0·75	0·65	0·65	1·3	
Front fork oil (cc/leg)	340	135	190	190	
Front tyre	3·00 × 21	2·75 × 21	3·00 × 21	3·00 × 21	3·00 × 21
Rear tyre	4·10 × 18	3·50 × 18	4·10 × 18	4·00 × 18	4·10 × 18
Front brake	sls drum	sls drum	sls drum	sls drum	sls drum
Rear brake	sls drum	sls drum	sls drum	sls drum	sls drum
Rear suspension	monoshock (4)	twin shock	monoshock (1)	monoshock (1)	monoshock(2)
Front suspension travel (mm)	250		170		236 (230)*
Rear suspension travel (mm)	250		135		224 (240)*
Rake (°)	27·5	30	31	31	31 (30)*
Trail (mm)	115	140	140	140	139 (133)*
Width (mm)	840	925	985	900	851 (864)*
Ground clearance (mm)	315	260	285	292	287 (295)*
Wheelbase (mm)	1420	1345	1410	1415	1410 (1420)*
Dry weight (kg)	87	80	86	86	88·5 (86)*
				*=Europe & Japan	*=YZ125E

Model	**YZ125F**	**YZ125G**	**YZ125H**	**YZ125J/K**	**YZ125L/N**
Year	**1979**	**1980**	**1981**	**1982–1983**	**1984–1985**
Chassis/engine id.	2X3/2Y5*	3R3/3N8*	4V2	5X4	39W/43M
Bore (mm)	56	56	56	56	56
Stroke (mm)	50	50	50	50	50
Capacity (cc)	123	123	123	123	123
Compression ratio (to 1)	8·3	8·5	8·1	7·7 – 9·8	8·0 – 9·9
bhp @ rpm	26 @ 11,000	26·5 @ 11,000			
Torque (kgm) @ rpm	1·71 @ 10,500	1·80 @ 9500			
Oil system	mix	mix	mix	mix	mix
Engine cooling	air	air	liquid	liquid	liquid
Carburettor (mm)	VM32SS	VM32SS	VM34SS	VM34SS	VM36SS
Ignition system	CDI	CDI	CDI	CDI	CDI
Ignition timing (mm)		2·27		1·88	(1·21)*
Primary drive gearing	3·83	3·83	3·44	3·44	3·33
Final drive gearing	43/12	48/12	48/12	46/12 (48/12)*	48/12 (52/12)*
Box gearing first	2·46	2·46	2·46	2·46	2·46
Box gearing second	1·88	1·86	1·86	1·86	1·87
Box gearing third	1·50	1·50	1·50	1·50	1·50
Box gearing fourth	1·25	1·25	1·25	1·25	1·25
Box gearing fifth	1·09	1·09	1·09	1·09	1·09
Box gearing sixth	1·00	1·00	1·00	1·00	1·00
Fuel (1)	6	6·5	6·5	8·2 (7·0)*	7·8 (7·5)*
Engine oil (1)	—	—	—		
Transmission oil (1)		0·7	0·8	0·85	(0·85)*
Front fork oil (cc/leg)		360		415	(540)*
Front tyre	3·00 × 21	3·00 × 21	3·00 × 21	3·00 × 21	90/90 × 21
Rear tyre	4·10 × 18	4·10 × 18	4·10 × 18	4·10 × 18 (4·25 × 18)*	12/80 × 18
Front brake	sls drum	sls drum	sls drum	sls drum	tls drum (disc)*
Rear brake	sls drum	sls drum	sls drum	sls drum	sls drum
Rear suspension	monoshock(2)	monoshock (3)	monoshock (3)	monoshock (4/5)	monoshock (5)
Front suspension travel (mm)	250	300	300	300	300
Rear suspension travel (mm)	230	290	300	310	310
Rake (°)	29·5	29	27·5	27·5 (28)*	27·5
Trail (mm)	128	125	119	118 (121)*	116
Width (mm)	950	950	850	870	815 (850)*
Ground clearance (mm)	290	340	335	350	350
Wheelbase (mm)	1410	1430	1450	1465 (1450)*	1450
Dry weight (kg)	88	85	90	91 (87·5)*	88 (90)*
	*=Europe & Japan	*=Europe & Japan		*=YZ125K	*=YZ125N

Model	YZ250A/B	YZ250C	YZ250D	YZ250E	YZ250F
Year	**1973–1974**	**1976**	**1977**	**1978**	**1979**
Chassis/engine id.	431/483	509	1W3	2K7	2X4
Bore (mm)	70	70	70	70	70
Stroke (mm)	64	64	64	64	64
Capacity (cc)	246	246	246	246	246
Compression ratio (to 1)	7·4 (7·8)*	7·69	7·8	7·3	7·9
bhp @ rpm		26·3 @ 8000	26·6 @ 8000	30 @ 7500	27 @ 8000
Torque (kgm) @ rpm				2·9 @ 7000	3·0 @ 6500
Oil system	mix	mix	mix	mix	mix
Engine cooling	air	air	air	air	air
Carburettor (mm)	VM34SC	VM38SC	VM36SC	VM38SS	VM38SS
Ignition system	CDI	CDI	CDI	CDI	CDI
Ignition timing (mm)	2·3			1·8	
Primary drive gearing	3·08	2·70	2·66	2·61	2·61
Final drive gearing	52/13 (50/13)*	50/13	54/13	50/13	50/13
Box gearing first	1·83	1·83	2·07	2·33	2·14
Box gearing second	1·41	1·41	1·56	1·81	1·81
Box gearing third	1·17	1·17	1·24	1·44	1·44
Box gearing fourth	1·00	1·00	1·00	1·22	1·20
Box gearing fifth	0·86	0·86	0·86	1·05	1·00
Box gearing sixth	—	—	—	0·92	0·87
Fuel (1)	7	8	7·6	8	8
Engine oil (1)	—	—	—	—	—
Transmission oil (1)	1·0			0·8	
Front fork oil (cc/leg)	194				
Front tyre	3·00 × 21	3·00 × 21	3·00 × 21	3·00 × 21	3·00 × 21
Rear tyre	4·00 × 18	4·10 × 18	4·50 × 18	4·50 × 18	4·50 × 18
Front brake	sls drum	sls drum	sls drum	sls drum	sls drum
Rear brake	sls drum	sls drum	sls drum	sls drum	sls drum
Rear suspension	twin shock	monoshock (1)	monoshock (2)	monoshock (2)	monoshock (2)
Front suspension travel (mm)	194	210	248	250	272
Rear suspension travel (mm)	105 (90)*	165	244	245	264
Rake (°)	30	31·5	30·5	30·5	29·5
Trail (mm)	129	138	134	134	128
Width (mm)	890 (985)*	900	851	898	851
Ground clearance (mm)	226 (240)*	256	286	317	315
Wheelbase (mm)	1420 (1425)*	1450	1450	1454	1450
Dry weight (kg)	94 (97)*	106	104	100	100

* = YZ250B

Model	YZ250G	YZ250H	YZ250J	YZ250K	YZ250L
Year	**1980**	**1981**	**1982**	**1983**	**1984**
Chassis/engine id.	3R4	4V3	5X5	24Y–100101*/ 24Y–000101	39X/43N*
Bore (mm)	70	70	70	68	68
Stroke (mm)	64	64	64	68	68
Capacity (cc)	246	246	246	246	246
Compression ratio (to 1)	8·1	7·9	7·5	7·4 – 9·2	7·8 – 9·5
bhp @ rpm	29·6 @ 8000		33·5 @ 8500		35·3 @ 8500
Torque (kgm) @ rpm	2·78 @ 7500		2·86 @ 8500		3·1 @ 8000
Oil system	mix	mix	mix	mix	mix
Engine cooling	air	air	liquid	liquid	air
Carburettor (mm)	VM38SS	VM38SS	VM38SS	VM38SS	VM38SS
Ignition system	CDI	CDI	CDI	CDI	CDI
Ignition timing (mm)	0·61	0·61			1·5
Primary drive gearing	2·63	2·63	2·63	2·63	2·63
Final drive gearing	48/14	48/14	45/13	48/13	48/13
Box gearing first	2·14	2·14	2·14	2·14	2·14
Box gearing second	1·81	1·81	1·81	1·75	1·75
Box gearing third	1·41	1·41	1·41	1·37	1·44
Box gearing fourth	1·14	1·14	1·14	1·10	1·20
Box gearing fifth	0·98	0·96	0·96	0·91	1·00
Box gearing sixth	0·87	—	—	—	—
Fuel (1)	9·0	7·0	9	9·5	9·5
Engine oil (1)	—	—	—	—	
Transmission oil (1)	0·8	0·85			0·9
Front fork oil (cc/leg)	387	604			550
Front tyre	3·00 × 21	3·00 × 21	3·00 × 21	90/80 × 21	90/90 × 21
Rear tyre	5·10 × 18	5·10 × 18	5·10 × 18	140/80 × 18	130/80 × 18
Front brake	sls drum	sls drum	tls drum	tls drum	tls drum
Rear brake	sls drum	sls drum	sls drum	sls drum	sls drum
Rear suspension	monoshock (3)	monoshock (3)	monoshock (4)	monoshock (5)	monoshock (5)
Front suspension travel (mm)	300	300	300	287	282
Rear suspension travel (mm)	300	310	320	312	320
Rake (°)	30	28·5	27·5	28·0	28
Trail (mm)	132	120	118	119	119
Width (mm)	935	880	870	820	850
Wheelbase (mm)	310	320	325	335	338
Ground clearance (mm)	1455	1480	1490	1470	1470
Dry weight (kg)	97	99	104	98·4	98
				* = Non-USA	* = Europe

Model	YZ250N	YZ360A/B	YZ400C/D	YZ400E	YZ400F
Year	**1985**	**1973–1974**	**1976–1977**	**1978**	**1979**
Chassis/engine id.		365/484	510/1W4	2K8	2X5
Bore (mm)	68	80	85	85	82
Stroke (mm)	68	70	70	70	75
Capacity (cc)	246	351	397	396	397
Compression ratio (to 1)	8·2 – 9·6	7·0	7·57	7·6	7·4
bhp @ rpm	36·1 @ 8500		34·4 @ 7500 (41 @ 7500)*	41 @ 7500	36·9 @ 7000
Torque (kgm) @ rpm	3·21 @ 7500		3·61 @ 6500	4·02 @ 7000	4·02 @ 6500
Oil system	mix	mix	mix	mix	mix
Engine cooling	liquid	air	air	air	air
Carburettor (mm)	VM38SS	VM34SC	VM38SS	VM38SC	VM38SS
Ignition system	CDI	CDI	CDI	CDI	CDI
Ignition timing (mm)	1·5	2·3	2·7	2·7	3·1
Primary drive gearing	2·63	3·08	2·70 (2·24)*	2·67	2·61
Final drive gearing	50/14	48/15	50/14	50/14	50/14
Box gearing first	2·14	1·83	2·29	2·29	2·38
Box gearing second	1·75	1·41	1·71	1·71	1·75
Box gearing third	1·44	1·17	1·30	1·30	1·32
Box gearing fourth	1·20	1·00	1·00	1·00	1·05
Box gearing fifth	1·00	0·86	0·79 (0·84)*	0·84	0·83
Box gearing sixth	—	—	—	—	—
Fuel (1)	9·5	6·8	8·0	7·6	7·6
Engine oil (1)	—	—	—	—	—
Transmission oil (1)	0·9	1·0	1·0	1·2	0·85
Front fork oil (cc/leg)	530	194	415	338	364
Front tyre	90/90 × 21	3·00 × 21	3·00 × 21	3·00 × 21	3·00 × 21
Rear tyre	130/80 × 18	4·60 × 18	5·00 × 18 (4·50 × 18)*	4·50 × 18	5·10 × 18
Front brake	disc	sls drum	sls drum	sls drum	sls drum
Rear brake	sls drum	sls drum	sls drum	sls drum	sls drum
Rear suspension	monoshock (5)	twin shock	monoshock (1/2)	monoshock (2)	monoshock (2)
Front suspension travel (mm)	280	194	215	250	270
Rear suspension travel (mm)	320	105	180 (215)*	250	265
Rake (°)	28	30	28·5 (30·5)*	29·5	29·5
Trail (mm)	120	129	139 (134)*	134	128
Width (mm)	850	889 (985)*	985 (838)*	910	935
Ground clearance (mm)	340	226 (240)*	255 (285)*	290	320
Wheelbase (mm)	1470	1420 (1425)*	1425 (1445)*	1450	1450
Dry weight (kg)	100	96 (98)*	105 (102)*	103	102
		* = YZ360B	* = YZ400D		

Model	YZ465G/H	YZ490J	YZ490K	YZ490L/N	IT125G/H
Year	**1980**	**1982**	**1983**	**1984–1985**	**1980–1981**
Chassis/engine id.	3R5/4V4	5X6	23X-000101/ 23X-100101*	40T/43R	3R9-000101/ 3R9-050101
Bore (mm)	85	87	87	87	56
Stroke (mm)	82	82	82	82	50
Capacity (cc)	465	487	487	487	123
Compression ratio (to 1)	7·0	7·0	7·4	6·9	8·1
bhp @ rpm	41·92 @ 7000	48·3 @ 6500	49·8 @ 7500	47·1 @ 6500	16·87 @ 9000
Torque (kgm) @ rpm	4·76 @ 6000	5·51 @ 6000	5·36 @ 6000	5·25 @ 6500	1·48 @ 8000
Oil system	mix	mix	mix	mix	mix
Engine cooling	air	air	air	air	air
Carburettor (mm)	VM38SS	VM38SS	VM38SS	VM40SS	VM30SC
Ignition system	CDI	CDI	CDI	CDI	CDI
Ignition timing (mm)	2·0	2·0	2·0	2·0	
Primary drive gearing	2·63	2·63	2·63	2·63	3·23
Final drive gearing	46/14	44/14	46/14	46/14	46/12
Box gearing first	2·14	1·75	1·75	1·75	3·09
Box gearing second	1·75	1·32	1·32	1·32	2·07
Box gearing third	1·32	1·05	1·05	1·05	1·50
Box gearing fourth	1·05	0·83	0·83	0·83	1·19
Box gearing fifth	0·83	—	—	—	1·00
Box gearing sixth	—	—	—	—	0·84
Fuel (1)	9·5 (9·0)*	10	9·5	10·5	8·5
Engine oil (1)	—	—			
Transmission oil (1)	0·8 (0·75)*	0·8	0·8	0·8	0·65
Front fork oil (cc/leg)	387 (604)*	606	578	530	
Front tyre	3·00 × 21	3·00 × 21	100/80 × 21	100/90 × 21	3·00 × 21
Rear tyre	5·10 × 18	140/90 × 18	150/80 × 18	140/80 × 18	4·10 × 18
Front brake	sls drum	tls drum	tls drum	tls drum (disc)*	sls drum
Rear brake	sls drum	sls drum	sls drum	sls drum	sls drum
Rear suspension	monoshock (3)	monoshock (4)	monoshock (5)	monoshock (5)	monoshock (2)
Front suspension travel (mm)	284 (300)*	300	300	300	180 (200)*
Rear suspension travel (mm)	298 (310)*	320	325	320	200
Rake (°)	30 (28·5)*	28·5	28·5	28·5	28·5
Trail (mm)	132 (120)*	120	119	120	120
Width (mm)	935 (880)*	870	850	850	
Ground clearance (mm)	310 (320)*	320	330	335	284 (300)*
Wheelbase (mm)	1480	1500	1500	1475	1365
Dry weight (kg)	103 (105)*	108	103	104	92·5 (91·5)*
	* = YZ465H		* = Non-USA	* = YZ490N	* = IT125H

Model	IT175D/E	IT175F	IT175G/H	IT175J/K	IT200L/N
Year	1977–1978	1979	1980–1981	1982–1983	1984–1985
Chassis/engine id.	1W2	2W6	3R6-000101/ 3R6-020101/ 4J0-000101/ 4J0-010101*	5X8*/5X9**/ 5Y0***	43G*/49T**/ 49U***
Bore (mm)	66	66	66	66	66
Stroke (mm)	50	50	50	50	57
Capacity (cc)	171	171	171	171	195
Compression ration (to 1)	7·4	7·5	7·9	7·7	8·4
bhp @ rpm	21·5 @ 9500	20·6 @ 8500	19·86 @ 8000	22·73 @ 8500	21·5 @ 7500
Torque (kg) @ rpm	1·73 @ 8000	1·78 @ 7500	1·88 @ 7500	2·08 @ 7500	2·19 @ 7000
Oil system	mix	mix	mix	mix	mix
Engine cooling	air	air	air	air	air
Carburettor (mm)	VM34SC	VM34SS	VM32SS	VM34SS	VM34SS
Ignition system	CDI	CDI	CDI	CDI	CDI
Ignition timing (mm)					
Primary drive gearing	3·23	3·23	3·06	3·06	2·90
Final drive gearing	41/12	41/12	44/12	44/12	44/12
Box gearing first	3·10	3·09	3·09	2·75	2·75
Box gearing second	2·06	2·07	2·08	1·86	1·86
Box gearing third	1·50	1·50	1·50	1·50	1·50
Box gearing fourth	1·18	1·19	1·19	1·25	1·25
Box gearing fifth	1·00	1·00	1·00	1·11	1·08
Box gearing sixth	0·84	0·84	0·82	0·91	0·86
Fuel (1)	9·5	9·5	11	12	11
Engine oil (1)	—	—	—	—	—
Transmission oil (1)	0·65	0·65	0·7	0·7	0·8
Front fork oil (cc/leg)					
Front tyre	3·00 × 21	3·00 × 21	3·00 × 21	3·00 × 21	90/90 × 21
Rear tyre	4·10 × 18	4·10 × 18	4·10 × 18	110/90 × 18	120/90 × 18
Front brake	sls drum	sls drum	sls drum	sls drum	sls drum
Rear brake	sls drum	sls drum	sls drum	sls drum	sls drum
Rear suspension	monoshock (2)	monoshock (2)	monoshock (3)	monoshock (4)	monoshock (5)
Front suspension travel (mm)	175	195	250	260	270
Rear suspension travel (mm)	175	210	250	285	270
Rake (°)	32	29·5	28·5	28·5	28
Trail (mm)	144	127	122	125	115
Width (mm)	851			805	820
Ground clearance (mm)	254	269	290	330	340
Wheelbase (mm)	1410	1375	1420	1430	1440
Dry weight (kg)	96	95·5	93·5	98	93
			* = Australia	* = US & Canada ** = Australasia *** = Europe	* = Australasia ** = US *** = Europe

Model	IT250D	IT250E	IT250F/G	IT250H/J	IT250K
Year	**1977**	**1978**	**1979–1980**	**1981–1982**	**1983**
Chassis/engine id.	1W5	2K9	2X7/3R7	4V5	25Y/29V*
Bore (mm)	70	70	70	70	68
Stroke (mm)	64	64	64	64	68
Capacity (cc)	246	246	246	246	246
Compression ratio (to 1)	7·84	7·8	7·9	7·8	7·7
bhp @ rpm		26·1 @ 7500	27·7 @ 8000	32 @ 7500	30 @ 7500
Torque (kgm) @ rpm		2·65 @ 7000	2·51 @ 8000	3·12 @ 7500	2·88 @ 7500
Oil system	mix	mix	mix	mix	mix
Engine cooling	air	air	air	air	air
Carburettor (mm)	VM36SS	VM36SC	VM36SC	VM36SC	VM38SS
Ignition system	CDI	CDI	CDI	CDI	CDI
Ignition timing (mm)	2·3	2·3			
Primary drive gearing	2·67	2·66	2·5 (2·61)*	2·63	2·63
Final drive gearing	46/15	46/14	48/13	50/13	48/13
Box gearing first	2·29	2·71	2·66	2·67	2·67
Box gearing second	1·71	2·07	2·00	2·00	1·93
Box gearing third	1·30	1·60	1·56	1·56	1·50
Box gearing fourth	1·00	1·26	1·25	1·25	1·20
Box gearing fifth	0·84	1·05	1·04	1·05	1·00
Box gearing sixth	—	0·92	0·87	0·87	0·83
Fuel (1)	12	12	12	13	13·5
Engine oil (1)	—	—	—	—	—
Transmission oil (1)	1·2	1·1	1·2	0·85	0·75
Front fork oil (cc/leg)	250	250	250		
Front tyre	3·00 × 21	3·00 × 21	3·00 × 21	3·00 × 21	3·00 × 21
Rear tyre	4·50 × 18	4·50 × 18	4·50 × 18 (5·10 × 18)*	5·10 × 18	140/90 × 18
Front brake	sls drum	sls drum	sls drum	sls drum	tls drum
Rear brake	sls drum	sls drum	sls drum	sls drum	sls drum
Rear suspension	monoshock (2)	monoshock (2)	monoshock (2)	monoshock (3)	monoshock (5)
Front suspension travel (mm)	210	210	230 (250)*	270	300
Rear suspension travel (mm)	180	180	205 (250)*	270	300
Rake (°)	31·5	31·5	29·5	29	28
Trail (mm)	142	142	122 (125)*	126	118
Width (mm)	832	832	860		
Ground clearance (mm)	240	240	275 (300)*	295	305
Wheelbase (mm)	1430	1430	1420 (1430)*	1450	1485
Dry weight (kg)	115	109	108 (106)*	106·5	108
			* = IT250G		* = Non-USA

186

Model	IT400C	IT400D/E	IT400F	IT425G
Year	**1976**	**1977–1978**	**1979**	**1980**
Chassis/engine id.	1K7	1W6	2X8	3R8
Bore (mm)	85	85	82	85
Stroke (mm)	70	70	75	75
Capacity (cc)	397	397	397	425
Compression ratio (to 1)	7·57	7·59	7·4	7·3
bhp @ rpm	32·5 @ 8000		36·7 @ 6500	36·95 @ 6500
Torque (kgm) @ rpm	3·1 @ 7500		4·09 @ 6500	4·23 @ 6000
Oil system	mix	mix	mix	mix
Engine cooling	air	air	air	air
Carburettor (mm)	VM38SS	VM38SS	VM38SS	VM38SS
Ignition system	CDI	CDI	CDI	CDI
Ignition timing (mm)		2·7		
Primary drive gearing	2·70	2·67	2·61	2·61
Final drive gearing	46/15	46/15	46/14	48/13
Box gearing first	2·54	2·54	2·67	2·67
Box gearing second	1·71	1·71	1·75	1·75
Box gearing third	1·30	1·30	1·32	1·32
Box gearing fourth	1·00	1·00	1·00	1·00
Box gearing fifth	0·77	0·77	0·79	0·79
Box gearing sixth	—	—	—	—
Fuel (1)	12	12	12	12
Engine oil (1)	—	—	—	—
Transmission oil (1)	1·0	1·2	0·8	0·85
Front fork oil (cc/leg)		250		
Front tyre	3·00 × 21	3·00 × 21	3·00 × 21	3·00 × 21
Rear tyre	4·50 × 18	4·50 × 18	4·50 × 18	5·10 × 18
Front brake	sls drum	sls drum	sls drum	sls drum
Rear brake	sls drum	sls drum	sls drum	sls drum
Rear suspension	monoshock (1)	monoshock	monoshock (2)	monoshock (2)
Front suspension travel (mm)	210	210	230	250
Rear suspension travel (mm)	180	180	205	250
Rake (°)	31·5	31·5	29·5	29·5
Trail (mm)	138	142	122	125
Width (mm)	864	832		
Ground clearance (mm)	250	240	275	285
Wheelbase (mm)	1425	1430	1420	1430
Dry weight (kg)	115	115	112	111

Model	**IT465H/J**	**IT490K/L**
Year	**1981–1982**	**1983–1984**
Chassis/engine id.	4V6	26A-000101/26A-100101/29W-000101/ 29W-003101*/045K-000101**
Bore (mm)	85	87
Stroke (mm)	82	82
Capacity (cc)	465	487
Compression ratio (to 1)	7·1	6·7
bhp @ rpm		34·65 @ 6500
Torque (kgm) @ rpm		4·23 @ 5500
Oil system	mix	mix
Engine cooling	air	air
Carburettor (mm)	VM38SS	VM38SS
Ignition system	CDI	CDI
Ignition timing (mm)		
Primary drive gearing	2·63	2·63
Final drive gearing	44/14	44/14
Box gearing first	2·67	2·67
Box gearing second	1·75	1·75
Box gearing third	1·32	1·32
Box gearing fourth	1·00	1·00
Box gearing fifth	0·79	0·79
Box gearing sixth	—	—
Fuel (1)	13	13·5
Engine oil (1)	—	—
Transmission oil (1)	0·8	0·8
Front fork oil (cc/leg)		
Front tyre	3·00 × 21	3·00 × 21
Rear tyre	5·60 × 18	150/80 × 18
Front brake	tls drum	tls drum
Rear brake	sls drum	sls drum
Rear suspension	monoshock (3)	monoshock (5)
Front suspension travel (mm)	267	300
Rear suspension travel (mm)	272	300
Rake (°)	28·5	28
Trail (mm)	122	118
Width (mm)		
Ground clearance (mm)	311	330
Wheelbase (mm)	1475	1485
Dry weight (kg)	112	112·7

* = Non-USA
** = Europe 1984

Model	XT125J/K/L	XT200J/K/L	XT250G/H/J/K	TT250G/H/J/K	XT250L/N
Year	**1982-1984**	**1982-1984**	**1980–1983**	**1980–1983**	**1984-1985**
Chassis/engine id.	15E[1]/12V[2]/15W[3]/ 16A[4]	15A	3Y1[1]/3Y2[2]/3Y3[3]	3Y0[1]/16E[2]	42U
Bore (mm)	57	67	75	75	73
Stroke (mm)	48·8	55·7	56·5	56·5	59·6
Capacity (cc)	124	196	249	249	249
Engine type	SOHC	SOHC	SOHC	SOHC	DOHC
bhp @ rpm	12 @ 9000	13·0 @ 8500	21 @ 8000	23 @ 8000	
Torque (kgm) @ rpm	1·0 @ 8000	1·61 @ 7000	2·0 @ 6500	2·15 @ 7000	2.5 @ 6500
Compression ratio (to 1)	10	9·5	9·2	9·7	9·5
Carburettor (mm)	TKY24P	TKY24PV	VM28SS	VM30SS	TKY22PV (YDIS)
Ignition timing R (*BTDC < rpm)	9 < 1300		7 < 1200	7 < 1200	12 < 1200
Ignition timing A (*BTDC > rpm)	29 > 2600			32 > 4800	34 > 5000
Ignition system	CDI	CDI	CDI	CDI	CDI
Inlet valve opens (*BTDC)	28	32	28	32	34
Inlet valve closes (*ABDC)	60	72	68	72	62
Exhaust valve opens (*BBDC)	64	68	64	68	70
Exhaust valve closes (*ATDC)	24	36	32	36	26
Primary drive gearing	3·32	3·32	3·13	3·13	3·13
Final drive gearing	50/14	48/15	46/16	51/15	52/19
Box gearing first	2·83	2·83	2·64	2·64	2·47
Box gearing second	1·79	1·79	1·68	1·68	1·81
Box gearing third	1·32	1·32	1·26	1·26	1·36
Box gearing fourth	1·04	1·04	1·00	1·00	1·08
Box gearing fifth	0·82	0·82	0·82	0·82	0·89
Box gearing sixth	—	—	—	—	0·78
Fuel (1)	7·3	8·5	8·25	7·2	12
Engine oil (1)	1·3	1·3	1·6	1·6	1·6
Front fork oil (cc)	249		269	318	319
Front tyre	2·75 × 21	2·75 × 21	3·00 × 21	3·00 × 21	3·00 × 21
Rear tyre	4·10 × 18	100/80 × 17	4·00 × 18	5·10 × 17	110/80 × 18
Front brake	sls drum	sls drum	sls drum	sls drum	disc
Rear brake	sls drum	sls drum	sls drum	sls drum	drum
Rear suspension	monoshock (3)	monoshock (3)	monoshock (3)	monoshock (3)	monoshock (5)
Front suspension travel (mm)	205	255	205	230	250
Rear suspension travel (mm)	180	175	180	205	220
Rake (°)	27·8	28·8	39·5	28·5	27·3
Trail (mm)	110	120	116	120	107
Wheelbase (mm)	1330	1335	1395	1400	1420
Ground clearance (mm)	265	265	265	280	275
Dry weight (kg)	98	103	113	113	120

1 = US XT125J/K
2 = European XT125J
3 = Canadian XT125J/K/L
4 = Australian XT125J

1 = US XT250G/H
2 = Canadian XT250G/H
3 = European XT250G/H

1 = TT250G/H
2 = TT250J/K

Model	XT350N	XT500C/TT500C	XT500D/E/F/G +	TT500D/E	TT500F/G/H
Year	1985	1976	1977–1980 +	1977–1978	1979–1981
Chassis/engine id.	55V	1E6/583	1E6[1]/3H6[2]/4R9[3]/ 1U6[4]/2H2[5]/3H7[6]	1T1	1T1/2Y0
Bore (mm)	86	87	87	87	87
Stroke (mm)	59.6	84	84	84	84
Capacity (cc)	346	499	499	499	499
Engine type	DOHC	SOHC	SOHC	SOHC	SOHC
bhp @ rpm	31 @ 7500	27·6 @ 5500	32 @ 6500	32 @ 6000	33 @ 6000
Torque (kgm) @ rpm	3 @ 7000	3·64	4 @ 5500	3·9 @ 5500	4·0 @ 5500
Compression ratio (to 1)	9·5	9	9	9	9
Carburettor (mm)	TKY24PV	VM34SS	VM32SS	VM34SS/ VM32SS	VM34SS
Ignition timing R (*BTDC < rpm)	12 < 1200	7 < 2250	7 < 1100	7 < 2250	7 < 2250
Ignition timing A (*BTDC > rpm)	34 > 5000	27 > 3000	27 > 3000	27 > 3000	27 > 3000
Ignition system	CDI	magneto	magneto	magneto	CDI
Inlet valve opens (*BTDC)	30	44	44	44	44
Inlet valve closes (*ABDC)	58	68	68	68	68
Exhaust valve opens (*BBDC)	66	76	76	76	76
Exhaust valve closes (*ATDC)	22	36	36	36	36
Primary drive gearing	3·13	2·57	2·57	2·57	2·57
Final drive gearing	55/19	44/16 / 52/15	44/16	50/15	50/15
Box gearing first	2·47	2·36	2·36	2·36	2·36
Box gearing second	1·81	1·56	1·56	1·56	1·56
Box gearing third	1·36	1·19	1·19	1·19	1·19
Box gearing fourth	1·08	0·92	0·92	0·92	0·92
Box gearing fifth	0·89	0·78	0·78	0·78	0·78
Box gearing sixth	0·76	—	—	—	—
Fuel (1)	12	8·7	8·5	8·5	8·5
Engine oil (1)	1·6	2·5	2·4	2·5	2·4
Front fork oil (cc)	319	217	238	223	247
Front tyre	3·00 × 21	3·00 × 21	3·00 × 21	3·00 × 21	3·00 × 21
Rear tyre	110/80 × 18	4·00 × 18/4·60 × 18	4·00 × 18	4·60 × 18	4·60 × 18
Front brake	disc	sls drum	sls drum	sls drum	sls drum
Rear brake	sls drum	sls drum	sls drum	sls drum	sls drum
Rear suspension	monoshock (5)	twin shock	twin shock	twin shock	twin shock
Front suspension travel (mm)	255	195	195	195	195
Rear suspension travel (mm)	220	145	160	159	159
Rake (°)	27·2	30·5	29·5/29	30	29·4
Trail (mm)	107	135	135/123	132	125
Wheelbase (mm)	1420	1420	1420/1415	1426	1420
Ground clearance (mm)	274	216	225/215	235	230
Dry weight (kg)	133	138/123	139	123	123

1 = US XT500D/E/F
2 = US XT500G
3 = US XT500H
4 = European XT500D/E/F
5 = Canada/Australia XT500E/F
6 = Canada/Australia XT500G

Model	XT550J/K	XT600L/N	TT600K/L/N	HL500
Year		1984–1985	1983–1985	1978–1979
Chassis/engine id.	5Y1[1]/5Y2[2]/5Y3[3]/5Y4[4]	43F[1]/49L[2]/49M[3]/49N[4]/49R[5]	34K[1]/36A[2]	3K4
Bore (mm)	92	95	95	87
Stroke (mm)	84	84	84	84
Capacity (cc)	558	595	595	499
Engine type	SOHC	SOHC	SOHC	SOHC
bhp @ rpm	33 @ 7100	44 @ 6500	22 @ 6000 (*)	
Torque (kgm) @ rpm		5·05 @ 5500	43 @ 2000	
Compression ratio (to 1)	8·5	8·5	8·5	9
Carburettor (mm)	TKY26 (YDIS)	TKY27PV	TKY27PV	VM36SC/VM38SC
Ignition timing R (*BTDC < rpm)	12 < 1200	12 < 1200	12 < 1200	
Ignition timing A (*BTDC > rpm)	35 > 6000	36 > 4500	36 > 4500	
Ignition system	CDI	CDI	CDI	magneto/CDI
Inlet valve opens (*BTDC)	30	28	30	
Inlet valve closes (*ABDC)	66	64	66	
Exhaust valve opens (*BBDC)	66	64	70	
Exhaust valve closes (*ATDC)	30	30	34	
Primary drive gearing	2·53	2·39	2·39	2·57
Final drive gearing	42/15	40/15	50/14	48/15
Box gearing first	2·31	2·58	2·31	2·36
Box gearing second	1·59	1·59	1·56	1·56
Box gearing third	1·2	1·2	1·2	1·19
Box gearing fourth	0·95	0·95	0·96	0·92
Box gearing fifth	0·78	0·78	0·78	0·78
Box bearing sixth	—	—	—	
Fuel (1)	11·4	11	11	5·5
Engine oil (1)	2·4	2·4	2·4	2·7
Front fork oil (cc)	369	483	578/589	364
Front tyre	3·00 × 21	3·00 × 21	100/80 × 21	3·00 × 21
Rear tyre	4·60 × 18	4·60 × 18	140/80 × 18	5·00 × 18
Front brake	sls drum	disc	tls drum/disc	sls drum
Rear brake	sls drum	sls drum	sls drum	sls drum
Rear suspension	monoshock (3)	monoshock (5)	monoshock (5)	twin shock
Front suspension travel (mm)	205	255	300	250/270
Rear suspension travel (mm)	190	235	270	250/260
Rake (°)	28·2	28	28	30
Trail (mm)	115	107	118	130
Wheelbase (mm)	1400	1435	1485	1430
Ground clearance (mm)	260	260	300	330
Dry weight (kg)	136·5	137	124	115

1 = US XT550J/K
2 = Canadian XT550J/K
3 = European XT550J
4 = Australian XT550J/K

1 = European XT600L
2 = Australian XT600L
3 = Canadian XT600L
4 = American XT600L
5 = American XT600N

1 = US/Canada TT600K/L
2 = Australia TT600K/L
* = European spec for homologation

191

Port profiles and dimensions

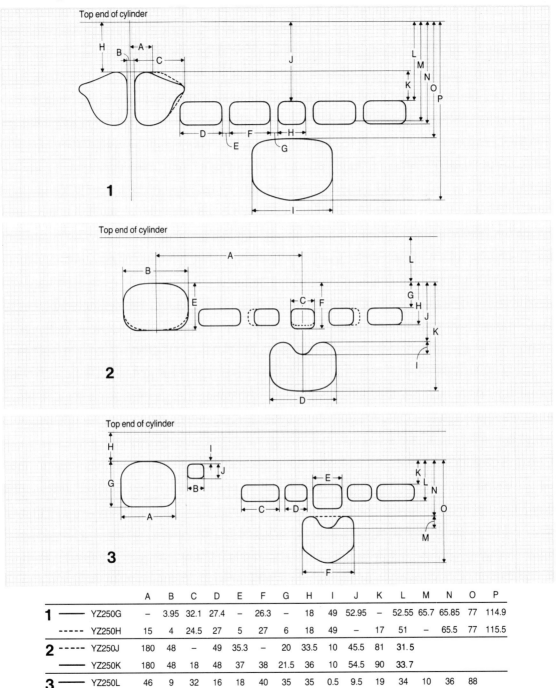

		A	B	C	D	E	F	G	H	I	J	K	L	M	N	O	P
1	—— YZ250G	–	3.95	32.1	27.4	–	26.3	–	18	49	52.95	–	52.55	65.7	65.85	77	114.9
	---- YZ250H	15	4	24.5	27	5	27	6	18	49	–	17	51	–	65.5	77	115.5
2	---- YZ250J	180	48	–	49	35.3	–	20	33.5	10	45.5	81	31.5				
	—— YZ250K	180	48	18	48	37	38	21.5	36	10	54.5	90	33.7				
3	—— YZ250L	46	9	32	16	18	40	35	35	0.5	9.5	19	34	10	36	88	
	---- YZ250N	46	9.5	31.7	16.9	18	40	35	35	–	7.5	19	34	–	52	88	